Presented to
Dr J D. Parkhurst
by J W Caughlan

REV. THOMAS A. MORRIS,

Bishop of the Methodist Episcopal Church

MISCELLANY:

CONSISTING OF

ESSAYS, BIOGRAPHICAL SKETCHES,

AND

NOTES OF TRAVEL.

BY

Rev. T. A. Morris, D. D.,

ONE OF THE BISHOPS OF THE METHODIST EPISCOPAL CHURCH.

Gather up the fragments that remain, that nothing be lost.—John vi, 12.

Cincinnati:

PUBLISHED BY L. SWORMSTEDT & A. POE,

FOR THE METHODIST EPISCOPAL CHURCH, AT THE WESTERN BOOK CONCERN,
CORNER OF MAIN AND EIGHTH STREETS.

R. P. THOMPSON, PRINTER.

1854.

PREFACE.

For many years I have occasionally employed fragments of time in writing for our Church papers. My articles are thinly scattered over a broad surface of periodical literature, some of them in papers which, at the time those articles appeared, had but a limited circulation. These papers are now rapidly going to waste, and most of their early readers have already disappeared from among the living. I am not quite willing that all of my articles should remain a dead letter, as I have often been requested, by different individuals, to republish some of them. And the only hope now of rescuing them from oblivion, is to republish them in a convenient and permanent form. In concluding to adopt this plan, I act in accordance with the counsel of some of the wisest and best of men within my knowledge.

This volume, as its name suggests, consists of different sorts of compositions, though it embraces only a small proportion of what I have written and published. The work is divided into three parts, for the convenience of readers.

The first part contains short essays on various literary, moral, and religious topics of a practical bearing, to the exclusion of speculative theology.

The second part is filled with brief biographical sketches of pious individuals, whose character, life, and death, I have, at different times, had occasion to notice, and whose example may encourage the living in their Christian course.

The third part consists of notes of travel. These are not in the form of a diary, or regular journal, for I have not kept any thing of the kind, but are made up mostly of journeys, incidents, and observations which transpired at various periods during my itinerant life. Among others will be found the report of a land trip from St. Louis to Texas, A. D. 1841–42, in the form of a familiar correspondence. Also, a similar report of a trip to the Indian country, west of Missouri and Arkansas, in 1844.

It is hoped that this small Miscellany may prove both safe and profitable for plain readers in general, and especially among the young; and as there is no necessary connection between the general parts of the volume, such as have but little time for reading, can examine the table of contents and select for themselves.

T. A. MORRIS.

CONTENTS.

PART I.

Essays.

PART II.

Biographical Sketches.

PART III.

Notes of Travel.

Part First.

ESSAYS.

MISCELLANY.

Essays.

THE BIBLE.

In reading mere human productions, however excellent, the mind becomes weary. The most attractive work among them, on the second or third perusal, begins to lose its interest. But not so of the Bible. Drawn from the fountain of all wisdom and goodness, its themes are sublime, its depths are fathomless, and its variety is infinite. The oldest, closest, and most uniform readers pronounce it always new and ever fresh. Each repeated perusal leads to the discovery of new beauties and unknown excellences. The more they read, the more they desire to read it; and the longer they read, the better they love to read it. The Bible is emphatically the Book—the Book of books—yea, the Book of God. It is a rich boon from our heavenly Father, to his children of all ages and nations—the people's book—the heavenly chart, with which alone life's boisterous seas can be safely navigated. Its precepts are so simple that the most ignorant may understand them, while its mysteries are so profound that the most learned could never have invented them. If the Bible were perfectly comprehensible in all its parts, by one human mind, that might suggest doubts of its being a revelation from heaven, for all the world of intellectual beings. Its sublime mysteries, so far from discrediting, only confirm its claims to a divine origin. Many of the precious truths of this sacred volume, such as that of the resurrection of the body, are purely matters of revelation, and could never have been discovered by the light of reason. The same may be said of all things future, which the prophets have made known; "For the prophecy came not in old time by the will of man; but holy men of God spake as they were moved by the Holy Ghost." Hence, the authority of its commands, the terror of its denunciations, and the consolation of its promises. While all things in the Bible, essentially connected with doctrine, experience, and practice, are sufficiently plain for ordinary readers, its resources are so boundless, as to call into requisition all the research of the learned, directed by the strongest intellect, without exhaustion. What are all the treasures of classic lore compared to the "word of life?" For depth of wisdom, beauty of style, and sublimity of thought, it surpasses the sages of Greece, the orators of Rome, and all the literati of modern times. The far-famed British, and other poets, are thrown into the shade by the book of Job, the Psalms of David, and the prophetic visions of Isaiah. All the works of fiction, by the most popular authors, may be safely challenged to produce one single essay that would bear any just comparison to the simple, veritable, and pathetic narrative of Joseph and his brethren. As to the sermon upon the mount, and all other discourses of our Lord and Savior, it is enough to recite the concession of his enemies: "Never man spake like this man."

Why should a man expend thousands of dollars for a mass of books, and commit himself to the toil of a lifetime in examining them, when, for a few shillings, he can obtain the Book which contains more wisdom, and is of infinitely more importance than all the libraries in the world? Nor is this saying too much for the Bible, which dates back near two thousand years beyond the oldest history extant, and by prophecy extends forward to the end of time. If all human productions, from the first imperfect scrawl on bark or skin, down to the ornamented volumes of 1850, be placed in one scale, and a single, plain copy of the Bible in the other, in point of real value, it outweighs them all. Would you learn the origin of the world, and the years of its existence? Instead of resorting to geology, and dealing in uncertain conjecture and inference, go to Genesis, and read an authentic history of the creation of all things from nothing. The earth first arose, without form, and void, and darkness covered the face of it; but, under the plastic hand of the Creator, assumed its proper shape and function. "And God said, Let there be light: and there was light." The sun took his appropriate position, and the rolling planets were distributed around him, so as to receive his light and heat. The whole system was then put in motion by its Author; and, for near six thousand years, has never, for one moment, ceased to move. As yet there were none to till the earth, or rule the multitude of its living creatures; but the Lord God formed man out of the dust, breathed on him and he lived, having dominion over every living thing on the earth. From his rib, God made woman, to be the companion and helpmeet of man. And from them have descended all the babbling tribes of humanity. Would you know whence came death and all the woes of man? Read it in the history of the fall. Do you desire to learn what is the only remedy for sin and its miseries? It is all comprehended in this, Christ died for our sins and rose again for our justification. Are you still prostrated, fettered, and powerless under the bondage of sin? Accept of his free, unmerited advocacy, nothing doubting, and you are "redeemed, regenerated, and disinthralled." Such are the history and doctrine of the Bible. It guides the pilgrim stranger through this howling wilderness, in the path of safety. It hangs out the lamp of its exceeding great and precious promises, to pilot him over the gulf stream of death; and leads him forth with songs of deliverance to join his friends in the deathless regions of immortality, where the river of life glides forever, amidst the beauties of perennial spring.

Now, the Bible, which alone affords any satisfactory information of our origin, duty, and end, or any assurance of a higher and happier state of existence than the present, is alike suited to all classes of society, and to all the circumstances of human life. It is the plain Christian's manual, and the learned man's text-book; the rich man's monitor, and the poor man's treasure; the traveler's guide, and the mariner's chart; the widow's companion, and the orphan's guardian. It is the basis of legislation, and the standard of morals; it binds over the witness, juror, attorney, and judge to a future reckoning, and requires the administration of universal justice, according to the golden rule, of doing unto all men as we would they should do unto us. It checks the turbulent passions of the wicked, protects the rights of the innocent, and enjoins peace on earth and good will to man. It tunes the harp of the musician, furnishes the song of devotion, and kindles the fires of eloquence. It imparts light to the ignorant, and peace to the broken-hearted; relieves the oppressed of their burden, and breaks the wizard spell of superstition. It is the sick man's consolation, and sustains the dying man's hope. The final inference is, there should be, at least, as many Bibles in the world as there are rational beings, and every man, woman, and child should own a copy.

THE PRESS.

THAT printing machine is a wonderful invention. Nothing could supply its place in the dissemination of knowledge. Through its agency one individual may speak to millions, not only while he lives, but when sleeping in his grave. Thoughts committed to paper, and printed in books centuries ago, are still in existence, and familiar to reading men of this generation. Thus, by the power of this simple engine, distant ages are brought together; and, with the aid of translators, men of all languages may converse and become acquainted with each other's laws, customs, and religion, through the press. When the world was dependent on scribes to multiply copies of manuscript, only limited scraps of history could be preserved, and the knowledge of them was necessarily confined to a few individuals, who might obtain access to the huge rolls of parchment on which they were written. We are indebted to the press for the abundance and cheapness of reading in this age. Had not the art of printing been discovered, "even the word of life," contained in the records of salvation, would still be locked up in the archives of the university, and read only by a few learned doctors of the law. The press, under a wise and gracious Providence, has thrown the Bible among the multitudes of common people, and made it at once the parent's companion and the child's school book. Thus, the people generally in this favored land may have access to the fountain-head of knowledge, which is able to make them wise unto salvation, through faith which is in Christ Jesus. So it is in all Protestant countries, and so it should be in all the world. To expect the people to find their way to heaven without the holy Scriptures, is as unreasonable as to require mariners to navigate the high seas without chart or compass. Every intelligent Christian can adopt the sentiment thus figuratively expressed:

"The Bible is my chart,
By which the seas I know;
I can not with it part,
It rocks and sands doth show;
It is my chart and compass too,
Whose needle points forever true."

Whenever the people of any country shall be furnished with the Bible, and sufficient knowledge of letters to read it, they will soon understand their chartered rights, both as Christians and citizens, and will have courage to assert them, too, in defiance of popes and tyrants. They, whose usurped authority rests upon the slender foundation, "Ignorance is the mother of devotion," have important reasons for withholding the Bible from their deluded subjects. And, to them, nothing is more troublesome than the press: it is difficult for them to exclude from their limited dominions all the light which it sheds upon the world around them. How important, then, is the press in multiplying copies of the sacred writings, and removing obstructions to their circulation! Just in proportion as pure Christianity progresses and prospers in the world, sound learning, civil liberty, and all the blessings of social life will advance among the nations of the earth, and no faster. "Righteousness exalteth a nation; but sin is a reproach to any people," is as true now as it was when Solomon wrote it.

But the press, like all other benefits conferred upon man, is liable to be abused and perverted to improper use. While "the liberty of the press" is to be maintained by every Christian and patriot, care should be taken to restrain it within proper bounds. There is certainly a marked difference between the liberty of the press and the licentiousness of it, whether viewed in the political, literary, or religious department of its operations.

The political press should teach the rights of man, expound international law, advocate the principles of our free institutions, keep the people advised of the state of commerce, and publish general intelligence. But it should never be enlisted in the cause of mobocracy, or demagogism, or such party measures as conflict with the general good of the country; nor should it ever be degraded by dealing in slander, or personal invective, or any disgusting details of private scandal. This standard is evidently none too high. But if every political newspaper which falls below it were expunged from the catalogue, how few of them would be left! How many political papers are there in the United States which do not evince more zeal for their respective leaders and parties, than they do for their country? Which of them will not abuse a political opponent to prevent his elevation, or flatter a political friend for the remote prospect of obtaining office? Nay, which of them will not publish fulsome notices of a masquerade, a theater, a circus, a horse-race, or a tippling-house for the paltry sum of a few cents? "Straws show which way the wind blows," and these objectionable items but too clearly indicate the spirit of the political press. In vain may it attempt to reform the people till it reforms itself.

The literary press operates in a milder atmosphere, sustains a relation less exciting, and occupies a position less perilous, and, consequently, is, in a great measure, clear of the objections above named. That it has its toils, perplexities, and discouragements to contend with, is admitted; but being free from the contaminating influence of office, and from the agitation of evil passion, it meets these difficulties calmly, patiently, and in hope of ultimate success. Beside, its toil is pleasant. What delightful labor, to store the mind with knowledge, and then employ it in erecting monuments of science, and strewing the garlands of literature along the path of life for the benefit of those who come after! Such employment, though it may promise but little wealth, and no sensual pleasure, has the advantage of being free from the corrupting influence of vicious associations, and threatens no remorse of conscience to be endured in the evening of life. Still, the literary press is only less liable to abuse than the political, and not wholly secure against it. The appetites of its readers are various, some of them quite vitiated by the use of improper aliment; hence arises a temptation to indulge their perverted taste to the injury of their judgment and general vigor of character. If proof be demanded, reference may be had to all the varieties of fiction, from the less offensive novel, down to the common-place love tale, written by a novice for some would-be literary periodical, and to the debilitating and contaminating influence which they exert upon the minds and characters of their deluded readers. All tales of wild adventure, whether in war or love, are highly injurious to young readers of both sexes. They not only lessen the inclination for study and the desire for the acquisition of useful knowledge, but they fix in the mind erroneous views of men and things, by portraying characters which never existed, and recording events which never transpired, and thus introducing them to a world very different from the one in which they live. Walker's definition of romancer is, "A liar, a forger of tales." And yet thousands of young females, whose minds are naturally sprightly and amiable, spend their days and nights in poring and weeping over these forgeries, as though they were credible and useful histories. Such a young lady has received an erroneous education. It has led her in the wrong path, and the sooner she retraces her steps the better. She is in danger of becoming an object of pity in the estimation of intelligent people. They who have encouraged her to take this delusive course in the pursuit of knowledge are justly censurable.

But what should be said of the religious press? Its responsibility is as much greater than that of all others, as our spiritual and eternal interests are higher than those of earth and time. Mistakes here may endanger the everlasting welfare of deathless spirits; yea, spirits redeemed by the blood of the Lamb, and already placed upon ground of possible salvation. The press which is professedly devoted to the interest of religion, should never become entangled with any question of worldly policy, or of popular excitement, or of personal or party conflict, or angry controversy on any subject whatever. All such errors tend to weaken public confidence in the religious press, and to divert its patronage into other channels. It is worse than useless to teach religion in theory, while its teachers contradict their own principles in spirit and practice, as the conclusion which naturally follows is, their religion makes them no better than their neighbors. The common sense of mankind will estimate the real value of every system and every enterprise by its practical results. If a press, though professedly religious, kindle the fire of contention, raise the storm of angry passion, and indicate a spirit of malevolence, it will be justly regarded as an engine of evil, sowing the seeds of discord and persecution. Religion would be far better off without any press, than with one which only betrays her interest, by practically renouncing her own principles, or with any number of presses which exhaust their energies by combating one another. What folly it is for those who are professedly aiming to accomplish the same great and good object—the conversion of the world—to turn aside from their high and holy calling, and wage a war of mutual extermination! Every consistent Christian sighs and weeps over such an exhibition of human depravity. Let the religious press be restricted to its appropriate work, and it will find ample employment for all its time, strength, and resources, without assuming any needless responsibility. The main design of it should be to impart a knowledge of that religion which brings "glory to God in the highest, and on earth peace, good will toward men." And whatever tends to the accomplishment of this result, should be encouraged by it. Here an almost boundless field of useful enterprise opens to view. It embraces the regular Christian ministry with all of its intense interest, the progress of revivals under the ministration of the Gospel, foreign and domestic missions, plans for the instruction of youth and childhood, sanctified learning, and all benevolent associations which have for their object the glory of God and the happiness of man. All of these interests are to be noticed, explained, defended, and encouraged, by presenting the truth in love, and in meekness of wisdom. Surely there is much land to be possessed and cultivated by the religious press before the peaceful reign of Christ shall be universally established and acknowledged. Beside, this press is expected to furnish the whole world with all the religious reading which it needs, or may need, in the form of books, duly assorted, distinguishing between the good and evil. The work is vast and increasing, both in extent and importance; but the means for its accomplishment, if not yet abundant, are, at least, accumulating. The gold and the silver are the Lord's, and his treasury is increasing. Presses are multiplying, and they are moving under a full pressure of steam-power, so that a copy of the Bible can be printed in a minute; and missionary ships are bearing off the old and new covenants to heathen lands by the ton. Only let the religious press not be turned aside from its own proper work, and it will prove itself an invaluable auxiliary to the Christian ministry, in subjugating the world to the "obedience of Christ," and raising it to holiness, happiness, and heaven.

HOUSES OF WORSHIP.

There has been perceptible improvement in church building, within the last few years, in several particulars. Under the old dispensation, it was supposed that some difficulty in reaching the place of worship was a necessary sacrifice for the privilege of attending. Hence, village churches were located in the country, and frequently over a creek, and on top of the highest hill in the neighborhood. But, of late years, it has been ascertained that it is easier to get the house to the people than the people to the house; and now village churches are generally erected as near the center of population as practicable. It is far better to pay the full value of a church lot in the proper place than to have one for nothing in the wrong place. Let all concerned remember it.

Overgrown houses are found to be inconvenient and unprofitable. A medium-sized house is much better. When it becomes crowded by increase of population, instead of removing it to make way for one of mammoth dimensions, let it stand as long as it is comfortable, and build another the same size; and when the second is full, then a third, and so on. Again: it has been fully tested, that cellars do not answer for lecture-rooms, Sabbath school-rooms, or class-rooms, because of the dampness of them. The basement-story should be entirely above ground to be comfortable and useful. Side galleries obstruct both sight and sound; they are the usual resort of rude boys and other comers and goers during public service, and a fruitful source of disturbance, and may well be dispensed with. But an end gallery over the vestibule, to hold the Sabbath school during sermon, is a convenience to the teachers and classes, as it affords them comfortable seats, where they can see and hear, and to which they have free access in a body, without disturbance to any one, leaving the lower floor for the balance of the congregation. The old style of circular pulpits, ascended by winding, narrow stairs, and running a minister's head nearly up to the ceiling, so as to require him to look down and the people to look up to see and hear, were a remarkable instance of the want of judgment. It is cause of thanksgiving that their days are numbered, and that ministers are allowed to speak horizontally, with room to turn round. And it is equally fortunate that the high fronts, constructed originally for reading sermons, which concealed the speaker's person, except his head and neck, have passed away, allowing the minister to be seen, and to use his hands without raising them overhead. As to the position of the pulpit, it should always be at the far end from the doors, not between them; otherwise there will be much inconvenience.

But while much has been done to render our houses of worship comfortable, much remains to be done. Outside steps, high enough to land the people on the floor of the church proper, are not only expensive, if made durable, but frequently mar the beauty of the building. A still greater objection is, they are always inconvenient to ladies, soiling their Sabbath dresses in passing up and down the muddy steps; and, when there is ice or sleet, they are dangerous. It is a much better plan to pass from the street into the lower vestibule; thence, by inner stairways, which are always dry, to the upper vestibule, and into the church proper. Church windows, in all cases, should be so constructed that the lower sash could be raised in hot weather, and the upper sash lowered, when necessary, to admit fresh air in cool weather, without letting streams of cold wind directly on to the people. The light should be let in sufficiently for all to read by without difficulty, and to produce a cheerful appearance, and yet it should be well diffused and mellowed, so as to be easy to the eye, changing the blinds as the sun turns, and avoiding the pain occasioned by concentrated sunbeams through one or two windows, while the shady side is all dark, when it alone should be open. At night, in the absence of gas-light, the house should be thoroughly illuminated with lamp-light, relieving the minister and his hearers from the intolerable annoyance of a sexton passing round in time of sermon to snuff candles, which he is almost certain to inflict just at the greatest point of interest in the discourse. A church, to be healthy and agreeable, should be kept clean, and well aired, relieving it, after each service, of the contaminated atmosphere so often inhaled and breathed, and supplying it with fresh. Beside all this care, every church should have a ventilator in the upper ceiling, allowing the heated and putrid air to escape as it accumulates, which would prevent one-half of all the stupor and drowsiness so common in our crowded assemblies, and keep all lively and vigorous.

One of the most essential things to comfort in church, is to have it just warm enough, and not too warm. When people are suffering with cold, and thinking of being made sick by it, they can not enjoy preaching or engage in prayer or praise to much profit; and when they are nearly suffocated with stove heat it is still worse. How often does the minister find himself, of an evening, where the stove heat has been kept up all day in the same dry, contaminated air, destitute both of physical and mental energy, with a dull, drowsy congregation before him, simply owing to the state of atmosphere in the house! During the service, he is covered with a clammy sweat, and when he steps out into the fresh air, he feels as if a bucket of cold water was poured upon his head, and running all over him. No marvel that he should have bronchial disease, or something worse. Such exposures destroy the health of many excellent ministers, and even the lives of some, thus cutting them off in the midst of their usefulness. "How may this great evil be remedied?" is a question worthy of serious consideration. Perhaps the following suggestions might be of some use. Let sextons be told, what very few of them seem to know, that there is a difference between a moderate day and a very cold one in this changeable climate, and that less fuel is requisite on the former than the latter. Let it be explained to them, and repeated till they understand it, that there is really such a principle as animal heat in the human system; and, consequently, if a church be made comfortably warm, as it always should be before the congregation assemble, and then filled with living men and women, and the doors shut, it will certainly remain warm till they disperse, without adding any more fuel. There can be no mistake in this matter. If the sexton can not find a lodgment for these simple facts in his cranium, so as to regulate the temperature of the house, hang up a large thermometer in it, and tell him when the mercury rises above a certain mark, to lower the heat, and when it sinks below a certain other mark, to raise the heat. No matter about his comprehending the principle, if he can only learn the use of the instrument. Finally: let the trustees provide the proper number of stoves, and put them up in the right place. Medium-sized churches, containing say eight hundred people, require two stoves, which should be placed near the doors; the further from the pulpit the better, if they be only in the house. Heated air rises.

If the stoves be near the pulpit, the heat strikes the speaker in his elevated position so forcibly as to embarrass and afflict him. Recently, I preached in a church containing four stoves, two of them near the altar, one on each side. It was a mild and beautiful Sabbath, preceded by several rainy, disagreeable ones. The sexton anticipated what was realized, a full house, and, therefore, filled all the stoves with fuel about the time the people began to assemble. By the time I got fairly under way preaching, the fire took effect in earnest, and turned my face near its own color; for the blood rushed to the brain, and I felt like falling; so that I had to desist from preaching, and commenced begging for less fire and more air. The doors were thrown wide open, and let sluices of fresh air on to the congregation, greatly to the relief of some; but a few invalids took fright, and, lest they should catch cold, left for home, and we saw no more of them. I sat down till the house became cool enough to close the doors, and the people composed, and then resumed the discourse. Perhaps a thousand people were incommoded, and the sermon interrupted by that piece of indiscretion, which, however, was nothing but might occur frequently, where the sexton supposes that he must build the largest fire when the weather is finest and the house fullest, and the least fire when the day is stormy and few attend—the rule by which most sextons practically operate in their line of business. In regard to this subject we need a reformation, and must have it, or the interests of public worship will suffer immensely.

LOUD PREACHING.

The object of preaching is to persuade men, women, and children to be good, that they may be happy. To accomplish this object, every preacher should aim to instruct and impress his hearers by a proper use of divine truth. To assist our preachers in the performance of these duties, sundry directions are given in the Discipline, recommending some things as proper, and pointing out others as improper. Among the latter is that of "speaking too loud." But in ascertaining what is too loud, reference must be had to many things; such as, our experience as speakers, our observation as hearers, the collected sense of enlightened Christian assemblies, and the natural peculiarities of the persons speaking. By attention to these several particulars, we may arrive at conclusions sufficiently correct. Experience will teach us what neither books nor men can satisfactorily explain; that is, how to use our strength to the best advantage. By observing both good and bad speaking in others, we will be assisted in correcting our own faults. The opinion of an enlightened community will aid us in deciding on the relative advantages and disadvantages of the different methods of speaking. And strict attention to natural peculiarities will enable us to judge charitably of our brethren. To require all men to speak alike is as unreasonable as it is unprofitable. Some men naturally speak loud without any painful exertion. These have a decided advantage over others, provided the gift be well cultivated; but unless they are careful they will become so boisterous as to be unpleasant. Others speak low, and can not do otherwise, without speaking unnaturally, which is far worse; hence, it follows, what is too low for one may be too high for another.

It will be of some service to read and study the various rules of rhetoric, especially in correcting improprieties; but whoever adheres implicitly to them, will be a dull speaker all his life—a mere imitator of school oratory. A few years' experience and observation are worth the whole of them, to any man of good taste and sound discretion.

As far as public speaking can be controlled by rules at all, those rules should be agreed on with reference to the convenience of the speaker as well as the hearer. The rule which requires the speaker to commence just so that the farthest person in the assembly can hear distinctly, can be enforced only when there is a correspondence between the size of the congregation and the strength of the speaker's voice. If the assembly be large and the voice of the speaker feeble, he can not practice on this rule, without commencing on a key too high for him to sustain; and the certain consequence will be a failure throughout. It would be better for the remote hearer to lose a score of words at the commencement, than for both speaker and hearers to be pained all the way through. Even in a large assembly, the speaker should commence at the middle of his voice, at that key on which he speaks most naturally and easily. As no one can sing with facility and pleasure when the tune is too high or too low, neither can any man speak with ease and energy unless he start with the right pitch of voice.

From these reflections we may arrive at the following conclusions:

To "speak too loud," is to speak louder than is necessary, to be heard by all present. For instance, if a man be preaching or praying in a private room, or a small, close chapel, where the voice is easily heard, to extend it to the utmost is not only useless, but highly injurious, producing such a roar and confusion of sounds as to destroy the sense of the words and bewilder the hearers. Such a method of preaching, even if it could be performed with convenience to the speaker, is only tolerable to the hearers in open space, say under a grove at camp meeting. In a close house it is extremely unpleasant; and if to a noisy be added a hurried method, it is scarcely to be endured.

A man speaks too loud whenever he assumes a tone beyond his natural strength, be that much or little. He that speaks with painful exertion to himself, never fails to produce painful sensations in his audience. Speaking in an easy, natural tone, with suitable earnestness, on a religious subject, will often melt and move a whole assembly; while the same words, delivered with unnatural screaming, by the same minister, to the same hearers, will only produce hardness and disgust. This fact is known to all who have attended strictly to these things, and may be known to any that will be at the trouble to examine for themselves.

What, then, is the use of hallooing? It affords no proof that the preacher has more skill; that he is more prayerful, or even that he is more zealous than others, who let their moderation be known to all men; for noise is no more essential to true Christian zeal, than fine style is to humble, sincere prayer. Again: hallooing is not essential to a minister's success, but often injures it; souls are not converted by physical force, nor is the Church built up by empty sound; but men are saved through faith in Christ, regenerated by the Holy Spirit, and edified by a faithful exhibition of Gospel truth. When preaching the Gospel, it is necessary to speak loud enough to be well heard under all ordinary circumstances, and to give force to the sentiment delivered; all beyond this is not only superfluous, but subversive of good teaching and devotional feeling. If the preacher would elevate the feelings of his audience, he must restrain his own within proper bounds. He may enter the pulpit with feelings excited by his own reflection on the message to be delivered; but those of the people are undisturbed; their attention must be fixed, and their judgment convinced, before their sensibilities can be reached. This done, heart responds to heart, sympathy intermingles with sympathy, as the drops of water run together, and the warm-hearted preacher carries his congregation with him wherever the practical bearings of the subject direct his course. This conquest, however, is not the effect of noise, but of simple truth, attended by the Divine blessing. In this state of excitement the preacher may extend his voice as much as it will bear, without throwing any damper on the feelings of the people, because they now feel noisy themselves; but whenever he gets beyond the strength of his voice, and loses the control of himself, he will no longer maintain the control of the people. Any minister who will make a fair trial, may satisfy himself, in a short time, that he can dispense with his screaming without any diminution of zeal, faith, comfort, or usefulness, besides promoting his own health and good standing among all the judicious of his flock.

The evils of speaking too loud are numerous, and apparent to all well-informed people. Allow me here to name a few of them for the benefit of all concerned.

The speaker becomes embarrassed by his own vehemence, which carries him beyond the feelings of his congregation.

His countenance being distorted by painful effort, renders his appearance disagreeable.

The sweet, musical tones of his voice, which would exert a favorable influence on his hearers, are exchanged for ravings that secure his own confusion and the disappointment of his audience, who are pained for the preacher, when they would be impressed with his subject if rightly managed.

By an imprudent waste of strength in the forepart of the discourse, the speaker is left without any where he needs it most; that is, in the application.

The preacher's lungs are tortured, his nervous system shattered, his spirits, after undue excitement, become depressed, his general health impaired, his life shortened, his usefulness cut off, and he dies a martyr to his own imprudence.

In the autumn of 1824 brother H. was appointed as junior preacher with me on Red River circuit, in Middle Tennessee. He was a young man of great promise to the Church, in almost every respect, except the unfortunate habit of screaming in his pulpit and other public exercises. In a short time he complained of a pain in his breast. He was faithfully admonished by myself and others to let his moderation be known to all men, or he would shorten his days and destroy his usefulness. He, however, pleaded that reformation in his case was impracticable, and continued to preach, exhort, and pray at the top of his voice with as much effort as a drowning man would halloo for help. The consequence was, his lungs became diseased, so that he broke down that conference year, and shortly after died, and, as I was informed, lamenting his intemperate exertions. Some may wear longer than others, but all habitual screamers, sooner or later, destroy their health and prospect of usefulness. The maxim, that a minister is immortal till his work is done, admits of one exception at least; that is, he may kill himself under a mistaken idea that his success depends on loud speaking.

PARENTAL DUTY.

It is the duty of parents to nourish their children with food convenient for them. In all practicable cases, they should first have what the Creator designed, the wholesome fluid of their mother's breast; and subsequently what agrees with them best—not candy, preserves, or rich cake, which only injure their health and vitiate their taste—but plain, simple aliment, such as bread, milk, and fruits, and digestible meats, dealt out at regular, stated times, and in reasonable quantities.

Parents should clothe their children comfortably. Very many injure the health of their infants, by keeping them too warmly clad, and too much excluded from the air, not observing that the animal heat in children is much greater than in older persons. This evil should be guarded against, as a slight injury, inflicted on the constitution in infancy, may be lasting as life. Another error, quite too common among parents, is, dressing their children in gay and costly style, with red shoes, shining buttons, fringes and ruffles, tassels and feathers, as if they were young officers in the navy or army. This is all wrong, being not only a waste of money, but injurious to the children, by pampering the natural pride of their hearts, and giving them false notions of their personal importance. Their clothing should be cheap and plain, but neat and comfortable, according to climate and season. They should be made to fit easy, and be kept whole and clean; for rags are disgraceful, and filth is loathsome. Some apologize for not keeping their children clean on the ground that dirt is healthy; but this is a mistake. The reason why the children of the poor are usually more healthy than those of the rich, is not that they are more dirty, but because they live on simple diet, and have plenty of exercise, without which no one can enjoy perfect health. Children should be kept just as clean, both in their person and apparel, as is consistent with plenty of exercise in the open air daily, and no more; for to confine them to their chairs and chambers by the week, lest they should get their aprons soiled, is to ruin their health for the sake of appearance.

Another duty of parents is, to protect their small children from danger. Whatever comes into the hand of a child is immediately transferred to his mouth; therefore, nothing should be left within his reach which will poison or strangle him; nor should he be left unguarded, where there is danger of falling, or being trodden under foot, or burnt, or scalded, because many, by these means, are destroyed, and perhaps some through the carelessness of those in charge of them. When large enough to run, they should not be allowed to wander alone into the streets or highways, lest they be run over by horses and carriages; nor should small children ever be allowed to go alone to rivers, lakes, or mill-ponds, lest they be drowned; or to a barn-raising, boat-launching, or the like, for fear of being crushed to death.

It is also the duty of parents to take care of their children in sickness. This implies timely prescription and proper remedies duly administered, to the exclusion of all doubtful experiments, whether of quackery or ignorance; also watching with diligence, and nursing with care, which are often of more importance than medicine. There are but few things, if any, in all the catalogue of parental duties which draw so heavily upon the sympathies and the constitution of parents, as taking care of their afflicted offspring; and yet no duty is performed with such interest and perseverance, because parental affection takes no account of sacrifice when the life of a beloved son or daughter is in peril. If health be restored, the parents are compensated for all their toil and care; and, should death ensue, the effort to save, though ineffectual, is not regretted.

Another duty, which parents are very generally anxious to perform, is, providing for the wants of their children in future. Beside making provision for their present comfort, it is desirable for children to have a small capital with which to commence the permanent business of life, and a moderate outfit when they get married and assume the responsibility of housekeepers. This, in many instances, they may be put in a way to earn for themselves by the time it is needed; but when that can not be done, then it is right and proper they should be aided and encouraged in the commencement. But more than a moderate sum to help in the outset is useless. And as to giving them large fortunes, it is a real injury, and in most instances a ruinous misfortune; because it leads to extravagant calculations and outlays of money, carelessness in business, or perhaps to dispense with all business, and resort to traveling and pleasure, till they become bankrupts, and are doomed to misery for life. Let this be remembered by those who are laying up largely for their children, while they are indulged in idleness and prodigality; for such a course, though intended as kindness, is cruelty to them. And, beside all this, no man can hoard up great estates for his children, to the neglect of the claims of charity and religion, without endangering his own salvation: "Woe unto you that are rich! for ye have received your consolation."

One of the most important duties of parents is, to govern their children. Family government was the first ever instituted for the well-being of human society, and it is still the most important, because the whole race of man is divided into families; so that, if each family be governed, all will be brought under domestic rule and order, and thereby prepared for civil and ecclesiastical government. Indeed, so far as children are concerned, and all are children at first, there is none but domestic government; and if they be not learned to render obedience to their parents in childhood, it will be difficult for them, in after life, to become obedient subjects of any government. By a wise arrangement of our Creator, it is made the duty of parents to rule and children to obey; and a mutual performance of these duties constitutes a well-ordered family, while the neglect of them leads to disorder and misery. Young children should be controlled by kindness and persuasion, if practicable; but when such considerations fail, resort should be had to force, discreetly exercised. We are not in favor of using the rod frequently, freely, or for small offenses; nor is it necessary to secure proper obedience; indeed, they who whip most usually govern least, because they thereby lose the affection of the child, and with it all controlling influence, except the fear of punishment. But, by some means, the child must be learned at first, and never allowed to forget the lesson, that he must obey his parents in all things. And let it be remembered, any attempt to enforce obedience which fails of the object in view, is worse than no effort at all. The point must be gained; and when subjection is once secured it is easily maintained.

So soon as children are capable of understanding the ground of their responsibility, moral considerations should be brought to bear upon them. Much can be done in securing the ends of good government, by teaching children the first principles of religion, and especially by letting them know that God requires them to honor their parents: "For God commanded, saying, Honor thy father and mother: and, He that curseth father or mother, let him die the death." Parental authority, then, is of so much importance, that we must maintain it, or give our children over to the righteous judgments of Heaven. Again: Solomon says, "The rod and reproof give wisdom: but a child left to himself bringeth his mother to shame." That is, timely correction and suitable admonition make a child obedient and happy; but if left to follow his own perverse inclination, without restraint, he disgraces himself and best friend. The truth of this maxim is verified constantly in our own day and country. Who does not know that ungoverned families afford our chief supplies of street loafers and vagabonds, our horse-racers, blacklegs, prostitutes, and felons? Parents should exert all their authority and influence over their children when young, to prevent the formation of those habits of insubordination which lead to such calamitous results; for when children once become habitually disobedient, they are ever after impatient of restraint, and the very worst consequences may be expected. On the other hand, every thing commendable may be anticipated of those who, being ruled with parental authority, tempered with love, learn to submit with pleasure and gratitude. They have the promise of a long and happy life, which, for their encouragement, is here inserted: "Children, obey your parents in the Lord: for this is right. Honor thy father and mother, (which is the first commandment with promise,) that it may be well with thee, and thou mayest live long on the earth."

It is a very prominent duty of parents to educate their children for usefulness in this life. The first material part of such an education consists in forming *industrious habits*, by regular application to some lawful business. A child who is allowed to be habitually idle, and select his own amusements, will very probably be a lazy man, and, consequently, unfit for any department of life. No man of indolent habits succeeds in any calling or profession, either in Church or state. Those who think it a disgrace for their children to labor with their hands for a living, are training them for drones in society. Every male and female should be, early in life, put to regular manual labor. It would be good for their health and fortunes, as well as their reputation and happiness. Boys might labor to advantage in the agricultural or mechanical branches of business, and girls in the domestic department. But any lawful business whatever is preferable to idleness; for idleness is the school of vice, and the way to ruin.

There is no good excuse for any, rich or poor, except the want of health; and every child should be taught the apostle's doctrine, "That if any would not work, neither should he eat."

Another material part of a useful education consists in being learned to *think*, which is of more practical importance than a diploma from a college. Many young men seem to be borne along through a college course, by their classmates and teachers, with but little knowledge of their text-books, and still less of any thing by way of preparation for future action, who are never of much use to themselves or the world. They go forth without constitution, without energy of character, or practical knowledge of life, to sink into obscurity; while poor boys, who are taught to work and think for themselves, with but a common school education, often rise to great eminence, as statesmen, scholars, jurists, or divines. I allow that such as obtain a classical education, without the loss of health, or of their industrious habits, have an advantage over others; but they appear to be comparatively few; and it is chiefly owing to the bad management of parents, in keeping them six or seven successive years wilting in the shade of a college, instead of requiring them to labor a part of each. One year employed in training a boy to think and apply what he knows to some useful purpose, is worth more than two spent in memorizing and reciting.

There is, in most instances, much error committed in the education of girls, it being conducted on the principle of gloss and show, without proper regard to practical usefulness. What is a young lady fitted for who has no constitution, no industry, no practical knowledge of domestic duties, and can only dress, perform on the piano-forte, repeat a French dialogue, and figure at fashionable parties? She may answer for a plaything, a mere subject of pastime; but how could she fill the responsible station of a wife and mistress of a family? A part of the education of every female should be given in the dairy and kitchen, where she may acquire a vigorous constitution, and much useful knowledge for the after part of life. Then, when thrown upon her own responsibility, as the mistress of a family, she will know what is to be done, and how to do it, or have it done. And, connected with this, should be a sound literary course, such as imparts not ornament merely, but useful knowledge on every subject pertaining to her appropriate sphere of life, so that she may examine for herself, and form an opinion of her own respecting every important matter.

Another important part of useful education, for both sexes, consists of a well-formed system of manners, which should be taught them from childhood up to maturity. By this, however, I do not mean a perpetual round of bowing and courtesying, which is just the reverse of agreeable manners, but a familiar acquaintance with the rules and usages of good society, and an easy conformity to them, so as to feel pleasant and unembarrassed in every genteel company, and help others to feel so too. To this end, young people should not only be instructed at home, by precept and example, but be allowed, under proper limitations, to mix in good society abroad, where they can learn by experience and observation. Social intercourse between the different sexes, on safe and well-regulated principles, is of great use in forming agreeable manners. And let no one suppose that it is of small consequence to be able to pass pleasantly in every sort of respectable society into which we may be thrown by the duties and changes of life; it is an accomplishment, not only convenient for them who possess it, but which imparts pleasure to others.

The most important of all parental duties, and the last one assigned to this article, is, training their children for happiness in the life to come, by a genuine religious education, and imploring the blessing of God upon the effort. "And these words which I command thee this day shall be in thine heart: and thou shalt teach them diligently unto thy children, and shalt talk of them when thou sittest in thy house, and when thou walkest by the way, and when thou liest down, and when thou risest up." From this authority it appears that the chief qualification for teaching our children the words and commands of God, is to have them written upon our own hearts, or to be experimentally religious ourselves; and then they are to be enforced by example, as well as precept, talking of them in doors and out, morning and evening. The Bible abounds with similar injunctions. Solomon says, "Train up a child in the way he should go: and when he is old, he will not depart from it." This is found to hold good, at least as a general rule, and might universally, if properly complied with. The principles of an early religious education are scarcely ever effaced from the mind; and though they may be violated for a time, amidst the follies of youth, they are almost certain to regain the ascendency afterward. The good seed sown in the heart of little children, by the pious mother, may lie dormant a long time, then vegetate under the showers of grace, and the genial rays of the Sun of righteousness, and produce fruit unto holiness, and the end be everlasting life. But the responsibility is not all with the mother; for Paul says, "And, ye fathers, provoke not your children to wrath: but bring them up in the nurture and admonition of the Lord."

The means afforded us for the religious instruction of our children are various. One of the best of all is, reading daily select portions of holy Scripture to them, for their special benefit, accompanied with familiar explanations, adapted to their age and capacity. By this means they may become so interested, that what Paul said to Timothy might truly be said to many of them: "From a child thou hast known the holy Scriptures, which are able to make thee wise unto salvation through faith which is in Christ Jesus." Family worship, too, should be performed, at such times, and under such circumstances, that the children may be present, and in such manner as to interest them. They should be learned short, easy forms of prayer, to repeat morning and evening, till they become old enough, and sufficiently advanced in knowledge, to express their wants in their own words. Their parents should lead them to the closet, unite with them in private devotion, and so live daily as to say by their example, follow us as we follow Christ. They should be taken to meetings for social worship, and regularly to hear the Gospel preached, from the time they can understand the nature and design of public worship. Moreover, they should be thoroughly taught the Scripture catechism at home, and in the meeting of catechumen by the minister of Christ. They should likewise be sent regularly to the Sabbath school, where they may derive a vast amount of mental, moral, and religious instruction, which will greatly aid in the formation of sound principles, for the regulation of their conduct in after life. And, when their years and attainments shall have prepared them for it, they should be thoroughly trained in Bible classes, by competent teachers, conducted on such principles as will call their knowledge of the holy Scriptures into requisition, and afford exercise for their own judgment in the application of it. Now, all this may be done without interfering materially with their daily labor, or their regular school education; and it will be worth more to them, both in time and eternity, than all the rest of their literary attainments.

In the work of religious training there are formidable

difficulties. The greatest of these, and the one which lies at the foundation of all the rest, is that inherent depravity common to all mankind, and which develops itself at a very early period of life. Solomon says, "Foolishness is bound up in the heart of a child." This foolishness, or sinful nature, grows with his growth, and strengthens with his strength, and, unless counteracted by gracious influence, leads to innumerable personal transgressions, and ends in perdition. Another difficulty arises from the influence of vicious examples. This indicates clearly the necessity of keeping our children out of bad company. If our sons are allowed to mingle with the street rabble, attend horse-races, and resort to other places of dissipation and corruption, and if our daughters are suffered to attend balls, theaters, and other sinful amusements, all our efforts to benefit them, by a religious education, will be useless. A few days of indulgence in such folly would destroy all the fruit of our care and toil for many long years: "Be not deceived: evil communications corrupt good manners." I entreat all parents, as they love their children, and desire their present and everlasting welfare, to keep them away from all such evil associations, and, resisting every opposing influence with decision and firmness, persevere, to the end of life, in striving to lead them in the path of duty and safety. The obstacles in the way of this work, though numerous and discouraging, are not insurmountable. The Lord said, by the prophet Ezekiel, "Behold, all souls are mine; as the soul of the father, so also the soul of the son is mine." They are alike redeemed by the death of Christ, and children and parents may be saved together. The children may be indifferent on the subject now, but the Holy Spirit can soon awaken them to a proper sense of their danger. They are depraved in heart, but the blood of Jesus is sufficient to cleanse from all unrighteousness: they may have to contend with hardness and unbelief, as we did, but God will be faithful to his promise, to take away the heart of stone, and give a heart of flesh. To use the means belongs to us, yet none but God can convert and save; therefore, we should be instant in prayer for his blessing upon our labor of love. Let the father and mother unite in a perpetual covenant to pray for their children, and take encouragement from the sure promise of the Savior: "Again I say unto you, that if two of you shall agree on earth, as touching any thing that they shall ask, it shall be done for them of my Father which is in heaven." Never cease to plead this promise; and though you may see no fruit for a time, be not discouraged. The Lord will hear and answer in mercy. If your children be not saved while you live, they may be after you shall have gone to rest. Many cases might be adduced, and some of them within our own knowledge, to show that the prayers of pious parents have been answered in blessings upon their children, after those parents had gone to heaven. Indeed, it would be difficult for those whose father and mother lived and died praying for them, to shake off their solemn convictions, and resist the powerful motives to a life of piety set before them. For a long time Jacob supposed that his son was dead: who can imagine his joy on hearing, "Joseph is yet alive!" Yet what was his joy, compared with that of Christian parents, who, in answer to their prayers, after all their painful solicitude, find their sons and daughters in heaven!

THE DUTY OF FASTING.

THAT fasting is enjoined in the Bible as a religious duty, will scarcely be questioned by any who have carefully examined the subject. Still, there may be much difference of opinion among pious people as to what that duty is; by what authority it is made obligatory; how, and on what occasions, it should be observed; and what are its beneficial results. To arrive at safe conclusions on all these points, reference must be had to the law and to the testimony. In such questions, mere human authority is not sufficient: to settle them requires Scriptural precept and divine sanction. Whoever presumes to set up his own judgment in opposition to the sacred record, or to teach what it does not warrant, as essential to salvation, should not be regarded as a safe instructor of those who wish to find the path of life. "If any man speak, let him speak as the oracles of God."

The point of inquiry which requires attention first of all, is, What is fasting, in the sense of the inspired authors? On this subject various opinions have been, and still are, entertained and propagated; and among them is the singular one, that fasting is simply "refraining from sin." To refrain from sinning is in itself certainly right and commendable; but to insist on that as the sense of the term fasting, involves at least one serious difficulty. Fasting is not, and can not be practiced daily and continuously; it is only occasional; and if to fast is to refrain from sin, then we are required to refrain from sin only on fast-days, which would imply that on all other days we may sin with impunity; whereas the Bible, which enjoins fasting, forbids sin at all times and in every place, and that under fearful penalty. "Awake to righteousness and sin not;" "The wages of sin is death;" "The soul that sins shall die." It is declared of the Lord Jesus Christ, on the occasion of his temptation in the wilderness, "When he had fasted forty days and forty nights, he was afterward an hungered." Now, will any one presume to say that he, after abstaining from sin forty days, hungered for it? I trust not; and yet, to be consistent, all who contend that fasting is simply refraining from sin, would have to admit the blasphemous conclusion.

Another view of the subject, and one entertained by many who regard themselves as the only true Church of Christ, is, that fasting is merely a change in the manner of living, from the use of certain articles of food to the use of others. While their conscience, acting in the light of their creed, or, more properly, in the darkness of it, will not allow them, on any consideration, to eat meat during certain days of the week, and certain weeks of the year, it does strangely allow them, on the same days and weeks, to eat fish, butter, eggs, vegetables, fruits, and most luxuries of the country. It is really amusing to read over a printed bill of sumptuous fare, made out by a prelate who assumes to have the consciences of the people in his own keeping, for a forty days' fast. Serious as the subject is, to read of a "fish-dinner" on fast-day is enough to excite a smile. To us this appears to be a singular kind of fasting—one which requires but little sacrifice of taste or self-denial, and which need not diminish the strength or flesh of those who practice it, however long the fast may be protracted. Daniel and his fellow-captives, while receiving their court education, were sustained only on pulse and water; and yet, at the period of examination, "their countenances appeared fairer and fatter in flesh than all the children which did eat the portion of the king's meat" and drank of his "wine." And why should not any healthy individual gain both flesh and strength during "Lent," with all its various substantials and luxuries? Such feasting may justly be regarded as a burlesque on the Christian duty of fasting. How different was the case with the devoted Psalmist, when he said, "My knees are weak through fasting; and my flesh faileth of fatness," Psa. cix, 24.

To fast, in the proper sense of the term, is to abstain entirely from food and drink of every kind for a given time—the period of such abstinence to be determined by the circumstances of the individual, and the nature of the occasion which moves him to observe it. The king of Nineveh, under just apprehension of the judgments of the Almighty, proclaimed a general fast, saying, "Let neither man nor beast, herd nor flock, taste any thing: let them not feed, nor drink water," Jonah iii, 7. Saul, afterward Paul, when stricken down by the power of God, and brought under sore conviction of sin, "was three days without sight, and neither did eat nor drink," Acts ix, 9. Many other facts similar to these might be recited, going to prove, beyond all reasonable doubt, that fasting, in the Scriptural sense of the term, is neither refraining occasionally from sin, nor a mere change of diet, but entire abstinence from all temporal refreshments, of every sort, for a given time.

Having settled the meaning of the term fasting—very briefly, it is true, but, as I trust, satisfactorily, at least to such as believe the Bible—the next point which claims attention is the authority for observing this duty as above explained.

This authority, to be satisfactory, must be clear and unequivocal, and from a source entitled to universal respect. Such authority, I maintain, is abundantly furnished in the holy Scriptures, in the recorded examples of inspired religious teachers, and in plain and obvious precept. In regard to the first, it is in place to observe that the example of uninspired persons, however pious, is not good authority; and, therefore, may be imitated or not, according to our own conviction of duty, without involving the sin of omission. Uninspired men are as liable to be mistaken as ourselves. Perhaps most of the truly pious, from Moses to the present day, have fasted, and their example might be profitably imitated; but of itself it imposes no obligation upon us. But with inspired men the case is different. When a man was called of God to be a prophet, or an apostle, and was inspired by the Holy Ghost, he became an infallible teacher of religious doctrine, experience, and practice; and whatever duty he enforced by example, as an inspired man, was obligatory upon others, as far as applicable to their cases. The holy prophets of the Old Testament, and the holy apostles of the New Testament were all inspired men; as such they fasted, and did it understandingly, and thereby settled the practice of fasting as a duty in the Church, Jewish and Christian. They were not deluded fanatics, but holy men of God, speaking and acting as they were moved by the Holy Ghost; and, consequently, their example rested upon others in this respect, and now rests upon us, with the force of religious obligation.

In addition to the example of inspired men on the subject of fasting as a religious duty, we have the authority of direct Divine precept. That God required the Jews to fast on the day of expiation, and on other occasions, will probably be admitted by all careful Bible readers; and hence I shall not occupy the room which would be requisite for inserting the proofs. And it is equally clear that our Lord and his apostles taught the Christians to fast, both by precept and example, not at regularly-recurring periods, but as an occasional duty. Christ gave his disciples special directions how to perform the duty of fasting, and, therefore, by fair inference, gave it his sanction—as it can not be presumed that he would give them direction how to perform an act which was either unlawful or useless. The certain proof that our Savior did give such direction is found in sundry places, and, among others, in Matt. vi, 16–18, which I shall have occasion to cite hereafter.

Again: when interrogated by the disciples of John Baptist, why they and the Pharisees fasted frequently, while his disciples fasted not, "Jesus said unto them, Can the children of the bride-chamber mourn, as long as the bridegroom is with them? but the days will come when the bridegroom shall be taken from them, and then shall they fast," Matt. ix, 15. Here our Lord compares the season of his personal intercourse with his disciples to a festival at or after a wedding; which, being a time of feasting and rejoicing, was not a proper time for fasting; and hence it was not required of them at that time. But, alluding to the time when his personal intercourse with them on earth should cease, and to all after-times of conflict and trouble, he said, "Then shall they fast." Now, this last phrase, "Then shall they fast," is not to be regarded as a mere prophecy that such an event should transpire, but as an expressed sanction of it, and an assurance that it would be done; as if he had said, "Though I do not wish my disciples to fast while I am personally with them, I do approve of their fasting after I shall have been taken from them."

Moreover, our Lord taught that there were some evil spirits in man which could not be dislodged without fasting; saying, "This kind can come forth by nothing but by prayer and fasting." Of course, when other means have been tried without success, that of adding fasting to prayer should not be neglected: it comes in as the last resort. And what our Savior taught his disciples respecting the duty of fasting by word, he enforced by his own example, only with more severity on himself than they were capable of enduring: "When he had fasted forty days and forty nights, he was afterward an hungered." Now, in view of all these recorded facts—that our Lord Jesus Christ, who was "God manifest in the flesh," and "spake as man never spake," prescribed the manner of fasting, authorized his disciples to fast after he should be taken from them, and added his own personal example to enforce his teaching—it is difficult to account for the hesitancy of some people in admitting that fasting is a Christian duty, and their slowness of heart to believe it is required of them. It was not so with the apostles.

That the inspired apostles, who were eye and ear-witnesses of what Christ taught and did, regarded fasting as an important part of Christian duty, is certain from the following facts: 1. They practiced it themselves, "in all things approving themselves as the ministers of God, in much patience, in afflictions, in necessities, in distresses, in stripes, in imprisonments, in tumults, in labors, in watchings, in fastings," 2 Cor. vi, 4, 5. 2. They enjoined fasting on others, saying to husbands and wives, "Give yourselves to fasting and prayer," 1 Cor. vii, 5. And what inspired apostles practiced themselves, and required private Church members to practice, must certainly be regarded as a Christian duty by all who take the holy Scriptures for the rule of their faith and conduct.

I shall next turn my attention to the occasions of fasting. And here let it be premised, that stated fasts, at regularly-recurring periods, such as were practiced by Pharisees, and are still required by Papists, were not appointed, commanded, or practiced by our Lord or his apostles. The Pharisees fasted "twice in the week" statedly, on certain days of the week; but all the authority they had for doing so was the "tradition of the elders," which, Christ declared, "made void the commandments of God." The Papists pretend to observe, as regular fasts, certain days of the week and certain weeks of the year; but all the authority they have for that practice is found in the tradition of the fathers, the decrees of councils, the bulls of popes, and the proclamations of bishops—all which savors strongly of the work of supererogation, and is, therefore, not only without any Divine sanction, but is contrary to the Divine will, as revealed in the new covenant.

While considering this point, it is proper to remark, that, in the ecclesiastical polity of Methodism, "fasting, or abstinence," is included among the "general rules," but without designating any definite or stated time of fasting. Again: among the duties of a preacher in charge is the following: "He shall take care that a fast be held, in every society in his circuit, on the Friday preceding every quarterly meeting." The time of the quarterly meeting, however, is not regulated by the moon's phases, nor by a particular Sabbath in the month, nor any thing of the kind; but is appointed from quarter to quarter, with reference to convenience and utility, and the quarterly fast goes with it. All I claim for this rule is, that it is a "prudential regulation," not possessing the force of Divine law. As such, I approve and defend it, as one calculated to promote uniformity, and secure general attention on the part of Church members. The fast was appointed on Friday, because the framers of the rule intended the quarterly meeting to follow on Saturday and Sabbath—not because the New Testament Scriptures designate any particular day of the week as a day of fasting. It is likewise probable that our fathers fixed on Friday, in common with other evangelical Churches, as being suitable, because it was understood to be the day of the week on which our Savior suffered. All these considerations were proper in establishing a prudential regulation. I maintain that in regard to the duty of fasting, as well as in regard to other duties enjoined in the word of God, some things are left to be determined by circumstances. For example, Christ said to his ministers, "Go ye into all the world, and preach the Gospel to every creature;" but did not say the Gospel should be preached on the first day, or some other day of the week—that it should be preached in the forenoon, afternoon, or evening; nor that it should be preached in a house called a church, or some other building, or in the open air; but simply that it should be preached in all the world, and to every creature, leaving times and places to be settled according to circumstances. In like manner, Christians are required in the New Testament to fast; but it is not there determined whether they shall fast on Friday, Monday, or some other day of the week; nor yet that they shall fast yearly, quarterly, monthly, or weekly; but they are left to regulate their times of fasting as circumstances may render most proper. Fasting, therefore, is to be regarded as an occasional duty, to be practiced from time to time, as the necessities and interests of communities and individuals may require. And if it should be objected by any, that this view of the subject tends to weaken the obligation to fast, let all such objectors remember, that the obligation to fast exists in the word of God, and not in the time designated by Church authorities for discharging that obligation. The objection will be further obviated by carefully weighing what now follows respecting the occasions of fasting, which may and doubtless do come up in the history of nations and individuals.

A time of public calamity and general distress, in progress or in prospect, is a proper occasion for a general fast. When the deceitful and intriguing Haman had procured a decree from King Ahasuerus, that all the Jews in his extended provinces should be massacred on a given day, Mordecai the Jew communicated the sad intelligence to Queen Esther, who was also a Jewess, and she appointed a three days' fast to be solemnly kept by herself, her maidens, Mordecai, and their countrymen, as far as they could give notice, which by God's blessing proved successful in averting the fearful calamity. Perhaps we, as a nation, are in no immediate or apparent danger of a general massacre, by any organized or legalized system of persecution, at present, whatever may transpire hereafter. Still, we are expecting soon, and have good reason to expect, a return of that dreadful scourge of nations, the Indian cholera, in the epidemic form, which, if unrestrained by Providential interference, may sweep millions of this generation, and even hundreds of thousands of our own countrymen, from the face of the earth into the world of spirits. In anticipation of so terrible a visitation in our land, a day of general humiliation, fasting, and supplication would be highly proper. There could not be any occasion more suitable than that for a national fast; and as no human foresight can ascertain who shall be marked as its victims, every individual should consider himself or herself as personally and deeply interested; for, when the sweeping pestilence shall break upon us, it will probably, as on a former occasion, reach all classes of the community. In 1832–33, though distinguished medical men had prophesied that none but the dissipated, lewd, and filthy had any thing to fear from cholera, some of the most wealthy merchants, profound scholars, brilliant statesmen, skillful physicians, and godly ministers, as well as steady farmers and sober mechanics, with their wives and children, were seen suddenly to fall under its deadly grasp. So it may be again. Let all see to it that their peace be made with God, and to this end let them fast and pray, and use all the appointed means.

There have been, and probably will be, many local and private events of an afflictive kind which have formed, and will form, sufficient occasions for sectional and private fasts. The wicked city of Nineveh fasted, and thereby escaped general destruction; and every wicked city has abundant reason to adopt the same measure, lest it be destroyed by whirlwind, earthquake, flood, or flame. "Now consider this, ye that forget God, lest I tear you in pieces, and there be none to deliver," is as worthy of being regarded now, as it was when first proclaimed in the days of the Psalmist; for the author of that solemn warning is unchangeable. Again: when King David's child was stricken with mortal sickness, he betook himself to fasting, lay all night upon the ground, refusing to receive any nourishment, or to be raised up by his servants, or comforted by his friends, till informed the child was dead. Then he arose from the earth, washed himself, changed his raiment, worshiped in the Temple, ate bread, and appeared again among his friends. "And he said, While the child was yet alive, I fasted and wept: for I said, Who can tell whether God will be gracious to me, that the child may live? But now he is dead, wherefore should I fast? Can I bring him back again? I shall go to him, but he shall not return to me," 2 Samuel xii, 22, 23. Though the king lost his son, no doubt he felt better satisfied under his loss than he would have done had he neglected his duty. With this illustrious example before us, it would be safe and proper, while laboring under a sore visitation of family affliction, to betake ourselves to prayer and fasting, that God might avert or mitigate the evil, and sustain us through it.

Every man has a personal reason for fasting, in his own natural depravity and practical sinfulness, calling for deep, continuous humiliation before God. Have we sinned grievously? Does the guilt thereof rest heavily upon us? And, after much penitence and prayer, does our conscience still trouble and make us afraid? Then we should add fasting, that we may be more deeply humbled in the sight of Heaven, still pleading the atonement of our dying, risen, ascended, and interceding Savior, till we obtain the evidence of pardoning and renewing grace. Again: if inbred sin remain and trouble us, after we have prayed long and much for purity of heart, there is reason to fear that it is of a kind that "cometh not forth but by prayer and fasting"—which remedy should be applied in earnest: for though there is no merit in fasting, more than in any other means of grace, God's method of salvation is to bless in the use, and not in the neglect, of the means; and in extreme cases no one of them should be omitted—all should be diligently used; and having used all the means, we should then trust in Christ only for the end; for when we have done all we can, we are still unprofitable servants, having only done our duty. Whoever pursues this course, will soon rejoice in possession of a present, free, and full salvation: it has been tried in thousands of cases, and always with success.

Another very important point involved in this subject is the manner of fasting. It should be done in moderation, not carried to excess—not so as to injure health, much less to endanger life. There are some individuals, in a debilitated state from recent affliction, whose health would not admit of their fasting for the time being; and others, who have general poor health and feeble constitutions, who, at best, can scarcely receive nourishment sufficient to sustain them in active life: these should not impose upon themselves frequent nor rigorous fasts. Indeed, it is very questionable whether such individuals should fast at all, as it might prove injurious, if not fatal. Let it be remembered, God does not require murder for sacrifice. Still there is danger of extremes, both ways; and no doubt there are many more who fast too little, than there are who fast too much. The inconvenience suffered by invalids from fasting, is no excuse for us who are healthy to neglect it.

Again: we should not aim at miracles in the performance of this duty; the days of miracles have passed away. Moses and Elijah as types, and our Savior as the antitype, each fasted forty days; but those fasts were all miraculous, and therefore do not form any rule of practice for us. No mere human being could live half of that time without some nourishment, unless there should be an immediate and continuous exercise of the power of God in his case, which is not to be presumed on. Some fanatics have exercised that presumption, and have lost their lives in consequence—thereby leaving a solemn warning to all others against yielding to such madness. Of this description of superstitious devotees, were some members of a modern sect called Halcyons, which flourished in the western country about the close of the eighteenth century. They never became numerous, and are now extinct, as might have been expected.

Fasting should not be attended with any outward show of sadness, such as neglect of person, voluntary humility, or self-inflicted abuse of any kind. If a man should be seen during his fast sitting on the ground, with rent garments, long beard, and disheveled hair, sprinkling ashes upon himself, and setting up a doleful howl or hideous wail toward heaven, he might excite pity, but not admiration; he would be regarded as a deranged man, or a hopeless victim of fanaticism in its worst form. How signally the Savior of man rebuked such conduct: "When ye fast, be not, as the hypocrites, of a sad countenance: for they disfigure their faces, that they may appear unto men to fast. Verily, I say unto you, they have their reward. But thou, when thou fastest, anoint thine head, and wash thy face; that thou appear not unto men to fast, but unto thy Father, which is in secret: and thy Father, which seeth in secret, shall reward thee openly," Matt. vi, 16, 17, 18. From this authority it appears plainly that a Christian, on his fast-day, avoiding all false show of piety and all unworthy motives, should shave and wash himself, adjust his hair, put on clean apparel, and, acting as in the sight of God, maintain the dignity of a rational, accountable being. Such are the instructions of Him from whose authority there is no appeal.

Much light is shed upon this point of my subject—the manner of fasting—by the fifty-eighth chapter of the prophet Isaiah. The Jews murmured because their fast was not accepted of the Almighty: "Wherefore have we fasted, say they, and thou seest not? Wherefore have we afflicted our soul, and thou takest no knowledge?" These were presumptuous interrogatories, and God answered by reproving those who put them: "Behold, in the day of your fast ye find pleasure, and exact all your labors." What folly, to set apart a day for fasting, and then spend it as a mere holiday in worldly amusements, or in worldly business! Can a man pray and fast, and at the same time sport and feast? Can he afflict his soul, and mourn over his sins, and at the same time mingle jovially with the ungodly in a ball-room or theater? Can he employ his fast-day in lucrative business? Can he scheme and calculate, clamor and drive his hands to make money, and yet expect God to accept his devotions? Certainly not. But those complainers did even worse: "Behold, ye fast for strife and debate, and to smite with the fist of wickedness"—turning the solemn occasion into a scene of wrangling and violence, or perhaps praying for the death of enemies in war. No marvel that the interdict should follow, "Ye shall not fast as ye do this day, to make your voice to be heard on high." Having administered this wholesome reproof, the Lord further exposes their hypocritical pretensions, by asking, "Is it such a fast that I have chosen?—a day for a man to afflict his soul? Is it to bow down his head as a bulrush, and to spread sackcloth and ashes under him? Wilt thou call this a fast, and an acceptable day to the Lord?" No, verily. After exposing all these abuses, the Lord explains in detail the kind of fast which he would accept; saying, "Is not this the fast that I have chosen? to loose the bands of wickedness, to undo the heavy burdens, and let the oppressed go free, and that ye break every yoke? Is it not to deal thy bread to the hungry, and that thou bring the poor that are cast out to thy house? When thou seest the naked, that thou cover him; and that thou hide not thyself from thine own flesh?" From this more forcible presentation of the subject, it appears clearly that the fast which God approves, and has promised to bless, is attended with works of penitence, justice, and benevolence, as well as piety. We must loose the bands of wickedness, or repent of all our sins; we must undo the heavy burdens, whether inflicted by heartless creditors, or unjust task-masters, and let the oppressed go free from under the galling yoke of bondage. Oppression of our fellow-creatures is unjust and criminal in the sight of God, whether inflicted by cruel husbands, cruel parents, or cruel masters; whether inflicted by the assumed tyranny of political despots, or by that inhuman traffic—the slave-trade; and it is worse than useless for any one guilty of such oppression and cruelty to fast or pray, till he is fully determined to forsake the evil of his ways. The fast which God has chosen for us requires also works of charity, dealing bread to the hungry—at least as much as is saved by fasting—sheltering the homeless and friendless, and covering the naked with garments, so that the blessing of him who is ready to perish may come upon us. In a word, Christians should keep their fast-days as strictly as they are required to keep their Sabbaths, refraining from all sinful pleasures, and from all temporal business, except works of necessity and works of charity, and devote themselves to God in prayer and supplication, as well as in watchings and fasting.

The last general point to be considered is the beneficial

effects of fasting. They who practice the duty of fasting properly, as above explained, derive personal benefits thereby. It aids in subduing the natural enmity of the heart, mortifying the deeds of the flesh, of the carnal mind, that our souls may live; it cultivates humility, by showing us our depravity, unworthiness, and helplessness; it inspires us with gratitude for the mercies of God, so bountifully and constantly bestowed upon us. As we can scarcely appreciate general good health till we have lost it, so we can not properly estimate the value of our daily bread, and return suitable gratitude to God for it, till deprived of it long enough to feel the gnawing pains of hunger.

There are likewise relative benefits to be derived from a proper performance of the duty of fasting, or benefits accruing to others besides those engaged in it, on the same principle whereby one individual is benefited by the prayers of another. While Cornelius fasted and prayed, the Gospel was sent to the Gentiles, who knew nothing of the deep agony of his heart for them, the result of which was glorious. When King Darius had been insnared by Daniel's persecutors to sign an unchangeable decree, consigning him to the lions' den, and found that he could not prevail with his officers to have it reversed, so as to save Daniel, though he labored with them till the going down of the sun, he "was sore displeased with himself." It was with deep, heart-felt reluctance that he had the fearful sentence executed, but not without some hope that Daniel's God would deliver him. "Then the king went to his palace, and passed the night fasting: neither were instruments of music brought before him: and his sleep went from him." Early next morning the king was at the lions' den, and cried, "O Daniel, servant of the living God, is thy God, whom thou servest continually, able to deliver thee from the lions?" Who can imagine the joy which thrilled the heart of that monarch, when Daniel responded: "O king, live forever. My God hath sent his angel, and hath shut the lions' mouths, that they have not hurt me!" Thus, while wicked courtiers reveled over the death of the good man, as they presumed, their afflicted sovereign fasted and prayed for his deliverance; and God, who was for him, proved greater than all that were against him. Great encouragement is here afforded to the children of God, to fast and pray for the deliverance of their pious friends in the day of persecution and peril; and even for such as are in danger of falling into the hands of the tormentors, worse than hungry, ferocious lions, that they may be spared, awakened, and saved.

The beneficial results of fasting, in many cases, have been general, extending to whole communities. While Esther, and Mordecai, and their servants and maidens fasted, enlargement arose to the Jews, and large multitudes of men, women, and children were rescued from cruel massacre. The prophet Jonah was sent, by Divine appointment, to make proclamation, "Yet forty days, and Nineveh shall be overthrown." But the people, moved by Jonah's preaching, betook themselves to a rigorous fast. "And God saw their works, that they turned from their evil way; and God repented of the evil that he had said that he would do unto them; and he did it not." They changed their manner of life, and he changed his manner of dealing with them. Had they persisted in their wickedness forty days, he would have destroyed them; but they repented, and God relented.

In concluding this article, I take occasion to remark, that we, as a people, in these United States, have much reason to be interested in the subject under consideration. As a nation, though, perhaps, no worse than others, our sins are numerous and great. Profanity, disregard of the holy Sabbath, drunkenness, lewdness, fraud, and oppression exist to an alarming extent. Party political measures are often corrupt, and, sometimes, marked with violence—threatening even the disruption of our Union. The political press is prostituted to demagogism and slander, as a general thing, catering to the worst passions of men, and to party intrigue, instead of supporting the country and its noble institutions. Men in high places, who should be examples of virtue and piety, are too commonly degraded libertines. Even our Churches are too much conformed to the world, and too much involved in bitter controversy among themselves, when they have need to concentrate their united energy against the powers of infidelity and sin. Some who are set as watchmen upon the walls of Zion, to sound a timely alarm, are fast asleep; and many who once knew the way of righteousness have turned aside from the holy commandments delivered to them, so that their last state is worse than the first. All these things, and many others, cry to Heaven against us for vengeance. The judgments of God are abroad on the earth—famine, war, and pestilence move in quick succession, sweeping away multitudes of the guilty inhabitants of this sin-polluted world into a fearful state of retribution. Surely, then, such as have access to the mercy-seat, and power with God in prayer, should fast and plead with him, that we perish not in our sins as a people, but live and prosper, proving to all the world that "righteousness exalteth a nation." We have much encouragement to return to the Lord by penitence, prayer, and fasting, for there is forgiveness with him, that he may be feared. And here again I earnestly renew the suggestion, that a national fast, in 1849, would be both opportune and salutary as anciently. "Therefore also now, saith the Lord, turn ye even to me with all your heart, and with fasting, and with weeping, and with mourning: and rend your heart, and not your garments, and turn unto the

Lord your God; for he is gracious and merciful, slow to anger, and of great kindness, and repenteth him of the evil," Joel ii, 12, 13.

FOR BETTER, FOR WORSE.

PARTNERSHIPS for mere purposes of business and gain, may be dissolved whenever the interest, convenience, or pleasure of the parties requires. But there is a partnership for life. It blends names and fortunes, reputations and destinies, for better, for worse, for richer, for poorer, in sickness and in health, through weal and woe, till the parties are separated by death. No other union bears any comparison to this in point of importance. If formed suitably and on proper principles, nothing earthly contributes so much to smooth the rugged path of life, and strew it with the flowers of peace; but if otherwise, nothing is so fruitful in discontent, poverty, and wretchedness. When a man of honorable principle and fine sensibility gets taken in by the false appearance of one, who turns out to be an idle slattern, or busybody in other people's matters—by one who becomes a by-word and a proverb among her neighbors, and is shunned by the friends of her husband, he deserves the sympathy of all who know him. But of all the sights of woe, save me from that of a worthy, intelligent, and agreeable Christian lady, bound for life to a rough, ill-natured, unprincipled husband, without character, without means of support, or industry to acquire it. And if to all this be added gross intemperance, and its kindred vices, the case becomes quite intolerable. Yet there is no remedy for these oppressive evils, bad as they are, but to let patience have its perfect work, till death brings her the desired relief.

It is often said, in connection with this subject, "There is no accounting for taste." Perhaps it is so in some cases, especially such as those above described. Yet I am not sure but some things connected with the choice of companions, and generally regarded as mysterious, may be traced out and explained on natural principles. One thing, at least, appears to me, from long-continued observation, to be pretty well established, namely: There is, both in men and women, a natural proneness to fall in love with those who form a contrast with themselves; and in nothing is this principle so strongly developed, as in the choice of companions for life. Examples: Large men generally select small wives, and small men large wives; and as it requires two to make a bargain, it would seem that small ladies admire large husbands, and large ladies admire small husbands. A man of dark complexion, black eyes and hair, with heavy, black mustaches, and goatee beard—resembling that of the loathsome animal after which it is called—generally selects a wife with pale blue, or light hazel eyes, light hair, and fair complexion. If the husband has a long, narrow face, the wife has a short or round one—if the husband has a curving face, and receding forehead, then you may expect to see a wife whose face is straight, if not dished. Ladies who have dark hair and eyes, and brunette skin, generally marry husbands with sandy hair, light eyes, and white complexion. The pale and ruddy, the feeble and robust, are, also, prone to meet. To these rules there are, of course, some exceptions. And yet they hold good so generally, that one practiced in observation upon them, has frequently pointed out, in a mixed assembly, a wife whom he never saw before, nor heard described, by being previously introduced to her husband, and pointed out a husband, in the same way, by being previously introduced to the wife. Should the reader still doubt the existence of any such principle as the love of contrast, as developed in the choice of companions, let him apply the rule in a hundred cases, as they come, before he decides.

One natural consequence of this system of choosing husbands and wives is, the children are often dissimilar in their appearance; and when that is the case, as a general rule, the sons inherit the features of the mother, and the daughters those of the father. Another consequence is, the race of man is preserved in a proper state of equilibrity, and his human identity easily maintained. From all which it might, perhaps, be safely inferred, that this love of contrast, the practical operation of which brings together all these extremes of large and small, long and short, athletic and feeble, swarthy and fair, is wisely implanted in us by the benign Creator as one of the laws of our nature, and if restricted in its exercise to mere physical considerations, would be both innocent and useful. It may, however, be indulged to an injurious extent, and, like all other gifts of Heaven, be abused. Perhaps the love of contrast may have some agency, or, at least, exert some remote influence, in bringing together, under the sanction of an indissoluble union, those whose natural dispositions, social habits, moral principles, and religious creeds, are not only variant, but conflicting. The reserved and the frank, the loquacious and the taciturn, the close and the liberal, the meek and the irritable, the industrious and the idle, the moralist and the libertine, are often united in the enduring relation of husband and wife, the probable effects of which can be more easily imagined than endured. There is, also, among those who are generally regarded as strictly religious, frequently observed a want of suitableness in their marriage connections—Pedobaptists and Immersionists, Calvinists and Arminians, Episcopalians and Independents, Methodists and Presbyterians, blended together in matrimonial bonds. That these may all be experimental and practical Christians, and on their way to heaven, is admitted. Still, they must suffer some inconvenience from such connections. In the important matter of attending public worship, for example, they have to separate, or alternately attend each other's Church; while the children, it would seem, scarcely know to which Church they pertain. It would probably be better to adjust this matter, and guard against these difficulties in the outset, by becoming members of the same Church, wherever it can be done without sacrifice of principle or a good conscience. And, after all, while the true friends of Jesus marry within the pales of his evangelical Churches, though the husband and wife may belong to different denominations, there is but little ground of objection. If they are disposed to suffer the inconvenience arising to themselves and families from such connections, so let it be. But when they intermarry with those who are known, or believed to be the enemies of Christ, there are serious grounds of objection in the estimation of all the truly wise and pious. And among those grounds of objection are the following, which, I trust, will be duly considered by those concerned.

The intermarriage of practical Christians with unawakened sinners is *inconsistent*. In the enterprise of leading a pious life to gain heaven, we need to avoid every possible hinderance, and avail ourselves of all the help within our reach. The way to heaven is strait and narrow. Why, then, should we form any connection with those whose influence would bewilder and turn us aside? When we commenced the Christian race, we professed to lay aside every weight. Why, then, should we stop and take up a heavy burden on the way? As Christians, we can make no compromise with sin, without abandoning our principles and our blood-bought liberty, and, therefore, should form no alliance with sinners, lest we be entangled again with the yoke of bondage. As the children of God, our heavenly Father speaks to us on this wise: "Wherefore, come out from among them, and be ye separate, saith the Lord, and touch not the unclean thing; and I will receive you, and will be a Father unto you, and ye shall be my sons and daughters, saith the Lord almighty." This we have professedly done, by separating from all worldly associates, uniting with the Church of Christ, and claiming the promise of adoption; and will we now abandon our Christian calling, reunite with the enemies of the cross, and retrace our steps to sin and death? I trust not. Our baptismal vow requires us to renounce the world, the flesh, and Satan, and obediently keep God's holy commandments. How, then, can a pious female, with this vow upon her, deliberately promise, at the marriage altar, to "obey" one whose governing principle of action is the carnal mind, which is enmity against God? How inconsistent! The thought is too absurd to be entertained for a moment. She should dash it from her, and have done with it forever.

The marriage of a practical Christian to an unawakened person is *inconvenient.* "How can two walk together, except they be agreed?" But a Christian and an infidel are agreed in nothing pertaining to the subject of religion. Their belief, their principle of action, their habits, pursuits, pleasures, purposes, are all not only different, but opposite. And here let it be observed, that every unawakened and impenitent sinner is, practically, an infidel, though he may not be so professedly. He, of course, sees no necessity for his wife to be habitually serious and pious, or for her to attend Church every Sabbath, much less for her being punctual to her social meetings, and cultivating the fellowship of the saints. So far from aiding her to walk in Christ as she has received him, he is a hinderance of the worst kind—worst, because of his relation to, and influence over her continually. If he occasionally accompany her to the house of God, it is, perhaps, only to furnish himself with an argument to influence her, in turn, to go with him to a ball, or theater, or on a Sabbath-day's excursion of pleasure, that she may disgrace her Christian profession, be censured by her religious friends, and finally weaned off from them altogether. If she wish to have their children consecrated to God, sent to Sabbath school, and brought up religiously, he will probably prefer sending them to a dancing school, or leading them to places of fashionable amusement and sinful pleasure. While she would teach them to pray, he learns them, by example, to neglect it; while she would teach them to read and love the Bible, he furnishes them with silly romance. In a word, while she aims to be religious, get to heaven, and take her family with her, he is traveling the way to perdition, and, by example, if not precept, doing what he can to draw his wife, children, and friends after him. Now, with such opposite views and feelings, pursuits and practices, to say the least, there must be great inconvenience arising to the religious party from a connection so intimate and enduring.

For a Christian lady to be united in marriage to an unawakened husband, must be *unfavorable to her happiness*. It must be so almost of necessity, by having her wishes crossed continually in that which is to her of the greatest moment. For example, as a practical Christian, she wishes her house to be a house of prayer, with an altar, on which shall be offered daily the sacrifice of prayer and praise—a house where the weekly Sabbath shall be strictly kept, and where her religious friends may freely resort, and, without embarrassment, hold pious converse for mutual profit and consolation. But the head of the family being irreligious, there is no family prayer, no proper observance of the Sabbath, no pleasant religious association, none of the songs of Zion; on the contrary, her dwelling is made a place of resort for the worldly-minded and impious, by whom her religion is not appreciated, and by whom the name of her blessed Savior, if used at all, is used irreverently. In some instances the unawakened husband becomes the opposer, ay, the persecutor of his pious wife, trying to block up her way at every step, and venting his indignation upon her pastor, and all others who extend to her either aid or sympathy. Certainly, a wife, under such circumstances, can have but little enjoyment, except what comes from anticipation of deliverance in the hour of death. Yet thousands of our pious young ladies, from year to year, are heedlessly forming such connections and becoming victims to such like troubles. It is time for others to pause and think before they take the fearful step. That a few such husbands get awakened, converted, and become agreeable companions, is not a sufficient warrant for taking the risk. Too many, by marrying sinners, with the hope of their becoming saints, have ruined their prospect of happiness for life.

The marriage of a Christian lady to an unawakened and impenitent sinner is not only inconsistent, inconvenient, and unfavorable to her happiness, but exceedingly *dangerous*. Every individual is more or less influenced by his or her immediate associates, especially by one so intimately associated as a bosom companion for life. That influence is always good or evil. But, inasmuch as the natural tendency of the human heart is to evil, the religious party is much more likely to be worsted than the irreligious is to be bettered, and especially so, if the irreligious party is head of the family, claiming the right to rule his own household. Where the husband and wife differ essentially in their views and professions, feelings and habits, there must be some compromise, or constant liability to unpleasant misunderstanding; and that compromise is very likely to be made at a sacrifice, on her part, of privileges important to her religious prosperity and enjoyment. Let all concerned look well to this point before they bring upon themselves, by improper marriage, any necessity of compromise. Trust not too much to promises of future reformation. Voluntary professions of friendship for the Church, and vows of future alliance with it, made by unconverted men, anxious to obtain its fair and pious daughters for wives, have often been forgotten or violated after marriage, when it was too late to correct the error of listening to them. The united wisdom of our Church on this subject, gathered from experience and extensive observation, is thus briefly expressed in her Discipline: "Many of our members have married with *unawakened* persons. This has produced bad effects; they have been either hindered for life, or have turned back to perdition." This is, undoubtedly, true in general. There may be a few exceptions, occasioned by the early conversion of the irreligious party, and only a few, compared with the whole number. Most of our pious young females who have married with the unawakened, hoping thereby to bring them over on the Lord's side, have been sadly disappointed. It is a dangerous experiment, try it who will. How can pious parents give their religious daughter, nay, how can she give herself to an enemy of the blessed Savior—that Savior whom she ought to love above every thing in earth or heaven? How can she, as a child of God, promise to obey one whose heart is alienated from his Creator, whose mind is enmity against him, and whose life is one continuous act of rebellion against his sacred laws? Let her consider the following Scripture authorities, and then let conscience answer.

My first reference is to the sixth chapter of Genesis: "And it came to pass, when men began to multiply on the face of the earth, and daughters were born unto them, that the sons of God saw the daughters of men that they were fair; and they took them wives of all which they chose." That intermarriage of the pious and impious not only occasioned the Divine threat, "My Spirit shall not always strive with man," but led to a state of society in which "the earth also was corrupt before God; and the earth was filled with violence. And God looked upon the earth, and behold, it was corrupt: for all flesh had corrupted his way upon the earth. And God said unto Noah, The end of all flesh is come before me; for the earth is filled with violence through them: and behold, I will destroy them with the earth." Again: the prophet Nehemiah, after much fasting and prayer, was sent to Jerusalem to reform certain evils, and, among others, that of improper marriages, saying, "In those days, also, saw I Jews that had married wives of Ashdod, of Ammon, and of Moab: and their children spake half in the speech of Ashdod, and could not speak in the Jews' language, but according to the language of each people. And I contended with them, and cursed them, and smote certain of them, and plucked off their hair, and made them swear by God, saying, Ye shall not give your daughters unto their sons, nor take their daughters unto your sons, or for yourselves." But the New Testament rule, which bears more directly upon us, is still more decisive, and is enforced by reasons sufficient to satisfy every reasonable inquirer after truth on this subject: "Be ye not unequally yoked together with unbelievers: for what fellowship hath righteousness with unrighteousness? and what communion hath light with darkness? and what concord hath Christ with Belial? or what part hath he that believeth with an infidel?" This law is so appropriate and pointed, that no comment could render it either plainer or stronger.

Finally: this article is not designed to dissuade mem bers of the Church from marrying with those out of the Church, provided they be firm believers in, and true friends of our holy Christianity, properly informed respecting its obligations, and earnestly seeking salvation, but to discourage them from forming any such connections with the enemies of Christ. There are two evils against which I would here caution all who would be truly pious, useful, and happy. One is, marrying with impenitent sinners; and the other is, refusing or neglecting to get married altogether, lest they should have to linger out a tedious old age in solitude, and die unlamented. There is certainly no fatal necessity for falling into either dilemma. All Christians who will, may avoid the reproach of swelling the list of old maids and bachelors, without committing themselves to the tender mercies of the wicked, which are cruel. There are many promising candidates for matrimony in the Church, and perhaps some out of it; and if some of these do not suit exactly, others will. In regard to this important enterprise, there is a proper medium between indecent haste, on one hand, and total indifference on the other. Shunning both extremes, proceed as a Christian should do, make it a subject of little conversation with man, but much prayer to God; for it involves greater interest than any other act of human life. Be careful and prudent, wait patiently the opening of Providence, till there is an opportunity to form a safe and happy union, then improve it. And when such union is formed, let the parties make the best of it, for the glory of God, the good of society, and their own happiness.

HUMAN LIFE.

This life is a compound of good and evil, pleasure and pain, toil and rest, hope and disappointment. On one hand, before we are ushered into being, a universe is prepared for our reception and accommodation, which affords us aliment pleasant to the taste, crystal streams to quench our thirst, the balmy air to inhale, the sun to light up the path of our earthly pilgrimage, the sweet melody of nature to enliven our feelings, and many kind friends to sympathize with us in all our troubles. On the other hand, the day we begin to live we begin to suffer, and, in one sense, to die. From infancy we are the subjects of pain, sickness, vexation, anguish, and revenge, till exhausted nature sinks beneath the accumulated weight of evils, or till some of the multiplied thousands of diseases to which humanity is heir, bring us down to the house appointed for all the living.

It is well for us that, when we commence the journey of life, we are ignorant of what lies before us; for if we could then foresee all the plans, failures, treacheries, and losses, which come up in after life, that sight would so overwhelm us, as to paralyze all our efforts, and blast all our prospects. By a wise arrangement of Providence, we know not what a day may bring forth. The history of life is learned as it transpires. In the mean time, Hope is buoyant, and, though often disappointed, it is among the last of all our friends that forsake us. When the winds of adversity howl around and threaten to overwhelm us, Hope reaches within the vail of safety, and, like the mariner's anchor, is the most useful in a storm. When poverty blights our earthly possessions, or disease invades our domestic circles, and is permitted to spread the winter of death around us, Hope, like a smiling evergreen, rears its lovely form before the vision of our desolate hearts. Thus we are borne onward through the changing scenes of mortal life.

In contemplating human life, there is, perhaps, nothing which strikes us more forcibly, or admonishes us more frequently, than the thought of its brevity. After breathing for half a century, then reviewing the past, life appears as a dream when one awakes from his night slumbers; and should fifty per cent. be yet added to the years of his life, he would be but a breathing mass of physical and mental weakness, tottering on the verge of time, ready to launch on the dark ocean of death. And is our race so nearly run? and are we so little concerned about the end of it? Again: how many millions of our race, who came into being after we did, have gone to the eternal state! Neither childhood, youth, nor manhood has any security against the shafts of death. Of the nine hundred millions of human beings now upon earth, as nearly as can be calculated, there is one birth and one death per second, on an average. And are the children of men going into eternity at the rate of sixty per minute, or three thousand six hundred per hour, or eighty-six thousand four hundred per day, or nine hundred millions per one generation of thirty years? and is not our time at hand? Though the patriarchs lived for centuries, the life of man has, ever since their day, been gradually growing shorter, as he increases in the luxuries of civilized society. In the days of the Psalmist, the years of his life were reduced to threescore and ten, and, perhaps, now would scarcely average thirty years. How truly it is said, "Man that is born of a woman, is few of days and full of trouble. He cometh forth like a flower, and is cut down: he fleeth, also, as a shadow, and continueth not!" In view of all which, it follows, to consider our latter end, so as to prepare for it, is wisdom, and to neglect it is madness. "Seek ye the Lord while he may be found," Isaiah lv, 6.

Dying is truly a solemn event, but living is still more so, when properly considered. For every act of life we are accountable to the great Author of our being; but for the pains of death we are not accountable. It is not in death, but while living, that we adopt our principles, form our characters, and take our coloring for eternity. When a man dies in the order of Providence, he is not held responsible for the time, place, or circumstances of his dissolution; but, let it be remembered, the King of kings and Lord of lords has said, "For every idle word that men shall speak, they shall give account thereof in the day of judgment." Every day that we live we are laying up a good foundation against the time to come, or treasuring up wrath against the day of wrath, and the revelation of the righteous judgments of God. Our business in this world, therefore, is to get well through and safe out of it; and whoever does this, shall have accomplished the great end of living; but whoever fails herein, will have occasion to say, with the celebrated statesman, when dying, "Remorse;" and it would be better for such a delinquent if he had never been born.

In regard to the termination of life, that which should concern us most is to be prepared for it, and for what lies beyond it. Whether we sink under slowly-wasting disease, or break with sickness in a day—whether we die at home, surrounded with family and friends, or abroad amidst strangers, or entirely alone, is not material; but every thing depends on dying in Christ, and being saved with the power of an endless life. A few years ago, a young man, in the city of New Orleans, whose friends had assembled to witness his departure from this world, and catch the last whispers that might fall from his quivering lips, on reviewing the countless dangers through which he had passed, and surveying the crown of life, then full in view, amidst the agonies of death, exclaimed, "I am safe!" That young man was a Christian, and knew whom he had believed. Jesus has vanquished death. All that trust in HIM, whenever and wherever they meet the pale horse and his rider, shall "conquer through the blood of the Lamb."

TIME.

TIME is a particular portion or part of duration, which, to us, may be present, past, or future. Time, as it refers to this world, is measured by days, years, and centuries; therefore, it had a beginning, and will have an end. Hence, the definition of one author: "Time is a fragment of eternity cut off at both ends." Moreover, it is a revealed truth, that "time is short." When time will end is unknown to man or angel, as our Lord Jesus Christ informs us: "Of that day and hour knoweth no man; no, not the angels of heaven, but my Father only." But the manner of its termination is revealed, and is truly awful: "And the angel which I saw stand upon the sea and upon the earth, lifted up his hand to heaven, and sware by him that liveth forever and ever, . . . that there should be time no longer." So soon as that solemn oath shall have been administered, the heavenly bodies will cease to revolve, the planetary system will be dissolved, day and night, seed-time and harvest, will no longer succeed each other, and time will be lost in the boundless ocean of eternity.

The portion of time allotted to each human being, in this world, is extremely limited: "For what is your life? It is even a vapor, that appeareth for a little time, and then vanisheth away." And yet the events arising out of this short existence are of infinite moment to us. Their effects will remain forever. The Psalmist exclaimed, "Behold, thou hast made my days as an handbreadth, and mine age is as nothing before thee." Yet in this particle of time, which, in comparison of eternity, "is as nothing," and in this only, may we prepare for a state of endless being. About one-third of the period of life is spent in sleep and needful recreation for health and comfort. A man who lives sixty years, passes about twenty years in a state of insensibility, and in receiving the daily refreshments requisite to sustain his feeble nature. Much time is consumed in journeying and resting, and much more in useless ceremony, and light, commonplace conversation. No small proportion of time is wasted in the pursuit of novelties, and feasting our eyes on vain curiosities. But to designate all the means employed in the consumption of time, would be at once tedious and difficult. Consequently, the remnant of time left for useful pursuits is comparatively small. How appropriate, then, is the admonition of Solomon: "Whatsoever thy hand findeth to do, do it with thy might; for there is no work, nor device, nor knowledge, nor wisdom, in the grave whither thou goest."

Time, in anticipation of any desired event, seems long; but viewed in the past, it appears very short. It also appears differently to young and aged people. A week appears to be as long to an individual when youthful, as a month does when he is far advanced in life. This fact, which has the sanction of general experience, speaks volumes respecting the value of time, and the importance of improving it while we may. Yet under the influence of restless anxiety respecting some future event, or the wasting influence of discontent in general, time hangs heavily on hand. Many who are thus affected resort to various means of killing time, when they should be studying how to improve it to the best advantage. A lost day can never be recalled. Each precious moment, as it transpires, is irrecoverably gone, and bears to eternity some good or evil report of the use we have made of it. Instead of contriving new schemes for wasting time, we should by all possible means strive to redeem it for useful purposes. To this end, we should be systematic and punctual in all the duties of life. "He who lives not by rule, lives not at all," said Wesley; that is, he lives to no valuable purpose. By saving time enough to read a few chapters of the Bible each day, we may read the whole of it in a year, which would be of more real value to us than the self-indulgence of a lifetime. If one-half of the time which is spent in idle and unprofitable conversation were devoted to secret prayer, it would add vastly to our felicity in this life, and to our preparation for the life to come. No one ever regretted, in a dying hour, that he had employed too much time in getting ready for that solemn scene, but thousands have lamented to the last that they had devoted so little time to the accomplishment of that all-important object. When a life that has been chiefly spent in the pursuit of folly is nearly exhausted, how precious does lost time then appear! If it could possibly be redeemed, no consideration would be thought too great for the ransom. He who once sought how to kill time by the hour, now pleads for it by the minute, but pleads in vain. The ungrateful mortal who has wasted a lifetime in sinning against his Maker, deserves not to have his probation extended. How gladly would he then recall the hours sacrificed on the altar of sensual gratification, and convert them into seasons of prayer, if it were possible; but time with him is closing up, and he is just going "where hope never comes," to render an account of himself to the Judge of all the earth. If a lost spirit could enjoy one Christian Sabbath, with the privilege of hearing the Gospel, and its overtures for repentance, faith, and salvation, as he often did in this world, who can imagine the estimate he would place upon it? How, then, should we, who live in a "day of merciful visitation," and in "a time accepted," appreciate our privileges, and improve the golden moments as they pass, remembering that, with us, "the end of all things is at hand."

THINK OF DEATH.

The things which now employ our thoughts and excite our feelings, will soon pass away, and the most of them will sink down into that insignificance which justly belongs to them. Amidst all the business and bustle of the world, the clamor of political strife, the heated fumes of popular elections, and the recriminations of intemperate religious controversy, men almost forget that they are mortal. But, in the mean time, a period is fast approaching, in the history of our existence, when all these exciting matters will avail us but little; we mean the hour of *death,* which will exhibit the world in its true colors as "vanity and vexation of spirit." How many that are figuring on the stage of life, will never see the accomplishment of the plans which now enlist all the energies of their minds! Before the frosts of autumn shall arrest the march of disease, they will go the way of all the earth. The particular individuals are not to be now designated; but none are certainly exempted. No order of talents or pursuit in life forms any barrier against the king of terrors. Providence is not dependent on any man to carry on his wise and powerful plans in Church or state. It would be equally difficult to name the disease by which they will be removed. Nor is this of much importance; the consequence in reference to our future destiny is the same, whether we sink under lingering affliction, or are

"Broke by sickness in a day."

The change itself, from time to eternity, is a solemn thing, apart from the immediate circumstances attending it; but this consideration alone seems to exert too little influence on the mind of man, and a wise, just, and merciful Providence sends his judgments abroad that the people may learn righteousness. The words of Christ, "be ye also ready," though always appropriate to sinners born to die, seem to gather additional strength from circumstances for the last few years, and now again by the scenes of mortality in our country. Apoplexies have been frequent; the work of cholera is short but sad; its victims lie down at night, unconscious of any special danger, and are awaked by the attack of the mortal foe, to sleep no more, except the sleep of death. Others rise in the morning to resume their daily employments, but are seized by fatal disease, and, after a few hours of agony, which we have often witnessed but can not describe, sink under the cold grasp of death, before the shades of night come on.

Such a state of things, if nothing else, should teach men to "consider their latter end," and examine the ground-works of their hope for a better world. A state of *preparation* for death implies much; which, however, is soon told. It presupposes a thorough conviction and hearty repentance of sin; he who does not understand this experimentally has not taken the first step in preparing to meet God. A second indispensable part of the preparation is, a clear sense of the Divine favor received through faith in the blood of Christ, accompanied by the direct witness of the Holy Spirit. Third, the present enjoyment of this evidence, to the exclusion of unbelief, the dominion of sin, of all angry or bitter feelings, the willful neglect of any known duty, and, in a word, whatever is contrary to the love of God and man. In such a state of mind as this there is solid peace, which is not broken by outward fightings or inward fears. The subject of it is attended by the Divine presence wherever he goes. When he retires at night to rest, it is with the testimony of a good conscience; and when he rises in the morning, he can say, "Thou art still with me." With him, "to live is Christ, and to die is gain." But what peace have they who neglect these things? All they have for time and eternity is in jeopardy every hour. They know not at night that they will ever see another day, or in the morning that they will see another night but the night of death. Are they content to live as they list, die without hope, and take a leap in the dark? We trust not. There is mercy for them. Christ is ready to receive them, and do it now: "This is the accepted time; behold, now is the day of salvation!" To-morrow may be too late forever.

PRIDE.

"A man's pride shall bring him low," PROVERBS XXIX, 23.

INORDINATE self-esteem, haughtiness of spirit, and insolent manners, constitute pride, and are sad proofs of the fall of man. Of all the features of the carnal mind, pride is one of the most prominent and unseemly. How contemptible all its subjects appear in the estimation of sober, rational minds! And yet how generally this principle exists in the hearts of men, whether in high life, low life, or the middle ranks of society. The ruler and subject, master and servant, rich and poor, scholar and savage, nominal Christian and open infidel, all betray the symptoms of this moral disease. Formal confession is needless. The evidence appears in the look of self-importance, the affected air, tone of voice, wag of the head, and general movements of the individual who is thus depraved. The case of such an individual excites more pity than indignation, in the mind of a humble Christian.

But what has man to be proud of in his best estate? Is it wealth? This is but trash for the fire to burn, the moth to eat, the thief to steal, or the swindler to riot on. Is it office? This was given to him, perhaps, by designing men, who only wish to use him as a tool to accomplish their own unrighteous designs, and which, at most, he can enjoy but a short time. May be it is knowledge. If so, it only argues that he is still ignorant of himself, of his own weakness. If it be apparel, it is only borrowed. It was worn before, by the stalk, silk-worm, or sheep. Should it be his person, let him remember he is an animal, who subsists here only for a short time on vegetables and the flesh of other animals, by the humiliating process of digestion; that he is a mortal, liable to disease and death, destined to the putrefaction of the grave. Or if he be proud of his character in the world, the principle is the same; while he feeds the flame of inordinate self-love, by fuel gathered from the good opinion of his fellows; yet, being a proud man, he is but a criminal, already sentenced to eternal infamy, and is on his way to execution: for "pride goeth before destruction, and a haughty spirit before a fall." In proof of this, there are fearful examples in the sacred records. King Nebuchadnezzar walked in his palace with a proud heart, and said, "Is not this great Babylon, that I have built for the house of the kingdom by the might of my power, and for the honor of my majesty? While the word was in the King's mouth, there fell a voice from heaven saying, . . . The kingdom is departed from thee. . . . The same hour was the thing fulfilled upon Nebuchadnezzar: and he was driven from men, and did eat grass as oxen, and his body was wet with the dew of heaven, till his hairs were grown like eagles' feathers, and his nails like birds' claws." His pride brought him low.

We will add one more example: "And upon a set day Herod, arrayed in royal apparel, sat upon his throne, and made an oration unto them. And the people gave a shout, saying, It is the voice of a god, and not of a man. And immediately an angel of the Lord smote him, because he gave not God the glory: and he was eaten of worms, and gave up the ghost."

Surely these expressions of Divine indignation against the proud of the earth, should induce men to humble themselves under the mighty hand of God, while Jesus pleads their cause, and the Holy Spirit strives with them, lest, by persisting in their haughtiness, they fall to rise no more forever.

HUMILITY.

Humility is freedom from pride; modesty; abasement. It is of gracious origin; belongs not to our fallen nature, but to "the new man," and is one of the fairest ornaments in the Christian character. The children of God are exhorted to put on "humbleness of mind," that it may cover them as a garment. He who does this, will be enabled not to "think of himself more highly than he ought to think, but to think soberly."

He will not estimate himself below what he knows to be the truth, much less abuse himself before his friends beyond what he deserves; for this is voluntary humility, and is mostly used by such as wish to give others an occasion to speak in their praise; whereas genuine humility is modest, unassuming, not disposed to intrude its subject into public notice unnecessarily.

Yet it does not supersede real, moral courage, or stand in the way of duty. If a man possess knowledge, humility does not require him to profess ignorance, but to avoid making pretensions that are uncalled for, or mere display. If he be saved from sin, through faith in Christ, it does not require him to profess present guilt, but to acknowledge his dependence; nor does it allow him to bury his talent and destroy his usefulness, lest he be thought forward.

But all this is reconcilable to great self-abasement—another part of humility—on account of our innate depravity and consequent weakness—a sense of past unfaithfulness and present unworthiness. He who recollects his sins with pleasure, though committed "ignorantly in unbelief," before he professed conversion, has just cause to doubt his change of heart; and he who can think of his sins committed after such profession, and not abhor himself and repent, as in dust and ashes, has good reason to doubt his present safety. Even the joys of religion do not remove a man's sense of his dependence and unworthiness; but they save him from despair, both in reference to present acceptance and future felicity.

To sum all up in a few words, a humble man is neither haughty nor mean, but modest and yet manly. He does not blow the trumpet of his own fame or disgrace, but fearlessly performs his duty with a proper sense of his unworthiness and entire dependence on God. Such a character will always secure respect from such as know him. He may take the lower seat at the feast, but his brethren will lead him to the highest one; the less distinction he seeks, the more will be conferred upon him.

But, better than all this, the Lord of all pronounces him blessed: "He that humbleth himself shall be exalted," for "God resisteth the proud, but giveth grace unto the humble."

INEQUALITY IN PROPERTY.

The right of private property is not incompatible with the sacred Scriptures, nor is there any wrong in efforts to acquire wealth on proper principles, and from proper motives; yet, unless he keep a single eye, there is much danger to the Christian, both in the pursuit and use of wealth. While "the hand of the diligent maketh rich," let him remember "riches profit not in the day of wrath." Therefore, "if riches increase, set not your heart upon them." Christ says, "A rich man shall hardly enter into the kingdom of heaven"—meaning, it is with difficulty he can be saved. But no one who does his duty as a Christian, will be cumbered with much wealth. Whatever he has more than sufficient to render himself, his family, and those immediately dependent on him comfortable, together with what he needs to keep up their support by carrying on a reasonable share of business, he is bound to give for the support of piety and benevolence. Those who feel any interest in this subject, as it is connected with their soul's salvation, are referred to Mr. Wesley's sermon on the right use of money, in which he reduces all to these simple rules: *Gain all you can, save all you can, and give all you can.* If these rules were observed by all, none would suffer for the substantials of life. It is probable our heavenly Father has provided just enough of temporal blessings to meet the real wants of his creatures, taking the world at large. To say he has provided less, would impeach his mercy; to say he had provided more, would be a poor compliment on his wisdom. And the general distribution of these blessings by his providence, among the nations of the earth, when every thing is taken into the account, will be found nearly equal. But there is a more special distribution of these things committed to us, who, as stewards of our Lord's goods, will have to give an account of the use or abuse of them. Now, a failure to use the blessings of heaven, as required by Gospel rules, is what produces the extremes of intemperate feasting on one hand, and starvation on the other. Some have not enough, because others have too much. Some have nothing, because others have a superabundance. If the rich man, who was clothed in purple and fine linen, and fared sumptuously every day, had divided his income liberally with the beggar which lay at his gate among the dogs of his flock, half clothed with rags, and desiring to be fed with the crumbs which fell from his table, would there not have been enough to relieve the reasonable wants of both? Let those among us who roll in affluence and revel in luxury, think of the hungry orphan who cries for bread, the discouraged widow who has no income, no employment, and sits weeping over the forlorn prospects of her helpless children; let them remember the afflicted poor, destitute of medicine, nourishment, and fuel, without a cent of money, or a kind friend to whom they dare make known their wants. He that giveth to the poor, lendeth to the Lord, with whom the principal is safe, and the interest certain.

COMPARATIVE HAPPINESS.

All men are, in some degree, capable of happiness. All desire and pursue it in some form or other. None obtain it unmixed in this life; and but few enjoy it to any great extent. Yet some enjoy it more than others. These propositions are so obviously true, that it would be lost labor to attempt any proof of them. But the admission of the last, that some men enjoy more felicity than others, would seem to justify an inquiry as to those circumstances in life which are the most favorable to that desirable object. On this subject I will venture a few thoughts in reference to the following points: Property, residence, intellect, employment, and future prospects.

As regards *property*, he enjoys most contentment, who, like Agur, has "neither poverty nor riches." Extreme indigence renders a man too dependent, and much wealth brings too many cares; while a medium condition is measurably relieved from both.

Residence. An extreme frontier, with all its hardships and privations, is not a comfortable home to most people. A crowded city, with its plagues, its confusion, and moral pollution, is equally uncomfortable. They are both extremes not to be desired. A good country neighborhood, or neat village, while it is free from the objections above named, affords all necessary comforts and conveniences, and is the more desirable place to those whose circumstances and business allow them to make a choice.

Intellect. If one whose intellectual powers are very limited, enjoys but little rational pleasure, he has, at least, this consolation: he cares for but little, and has but little to answer for. A master spirit, or mind, of the very first order, need not be envied by those less distinguished.

His responsibility, in exact proportion to his strength, is sufficiently fearful to mar his peace. But being always overrated, it is impossible to meet the expectation of all; and he suffers mortification because of the disappointment of friends and clamor of enemies. A man whose ability is just sufficient for practical usefulness in his profession, or calling, without any attractive brilliancy, suffers less mortification and enjoys more real satisfaction, than one much distinguished by the splendor of his talents. For though the latter may occasionally receive great applause, this only prepares him for greater chagrin when he makes the next failure in an attempt at popular display.

Employment. Men do not receive any increase of happiness from being placed on prominent ground and exposed to public scrutiny: on the contrary, if they possess due sensibility, it greatly disturbs their repose. You may pity the slave of the planter, and envy the man put in high authority, but they are both slaves, with this difference: one is subject to the caprice of a single master, while the other has to please, or incur the censure of many masters, of various opinions and conflicting interest. Nothing but a sense of duty, or a desire of doing good, can reconcile any sensible man of experience to accept any office, either in Church or state, if he consult his own personal enjoyment. If any seek promotion at the expense of domestic happiness, for the "loaves and fishes," they pay dearly for them. So far as employment is concerned, those men are the most happy who live privately on the fruit of their own labor. Farmers and mechanics need not envy cardinals or demagogues, kings or conquerors.

Future prospects.—Much of our present enjoyment depends on our future prospects. Present possessions, held in uncertainty, or with the expectation of losing them in a short time, afford but little satisfaction. Hence, though a man may have wealth, a comfortable home, popular talents, and honorable employment, yet, if these be held in unrighteousness, without a reasonable expectation of future bliss, they suffice him not. One thought of eternity destroys all his comfort. Whatever a man may be otherwise, if he is a sinner against God, he carries a hell in his own heart, and shudders at the thought of a general judgment, when he allows himself to think at all. But if a man possess heart-felt religion, it not only sweetens all the pleasures of this life, but assures him of future bliss. With the love of God shed abroad in his heart, he has "the promise of the life that now is, and of that which is to come." Without this, nothing can make him truly happy; with it, nothing can make him really miserable.

CONTENTMENT.

CONTENTMENT is a virtue, the value of which may be inferred, both from the felicity it affords, and the misery that ensues from the want of it.

Happiness does not consist so much in outward things, as in the state of the mind. To be contented is to be happy. "A contented mind is a continual feast." And this may be enjoyed under every variety of outward circumstances, provided the heart is right.

But restless discontent is characteristic of our fallen nature. Most of the human family are dissatisfied with their earthly allotment, with their location, their calling, and their respective circumstances. Every relation in life, every position in society, has its own peculiar difficulties. Each individual seems to imagine that his is the hardest case. All that can be truly inferred from this, however, is that he knows more of his own, and less of his neighbor's difficulties. Hence, the world is full of complaints. They come from high places and low places, from public life and from private life—all indicating a destitution of contentment.

But from this extreme of restlessness, some are removed to the other—of stoical indifference. They manifest a listless indifference to all the events of life, right or wrong, pleasant or unpleasant. Evils are coming, dangers are threatening, poverty and real suffering are staring them in the face, ready to fall upon them and their families; but they are unmoved. Such indifference is not contentment, but criminal inattention to duty. "A prudent man foreseeth the evil, and hideth himself: but the simple pass on, and are punished."

Now, contentment is the happy medium between the extremes of restless discontent and criminal indifference. It brings rest, quietude of mind, not from ignorance of our real condition, nor from heedlessness, but from a consciousness of having done our duty, and a willingness to trust Providence for the result, and make the best we can of our actual circumstances, whatever they may be. If the means of bettering our condition be within our reach, we should avail ourselves of them; but if not, why should we afflict ourselves by fruitless regrets? "What can not be cured must be endured." And why not bear it with a "meek and quiet spirit?"

One very common source of discontent is an unreasonable anxiety for worldly gain. Each one, according to his avocation, prospects, and supposed ability for the acquisition of wealth, luxury, and fame, fixes his standard, and pursues his object with avidity. But unforeseen difficulties arise, many of his calculations fail, defeat succeeds defeat, till at length his fortitude forsakes him, and, stung with disappointment, he sinks down into the sullen gloom of despondency, dissatisfied with the world, with himself, and with every thing around him. Others, who are successful in gaining the first point aimed at, beholding other and higher objects ahead, become more anxious to secure them, than they were to reach the first, vainly supposing the more they acquire of wealth, honor, and influence, the more happiness will ensue. But in the end they learn that "a man's life consisteth not in the abundance of the things which he possesseth." On the contrary, the more wealth the more care, the more honor the more trouble, and the more influence the greater the responsibility and danger.

Most of our discontent, growing out of either penury or affluence, might be avoided, by adopting the prayer of Agur: "Give me neither poverty nor riches; feed me with food convenient for me." The contented man, so far as property is concerned, is he who is neither pressed with want, nor burdened with the care of a superabundance, but knows, from experience, that "godliness with contentment, [or the true religion, with a competency,] is great gain." He reasons thus: "For we brought nothing into this world, and it is certain we can carry nothing out. And having food and raiment, let us be therewith content."

Another excellent means of promoting contentment is comparing our own circumstances with those of other people, and also with what ours might be. If our health be poor, it might be worse. Our private and domestic trouble might be vastly increased. If we know little, there are others who know less. If our privileges be few, there are some people who have fewer. If we enjoy but few luxuries, there are multitudes wholly destitute of them. If we have but little of earthly store, there are many who have less, and some who have nothing, but are homeless, houseless, and friendless. Even our blessed Savior exclaimed, "The foxes have holes, and the birds of the air have nests; but the Son of man hath not where to lay his head."

> "But, lo! a place he hath prepared
> For me, whom watchful angels keep;
> Yea, he himself becomes my guard;
> He smooths my bed, and gives me sleep."

So far, then, from having any just cause of complaint, we have much cause of gratitude. Our comforts are far greater than we deserve. How reasonable and how appropriate is the admonition, "Let your conversation be without covetousness; and be content with such things as ye have;" or satisfied with the lot which Providence assigns you.

But perfect contentment can be secured and maintained only by that grace which reconciles us to the will of God in all things. Under its influence, Paul declared, "I have learned, in whatsoever state I am, therewith to be content." Happy are all they who attain to such knowledge. They have nothing to wish for and nothing to deprecate, only in accordance with the will of their heavenly Father. Relieved from all painful anxiety, in patience they possess their souls, and "rejoice evermore." With them it is an easy and pleasant task to live right and feel contented; and to them the words of the apostle are not grievous: "Be careful for nothing; but in every thing by prayer and supplication with thanksgiving let your requests be made known to God. And the peace of God, which passeth all understanding, shall keep your hearts and minds through Christ Jesus."

WESTERN STYLE OF LIVING.

I HAVE been carefully observing the mode of living among the people of the western states for a period of forty years. Great changes have appeared during that time. Of the fifty-seven years of my life, thirty-six have been spent in the employment of an itinerant preacher, affording me the best practical means of information. Moreover, I am the son of a western pioneer, who was in the celebrated battle at Point Pleasant in 1774, and subsequently identified with the Indian wars, till Wayne's treaty of 1795. Of course it is matter of much interest with me to note the changes in the society of the far-famed west; and it may be of some little interest to the reader to see some of those changes briefly pointed out. I shall limit myself chiefly to a few items pertaining to the style of living, which may serve to remind us that, while the real wants of man are comparatively few and simple, the imaginary ones scarcely have any bounds. I shall, however, not take into the account the wealthy aristocrat, with his costly mansion, Turkey carpets, silver plate, and thousand dollar carriage; nor the extremely poor man, who lives in a wretched hovel, on a floor of earth, and sleeps on his bundle of straw. They are both exceptions to the general rule. My few observations shall have reference to the great mass of western population.

What is now considered an ordinary outfit for housekeeping? A domicile with parlors, hall, chambers, sitting-room, dining-room, kitchen, and cellar. To furnish these apartments, there must be Scotch or Brussels carpets, hearth-rugs, brass-mounted andirons, window-blinds, ornamented or cushioned chairs, rocking-chairs, sofas, sideboards, bureaus, wardrobes, cloak-racks, wash-stands, elegant bedsteads, with testers or canopies, dressed with curtains and valance, dressing-tables and mirrors, breakfast-tables and dinner-tables, with their tea sets and dinner sets of China and Britannia, and silver spoons, beside cooking stoves, etc. Now, this may answer for a commencement, as far as it goes; but who would ever think of keeping house without a center-table, richly covered, on which to lay the nice little volumes done up in gilt and morocco? which, however, being intended as mere ornaments, are fortunately seldom or never read. Or who could endure to see a parlor so naked, and out of all fashion, as not to have some mantle ornaments, such as artificial flowers, with glass covers, or some specimens of conchology and geological formations? Beside, the walls must not only be papered, but beautified with portraits, landscapes, etc. These commonplace notions amount to quite a clever sum, though they are as few and economical as western people of this day, who make any pretension to being *stylish*, can well get along with. Indeed, they form only a part of the numerous and indispensable fixtures of modern housekeeping. Again: to procure the viands, such as are in keeping with this array of furniture, and maintain a force requisite to serve up and hand them round, and keep all the affairs of the household in order, will cost another round sum—to say nothing of parties and extras.

With this modern style I shall take the liberty of briefly contrasting the early style of living in the western country. When a young married couple commenced housekeeping, forty years ago, a very small outfit sufficed, not only to render them comfortable, but to place them on an equality with their friends and neighbors. They needed a log-cabin, covered with clapboards, and floored with wooden slabs, in western parlance called puncheons, and the openings between the logs closed with billets of wood and crammed with mortar, to keep all warm and dry—all which a man could erect himself, without any mechanical training, with one day's assistance from his neighbors to raise the logs. Usually, one room answered for parlor, sitting-room, dining-room, kitchen, and dormitory, while the potato hole under the puncheons, formed, of course, by excavating the earth for mortar, was a good substitute for a cellar. As to furniture, they needed a stationary corner cupboard, formed of upright and transverse pieces of boards, arranged so as to contain upper, lower, and middle shelf, to hold the table-ware and eatables. In order to comfort and convenience, it was requisite, also, to have the following articles: one poplar slab table, two poplar or oak rail bedsteads, supplied with suitable bedding, and covered with cross-barred counterpanes of home-made, one of which was for the accommodation of visitors; six split-bottomed chairs, one long bench, and a few three-legged stools were amply sufficient for themselves and friends; a half a dozen pewter plates, as many knives and forks, tin cups, and pewter spoons for ordinary use, and the same number of delf plates, cups, and saucers for special occasions; also, one dish, large enough to hold a piece of pork, bear meat, or venison, with the turnips, hominy, or stewed pumpkin. All this table-ware was kept in the corner cupboard, and so adjusted as to show off to the best advantage, and indicated that the family were well fixed for comfortable living. When the weather was too cold to leave the door or the window open, sufficient light to answer the purpose came down the broad chimney, and saved the expense of glass lights; and as for andirons, two large stones served as a good substitute. The whole being kept clean and sweet, presented an air of comfort to the contented and happy inmates. It is true the cooking was usually done in presence of the family, but was soon dispatched, when the Dutch oven and skillet were nicely cleaned and stowed under the cupboard, and the long-handled frying-pan hung upon a nail or peg on one side of the door, while the water pail was situated on the other, and the neat water gourd hanging by it. For mantle ornaments they had the tin grater, used in grating off the new corn for mush before it was hard enough to grind, and the corn-splitter, being a piece of deer's horn, very useful in parting large ears of Indian corn for the cattle. The parlor walls were sufficiently beautified by the surplus garments and Sunday clothes hung all round on wooden pins, the sure tokens of industry and prosperity.

In regard to property, if a man owned an ax, wedge, hoe, plow, and a pony to pull it, and a bit of ground to cultivate, or a few mechanics' tools, he asked no more; and if his wife had a spinning-wheel, a pair of cards, a loom, and plenty of the raw material of flax, cotton, and wool, she was content. In those days keeping her own house was a small part of a woman's work—it was only needful recreation from her steady employment; for she carded, spun, colored, wove, cut and made clothes for all the family. Ladies of the first respectability then vied in honorable competition, to manufacture the finest and most tasty dresses for themselves, and the most handsome suits for their husbands, sons, and brothers, in which they all appeared abroad with more exquisite pleasure than people now do in imported satin and broadcloth, and with far more credit to themselves and honor to their country. For coloring materials they used the bark of walnut, hickory, maple, and sycamore trees, together with copperas, indigo, sumach, paint-stone, etc.; and in carding for a fancy suit of mixed, they worked in scraps of colored flannel and silk to variegate the texture. Those were the days of pure republicanism, true patriotism, and real independence. All the money a man needed was enough to pay his tax and buy his salt and iron. When he needed marketing, he gathered fruit from his orchard, vegetables from his garden, and took a pig from the pen, or a lamb from the fold; or if he had neither, he took his gun and brought in wild meat from the woods. He raised his own breadstuff, and ground it on the hand-mill, or pounded it in a mortar with a sweep and pestle, and relished it the better for his toil in preparing it. Coffee was not then used, except as a luxury on particular occasions, by a few of the wealthy. Milk was considered far preferable. For tea they had sage, spicewood, mountain birch, and sassafras, which they regarded then, and which I still regard as altogether preferable to black tea, young hyson, or imperial, both for health and the pleasure of taste. Supplies of saccharine were easily obtained from the sugar-tree or bee-gum, and those who had neither, gathered wild honey from the bee tree. When medicine was needed, they obtained it from their gardens, fields, or forests; but they had little use for it. Children were not then annoyed with shoes and boots, or hats and bonnets—they went barefooted and bareheaded. It was no uncommon thing to see small boys trapping for birds or hunting rabbits in the snow without shoes or hats, and small girls playing about the yard in the same condition—all the very pictures of health. Reared under that system, young men were able to endure the toils of a frontier life, or brave the perils of a hard campaign in the service of their country. Young ladies needed no paint, the rosy cheek being supplied by the flush of perfect health. In those days I never heard of dyspepsy, bronchitis, or any of the fashionable diseases of this generation. Doctors were then scarce among us, and had but little to do. If a man was afflicted with pain or catarrh, and felt chilly, he drank herb tea, wrapped himself in a blanket, and slept with his feet before the fire. If he was sick, he abstained from food. If he had a slight fever, he drank tea of snakeroot, mountain ditney, or other sudorifics, till he started the perspiration. Or if he had a severe attack of settled fever, after exhausting his simple remedies, he laid himself in a cool place, drank abundance of cold water, his wife or sister fanned him with the wing or tail of a turkey, and he committed himself to the keeping of a kind Providence, without being plied with blisters or dosed with poison. Calomel, the Samson of fashionable remedies, was scarcely known here in those days, and people usually retained their teeth and jaw-bones unimpaired, even to old age, or while they lived.

Many people, such as would be thought Solomons of this day, assume that their fathers and mothers were deplorably ignorant, but without any sufficient proof or satisfactory reason. People possessed at least as much common sense forty years ago as their posterity do at present. If they had fewer opportunities for improvement, they made better use of them; if fewer books, they were better ones, or better read; so that, while our fathers and mothers knew less of newspapers, novels, and annuals, they understood more of the Bible, useful history, and practical life. One fact is palpable, and should not be overlooked nor forgotten; that is, the present generation, with all its rage for education and improvement, can not show any more eloquent preachers, learned jurists, able statesmen, or successful generals, than those which lived in the days of our fathers. What improvement there is in morals, if any, is attributable to the Gospel. That the "age of improvement" has produced vast changes in the manners and usages of society, is admitted; but whether for the better or worse, is another question, and one which would admit of much argument on both sides. While the modern style of living affords more luxury and elegance than the former style, it is attended with more expense and trouble, and exerts a more corrupting influence on society—leads to more idleness, vanity, crime, and wretchedness. The pleasure of social intercourse is, I believe, not increased, but diminished. One example on this item must suffice. Call on a friend at her own house, and she is locked up. You must first apply at the pull of the door-bell, or the knocker; then wait a long time for the servant;

and if not repulsed at once by the fashionable cant, "Too much engaged," or the fashionable falsehood, "Not at home," you must next send your name and request for an interview; and after waiting from a quarter to half hour longer, you may obtain an audience at last, though dearly bought with loss of time and sacrifice of feeling. Whereas, under the usage of former days, so soon as you knocked on the door, you heard the familiar response, "Come in;" then, by pulling the string which hung outside, you raised the wooden latch, stepped into the family circle, met with a welcome reception, received a hearty shake of the warm hand of friendship, and, being seated, felt perfectly at home as long as you chose to remain. Such were the days of simple-hearted, honest friendship, when social life was unembarrassed by the affected and heartless etiquette of modern times.

CHILD OF THE WEST.

The west is my native land. I love her for the vastness of her territory, her long rivers, capacious lakes, and extensive prairies. I love her for her lofty elevations and fertile valleys, her enterprising population and valuable productions. I love her for her cities and wastes, her schools and churches, her great men and great women, her hopeful youth and numerous children. That section of the United States is attracting the attention of all the civilized world, especially of the more enterprising portions. She exhibits much to interest the eye and stir the deep feelings of the heart. Among her native inhabitants is one of the most interesting characters of the nineteenth century—I mean the Child of the West, born in the Queen City, January, 1841. She is well grown for one of her age, but betrays nothing gawkish in her appearance, or confused in her manner. Her physical development and mental improvement are in advance of her years. She never engages in childish gambols like her neighbors' children, and has no relish for gewgaws, but dresses with neatness and good taste, changing her vesture as circumstances require, but not blindly following in the train of fashion. The ground of her vestal robe is a snow white, variegated with a small, dark figure, and trimmed with the most delicate hues of pink and straw. Her head-dress, curiously wrought, is grave, but beautiful, and varies to suit the season; now figured over with landscapes of cottages and herds, flowers and evergreens, and then ornamented with cascades and mountain scenery, and again with some monument of moral sublimity. Her form is a perfect model of symmetry, and her personal beauty at once striking and attractive. Her prudent demeanor and amiable disposition indicate maturity of all the moral virtues. She never betrays any ill temper or envious feeling, never participates in any exciting or angry dispute respecting political or ecclesiastical affairs, but is always frank to express her own well-formed opinion on every subject properly pertaining to her sex, age, and relation in life. Her mental capacity is confessedly of high order; and, though yet a mere child, she is a ripe scholar. In all the substantial branches of education, she is above criticism. No mistake in orthography, syntax, or even punctuation, can be detected in her ordinary compositions. Her memory is richly stored from the best ancient and modern authors, and her fancy highly embellished with brilliant poetry. Her summaries of history and biography have been eagerly read by thousands of the literati. Her mind is thoroughly instructed in the natural and moral sciences, and her reasoning faculty well developed by exercise in logical investigation. As to her belles-lettres accomplishments, they are unsurpassed by any of her age in the United States. She is a most agreeable companion in social life, and a general favorite among all the better classes of society having any acquaintance with her, especially such as have the advantage of a polite Christian education. Her friends are numerous and rapidly increasing. She has already very many admirers anxiously seeking her society in person or by correspondence. The choicest trait in her character is her piety. Though not a bigot, she is orthodox and firm in her religious principles, and lays all her brilliant attainments and commanding capabilities at the foot of the cross of Christ, thus teaching the fallen race of man "the path of life" by the force of example. I write the more confidently of this remarkable child, having known her from infancy. Indeed, her parents consulted me respecting her name and early education, being myself a personal friend of all her principal teachers. The name first suggested for her was, "Ladies' Monitor," but she was finally christened "Ladies' Repository." Child of the West, "many daughters have done virtuously, but thou excellest them all!"

ZEAL.

THIS is a very common term, but one that appears to be not generally well understood. The learned say, it comes from a word which, in its primitive signification, means heat; but when used figuratively, and applied to the mind, it means earnestness excited by ardent desire. *Religious zeal* is *fervent* love; in the absence of love there is no zeal, though there may be much religious frenzy. The zeal recommended in the Gospel does not depend on a man's ability, but on his earnest desire to do all he can for Christ. Nor on the strength of his voice, but the strength of his attachment and the whole amount of his exertion, on every score, according to his ability. "It is good to be zealously affected always in a good thing;" but we should take heed lest our zeal be "not according to knowledge." Some men would pass for zealous patriots, because they clamor for liberty and for the country, while they are slaves to their own passions, and violate the laws of their country by a daily course of licentiousness and profanity. In like manner, some men would impose themselves on community as zealous Christians, because they make a loud profession, and aim to be distinguished on all popular occasions, while their hearts are full of envy and bitterness. These only deceive themselves, by striving to deceive others.

There are some common rules for estimating true zeal, that are plausible and pass currently, which, nevertheless, are fallacious: such as those quick and strong feelings of the heart that are natural to some people, independent of any religious influence, or a bold, hurried, and boisterous method of speaking for or against any measure under consideration. We are far from supposing that true zeal can not, or does not often belong to such as possess these native properties; but we do suppose that the zeal of such is often overrated, while that of other persons possessing different peculiarities, is underrated by superficial observers. One preacher studies closely, prays much in secret, fasts often, visits the sick faithfully, watches over his charge diligently, preaches frequently, and, in a word, devotes his whole time, strength, and talents to the service of his Lord and Master, whom he loves supremely, and yet, with some people, he has no zeal; because he either has not strength, or does not think it advisable, when in the pulpit, to use *intemperate exertions* by screaming like the world was on fire, and as if he was sure he would never need any health, or strength to preach or pray at another time. Another preacher studies but little, prays less, lounges about, laughs and talks with the people about every trifle, and spends but little of his time and influence in promoting the cause of Christ, and yet he is esteemed, by many, a very zealous preacher; because he has a strong voice, a fluency of words, much native animation as a speaker, gets his feelings enlisted, and drives on like a raging storm that soon spends its fury, and is followed by a great calm.

The same distinction is apparent among private Christians. One is punctual to every duty, whether in the closet, family, class-room, or public worship. He is active to promote the benevolent enterprises of the Church by giving largely of his substance, and faithful to his neighbors, striving to lead them to Christ by pious example and holy conversation; yet he has no zeal, in the opinion of some, because he can not sing and pray as loud as others. But another member, who neglects all these, to a great extent, is thought to be very zealous, because he has a loud, shrill voice, and sings and prays with all his bodily strength.

We must not be understood as objecting at all to every man using his own proper gift, and adopting his own peculiar manner of using it, whether vehement or moderate; but at the same time we think to judge of a man's *zeal*, which is the thing under consideration, his whole course, and the whole amount of his exertion, according to his strength and ability, must be taken into the account. These thoughts have been suggested by much observation for many years on the movements of religious people; and though they are not intended to be applied to any particular individual, or individuals, we hope they may encourage some whose zeal is not sufficiently commended, and assist some reader to form a charitable judgment in the case. For a full and satisfactory explanation of the whole subject, we would refer the reader to Mr. Wesley's sermon on the nature and properties of true Christian zeal, second volume of his standard works.

BENEVOLENCE.

The social virtues often appear most lovely when viewed in contrast with their opposite vices. Both have their living examples. A man of misanthropic spirit may be strictly moral in his general deportment, and scrupulously honest in all his dealings; but the principle of his action is not benignity; it is selfishness. Philanthropy has no place in his heart. Like the snail in his contracted shell, he lives to himself, caring nothing for the happiness of others. But the benevolent man is influenced by a habitual feeling of good-will to his fellows, one which is indicated by gentleness of manner and tenderness of expression in all his intercourse with society, as well as by the free bestowment of charity where it is needed. It is not difficult to determine which of the two is more happy. A morose man is miserable in himself, and renders all about him unhappy, by his sullenness and selfishness; while the truly-benevolent individual enjoys felicity himself, and imparts the same to those around him, by breathing a spirit of cheerfulness and accommodation. One possesses so little confidence in his fellow-creatures, that he regards every man with suspicion till he proves himself worthy; the other allows every one to be innocent till he is proved guilty. And each of these opposite characters forms his estimate of others by the confidence he has in himself. Thus benevolence insures its own reward, and selfishness its own punishment. The former draws around itself the generous and good; the latter repels them, and seeks the misery it deserves. One is the offspring of heaven, and the other of sin.

Benevolence leads its possessor to imitate the Savior of the world, who "went about doing good" to the souls and bodies of men. It renders him more careful to learn the wants and miseries of human beings, than to ascertain the nation, sect, or party to which they pertain. He who is blessed with a benevolent heart, delights to direct the lonely stranger on his way, to supply the ignorant with the means of enlightenment, to encourage the poor in their honest endeavors to acquire a living, and the unfortunate in the pursuit of happiness. How joyfully he leads the unprotected orphan to the asylum of safety, points the inquiring youth to the fountain of knowledge, or administers a word of consolation to the broken-hearted! When the incautious and the simple-hearted are about to be insnared in the meshes of vice, or drawn into the vortex of dissipation, how promptly he warns them of their danger! Like Job, he can say, "Because I delivered the poor that cried, and the fatherless, and him that had none to help him, the blessing of him that was ready to perish came upon me, and I caused the widow's heart to sing for joy." Show him a fellow-mortal suffering with hunger, and he is ready to divide with him his last loaf of bread. When told of any that are afflicted, and in need of aid, how he hastens to their relief! Point out to him a human being borne down by sickness and poverty, and he waits not to inquire whether the suffering individual be Jew or Christian, Turk or Pagan, much less whether he be orthodox or otherwise. So far as the exercise of benevolence to the unfortunate is concerned, he regards every man as his brother. While some would seek excuse for withholding aid and comfort on the score of demerit, he only needs to know that the sufferer is now destitute and afflicted, and he is ever ready to relieve him to the extent of his ability. Many worthy persons have been left in a state of entire destitution, and others may be. But suppose the sufferer to have brought his misery upon himself, still, the voice of inspiration proclaims, "If thine enemy hunger, feed him; if he thirst, give him drink." How much more should we regard the cries of a suffering neighbor, or disconsolate stranger, that never offended us in word or deed! While the man of wealth enjoys his comfortable habitation, his cheerful fireside, and his well-furnished table, some of his worthy, but unfortunate neighbors, may be exposed to the winter's storm, howling round and driving through their frail tenements, shivering with cold, pinched with hunger, and wasting with despair. And why does he not fly as an angel of mercy to their rescue? Because benevolence and he are strangers to each other. Give him a heart imbued with that spirit of love, and he sleeps not till they are warmed and fed.

Inducements to the practice of benevolence are numerous and potent. None of us are fully assured that we shall never need the charity we now withhold from others; for no one knows to what extremities he may be reduced by reverse of fortune. "Therefore, all things whatsoever ye would that men should do to you, do ye even so to them; for this is the law and the prophets." No man is independent of this golden rule. Should we desire relief, if reduced to extreme poverty by adversity and protracted indisposition? Then let us extend it to others. And let no one suppose that he is loser by bestowing a portion of his wealth upon the Lord's poor—the very purpose, in part, for which it was placed in his hands. "He that hath pity upon the poor, lendeth unto the Lord; and that which he hath given will he pay him again." Other investments may fail; but all deposits made in the bank of heaven are both safe and productive; "for God is not unrighteous, to forget your work and labor of love." Another inducement to practice benevolence is, the happiness derived therefrom. While the obliged beneficiary enjoys pleasure, arising from the exercise of contentment and gratitude, in having his wants supplied, let it be remembered, that the giver has still higher enjoyment, from a conscious discharge of duty, in relieving the distressed. "It is more blessed to give than to receive." Who would deprive himself of such felicity, by holding on, with a miser's grasp, to the gold that perishes? and, what is still worse, subject himself to the fearful judgment, "Depart from me; . . . for I was an hungered, and ye gave me no meat," etc.? Again: the exercise of benevolence is encouraged by an offered mansion in heaven. "Make to yourselves friends of the mammon of unrighteousness; that when ye fail, they may receive you into everlasting habitations." When Washington, after successfully leading an army of patriot soldiers to conquest and American independence, returned from the conflict, covered with honors, and appeared among his grateful countrymen, with what enthusiastic delight they received him! But when the benevolent Christian, having so used his wealth as to secure the love and gratitude of the pious poor, dies and goes where they have gone, with how much more delight will they hail him welcome into mansions of heavenly bliss! The greetings of those redeemed spirits on the shore of endless life will surely be a full reward for feeding and clothing them on their journey thither

SELFISHNESS.

Selfishness is generally understood to mean, the exclusive regard of a person to his own interest or happiness. It originates in the depravity of our fallen nature, is nurtured by mistaken views of our own personal importance, and produces much evil in the world. When an individual abandons himself to the full operation of this inhuman principle, he reminds those around him of a surly mastiff that gnaws his bone and growls, lest another should get a taste. Selfishness is not a stranger, or new-comer among us. It is an old acquaintance in every land, and a busybody in nearly all communities, and thus renders itself as common as it is contemptible. This pest of society frequently creeps into a public coach, and is always contending for the best seat, to the annoyance of the company. It is often seen in the crowded steamboat, pushing and clamoring for the choice berths, scrambling for a prominent chair at the first table, and quarreling with the steward, unless waited on to the neglect of all other passengers. In no place, however, does selfishness render itself more prominent than on the highway, where an observing traveler may read, with tolerable certainty, the disposition and general character of all he meets. Every liberal, high-minded gentleman, in all possible cases, will give at least half of the road, while every selfish, unprincipled man drives right in the middle of the track, and compels you to turn off, without any regard to your convenience or safety. Having long observed the practical working of this rule, I am persuaded it may, in general, be relied on as correct.

Again: how common is selfishness among business men in the various departments of mechanism and commerce!

They too generally seem determined to promote self-interest, whatever may become of their neighbors. The maxim, "Every man for himself," governs the many; while the maxim, "Live and let live," governs the few. With the former class, the temporal prosperity of a fortunate neighbor occasions envy and regret; with the latter, it occasions respect and gratulation. One class of traders, who deal in intoxicating liquors, are so much under the influence of selfishness, as to deal out poison to the vicious for gain, without any concern for the health, morals, lives, or families of their customers. Some deal it by the barrel for bank notes, and others by the dram for coppers; thus inflicting human misery, wholesale and retail, for "filthy lucre." And does not selfishness have something to do with the principles and movements of professional men, at least some of them? Are there not lawyers that encourage strife and litigation among the people for the sake of getting a fee? Would not one school, or class of physicians, if in their power, monopolize the practice, and drive all others out of the land? But, unfortunately for the accomplishment of their object, the people have a right to make their own selection. Do politicians, in general, legislate for the country at large, or for the advancement of party interests? And when demagogues clamor for office, is the design to serve the "dear people," or to serve their own personal aggrandizement? That is the question, and it is easily answered.

It is doubtful whether all Churches, even, are free from the debasing principle of selfishness. It would seem that some of them, not content with laboring to build up their own cause by fair means, seek to do it foully, by endeavoring to pull down others. Ay, and some who are called ministers of the Gospel of peace, unable or unwilling to multiply hearers and converts by their own efforts, or the Divine blessing upon them, endeavor to do it by secretly proselyting those of their more successful neighbors. This is ungenerous and inglorious. I have long believed that deliberate, underhanded proselyting from one Church to another, is very near akin to sheep-stealing. If it do not fix upon a minister the charge of felony, it does, at least, show him to be selfish. No such proceedings, on the part of any Church, or its minister, will ever secure a healthy tone of action, or a permanent state of religious prosperity. We may not do evil that good may come. Paul said, "For our rejoicing is this, the testimony of our conscience, that in simplicity and godly sincerity, not with fleshly wisdom, but by the grace of God, we have had our conversation in the world, and more abundantly to you-ward," 2 Cor. i, 12. And it would be a fortunate circumstance for society in general, and the Church of Christ especially, if we could all say the same thing.

The rules and regulations of the Methodist Episcopal Church, if fully carried out, would go far toward counteracting selfishness, both in the ministry and membership. Methodist itinerancy, especially, is a self-sacrificing system, bearing alike upon the pastors and their flocks. The former engage not to choose their own fields of labor, and the latter not to choose their own pastors; but all agree to abide a regular interchange, according to the best judgment of the appointing power, under the prescribed rules and limitations enacted by the General conference. Every traveling minister, previous to his admission into full connection, consents to, and promises to keep the following, commonly known as the twelfth rule: "Act in all things not according to your own will, but as a son in the Gospel. As such, it is your duty to employ your time in the manner in which we direct; in preaching, and visiting from house to house; in reading, meditation, and prayer. Above all, if you labor with us in the Lord's vineyard, it is needful you should do that part of the work which we advise, at those times and places which we judge most for his glory." This rule being read or referred to, the candidate is asked if he has considered it, and whether he will keep it for conscience' sake; and an affirmative answer is one condition of his being received into full connection and elected to orders. This solemn pledge is given in presence of the conference about to receive him as a fellow-laborer. Most of the brethren throughout the connection, or union of conferences, sacredly keep this promise, and find it not grievous, but joyous. And if there be no selfishness at work among us to blind the mind, vail the heart, and impair the memory, how could any brethren, in view of this pledge, and their own professed creed, reconcile it to their conscience to maneuver for popular appointments? And a response, as if echoed from the tombs of our fathers, asks, *How?* On the other hand, the members of the Church, by assenting to the rules and promising to keep them, as one condition of being received into full membership, engage to receive and support the ministers regularly appointed to serve them as pastors from year to year. Consequently, when the brethren of any circuit or station reject the regular appointee from conference, they inflict an injury upon the rejected minister, violate their own rules, evince a revolutionary spirit, and seriously injure themselves in the estimation of their brethren, both of the ministry and membership. I am fully persuaded, however, that the people, as such, seldom or never do reject their ministers; but it is occasionally done by a few would-be-thought leading spirits, that not only do their own thinking, but modestly assume to think for all the rest. Those few brethren, in their own estimation, are the Church, the people, and two or three such often claim to speak for three, five, or seven hundred Church members and their friends that worship with them. In some cases they do this wholly unauthorized by any part of the Church; in other cases they profess to act as a committee appointed by the stewards, or trustees, or both jointly. Well, suppose they are appointed thus, where do stewards and trustees obtain any authority to think, feel, and act for three, five, or seven hundred Church members respecting their choice of a pastor? The membership, generally, wish to have ministers qualified to build up the Church, and get their neighbors converted, while stewards and trustees do not object to this, it is true, but often feel most concerned about the money; they want a minister that can raise the money, or, in other words, do his own work and theirs too. Thus the few that interfere with the difficult and responsible duties of the appointing power, more frequently mistake, and, therefore, misrepresent, the real wishes of the people generally, than otherwise. And it sometimes happens, that the few, failing to get their man, and disappointed in regard to their own purposes, raise a cry in opposition to the regular appointee from conference, get a few others to join with them, drive off the minister, and then make scape-goats of the people to carry their sins away, saying the people would not receive him. It is a mistake. The people know their own wants and preferences, but are generally well satisfied with our system of supplying them, untrammeled by committees; and, if left to their own course, the people would give little or no trouble on the subject. Moreover, I have good reason to believe that the people are very tired, in many places, of having their pastors nominated by committees, whether self-appointed, or appointed by a minority to act for the majority. It is an innovation on Methodist rules and regulations, one that originated in, and tends to selfishness, and in its effects decidedly hurtful to the common cause of Methodism. So I believe, and, therefore, have written.

CHRISTIAN PHILANTHROPY.

How cold-hearted is the charity of the world compared with that of the Gospel! He that confers a favor with the expectation of its being returned, or loves his friend because he is amiable and obliging, only acts on the principle of the ancient publicans, who were viewed as being among the greatest of sinners. Hence, Christ said to his disciples, "If ye love them which love you, what reward have you? do not even the publicans so?" Yes, verily, and so do the most irreligious of the present day. If we love a friend and hate an enemy, we come up to the standard of morals erected by the wisdom of the world, but afford demonstrative proof that we are not true disciples of Jesus Christ. He said, "Ye have heard that it hath been said, thou shalt love thy neighbor, and hate thine enemy: but I say unto you, love your enemies, bless them that curse you, do good to them that hate you, and pray for them which despitefully use you, and persecute you." This precept of the Savior shames all the boasted but meager systems of morality invented by man, and forms as great a contrast with the wisdom of the world, as noon does with night. It is worthy of its divine Author, "who loved us, and gave himself for us," not as affectionate children, faithful friends, loyal subjects, or profitable servants, but as enemies, as rebels; for "God commendeth his love toward us, in that while we were yet sinners, Christ died for us."

This commandment also affords one of the best rules by which to prove the genuineness of our claim to the Christian character; which may be applied thus: Hast thou an enemy? Then, as a disciple of Jesus, thou shouldst love, bless, and pray for him. "But he is a bad man." So much the more does he need thy sympathy and prayers, lest a soul perish for whom Jesus died. "But he has done me wrong." If so, thou art bound to forgive him, so soon as he repents. "But I can not forgive him; he has acted so cruelly toward me." Then thou canst not be forgiven of thy heavenly Father; for Christ said, "If ye forgive not men their trespasses, neither will your Father forgive your trespasses." These are hard sayings to an unregenerate mind; but to an individual whose heart is full of love to God, from a sense of pardon and adoption, they are not grievous. He can forgive, as he has been forgiven. The difference between the natural and the renewed man is this: The former hates his enemy, and seeks his injury; the latter loves his enemy, and prays for him. In performing this duty, he promotes his own felicity. Speaking against an enemy injures him, and inflames the worst passions of our hearts. Praying for him may do him good, and will certainly help us, by cultivating kindness, forbearance, and an ardent desire for his salvation, with which our own happiness, as Christians, is closely identified. Speaking evil of men, even when we confine ourselves to the truth, is wrong, and seldom fails to do mischief; but praying for them is always right, and never fails to do good either to them or to us, and generally to both.

This doctrine, however, does not require us to approve the conduct of bad men, which would place virtue and vice on a level; but it does require us to bear with them. While God bears with men, why should not we? Should we desire to take the rod out of his hand? No: "Vengeance is mine; I will repay, saith the Lord." We may hate sin, but we must love and pray for the sinner still, not forgetting that we too have sinned, and that Jesus "died for all." The Gospel allows us to esteem some men more highly than others, because they are better, and to select these for our associates and helpers in a life of piety; but not to hate or injure any. Though God exercises the love of complacency to none but good men, he extends his love of pity to all. In this we should imitate him. Is there a human being, however vile, wicked, or degraded, or malicious toward me, against whom I entertain a malignant feeling, or to whom I wish any evil? Then all is not right. "He that saith he is in the light, and hateth his brother, is in darkness even until now." Religion is love, and "love worketh no ill to his neighbor," but seeks to glorify God in the salvation of all men, and can not be indifferent to the wants of the poor or cries of the distressed.

VISITING THE SICK.

This is one of the plain duties of practical religion, which no Christian can entirely dispense with and remain guiltless, unless he be prevented by disability in himself. It belongs to that class of charitable works which are inseparable from true piety. "Pure religion, and undefiled before God and our Father, is this"—or it discovers itself in this—"To visit the fatherless and widows in their affliction, and to keep himself unspotted from the world." This duty is also classed with the fruits of faith, and is one of the evidences by which the genuineness of it will be determined at the last day, when the Judge shall say, "Come, ye blessed of my Father, inherit the kingdom prepared for you from the foundation of the world: for I was . . . sick, and ye visited me;" or, "Depart from me, ye cursed, into everlasting fire, prepared for the devil and his angels: for I was . . . sick, and in prison, and ye visited me not."

The object of visiting the sick is to afford relief to the bodies, and administer comfort to the souls of the afflicted. Keeping these points in view, on hearing that your neighbor is ill, go immediately and inquire if he needs any thing you can obtain for him, or any service you can render. And recollect your business is not to pay him a compliment, but to do him good. Therefore, decline no necessary service, or office of kindness, calculated to relieve or soothe the sufferer. If you only make a formal call, without affording any aid, it puts the family to the additional trouble of waiting on you, perhaps to the neglect of the patient, without receiving any benefit; and you had better stay away altogether than to make such a visit. If you have any reason to believe you can do any kindness to the sick, go and make the effort; and if they need nothing, still the interest you manifest will be grateful to them; and a good conscience will attend you on leaving the place, especially if you aim to improve the occasion to their spiritual edification. Do you object, "I know not that my sick neighbor needs me?" Go and ascertain the fact. If he has need, attend him; if not, you will feel clear of the sin of omission. "But the apostle saith, 'Is any sick among you? let him call for the elders of the Church;' and I have not been sent for." That respects the sick man's duty, not yours. The duty of visiting the sick is positive, and not on condition of being sent for; though this would increase the obligation by affording evidence that your service is necessary. "But I am so busy." Would this excuse from your friend be satisfactory to yourself, if in a suffering or dying condition? If not, dismiss it at once. "But it is a cross to go." Then take it up, and expect a blessing to follow.

The manner of performing this duty is important, and calls for the exercise of much prudence and firmness.

Go to the sick-room in the name of the Lord, and in all practicable cases, after specially asking his direction and blessing in private. When there, be serious, but cheerful; kind, but not loquacious; for it is distressing to most patients, distracting to some, and injurious to all who are very feeble, or very ill. Encourage, but do not flatter or deceive; be earnest, but not boisterous; it is wholly unsuitable for the chamber of affliction. If you converse, read, sing, or pray, be short, and to the point in hand; and let all your efforts be in favor of directing the sufferer to Christ, as a strong-hold in the day of trouble, and to trust in HIM alone for all he needs here, or expects hereafter. As to the time of performing this duty: go, if possible, when you are most needed, and when there is the least company. Those who attend the sick only on the Sabbath, because they are at leisure, and have on their best apparel, act an ungenerous part; they stand aloof when needed, and then throng the room as idle visitors, doing much more harm than good. Too much company about the sick is far worse than too little.

Let it not be supposed that this duty belongs exclusively to ministers. All who have the ability to relieve, serve, or comfort the afflicted, should engage therein. It is true, ministers should abound therein as a part of their official duty; but so should Church members as one of their Christian duties. Females are eminently qualified for this duty. Their refined sensibility, gentleness of manner, experience in nursing, readiness to alleviate, and their untiring attention amidst scenes of woe, make them the most valuable vigils of the sick-room. Yet their services do not supersede those of our own sex. Each one must render an account to God for himself respecting this duty. And that we may do it with joy, we should go to all whom we have any hope of benefiting, as far as practicable; but especially to the poor, for they need our services most. Christ has left them among us as his representatives, and any kindness bestowed upon the pious, afflicted poor, will be acknowledged by him as though conferred on himself: "Inasmuch as ye have done it unto one of the least of these my brethren, ye have done it unto me." What stronger inducement could be offered; what greater reward could be given for the performance of any duty, than such a sentence from the Judge of all the earth?

CHRISTMAS.

It is a question of some importance, whether the observance of this festive day does more good or harm, and consequently whether or not it should be perpetuated, under the sanction of Christian example. The origin of this festival, in reference to time, is doubtful, as the sacred Scriptures are silent on the subject. History, according to some authors, places it in the second, but according to others, in the third century. All seem to be agreed that it was observed before the days of Constantine. That it was well meant by those who first brought the usage into the Church of celebrating the birth of Christ, there is no good reason to doubt; but it might now, perhaps, be placed among the traditions of the elders, which, in their practical tendency, are calculated to make the commandments of God of none effect.

It is true that Christmas, considered apart from the dissipation now associated with it, is calculated to call up before the mind truths the most momentous, and mercies the most stupendous; and it might be rendered profitable by appropriate religious exercise and suitable expressions of gratitude to God, and love to each other as the subjects of his grace; but how strangely it is perverted by most people to purposes of sin and folly! It is an occasion on which very many take even unusual liberties for self-indulgence and sinful associations.

Hence, not a few, who at other times appear to be rational, sober, discreet, are known, during this festival, to give or attend Christmas wine-parties, Christmas balls, Christmas amusements, games at cards, Christmas horse-races, or shooting-matches, where all spirits are sufficiently enlivened by the presence of "King Alcohol." Boys are induced by such examples to assemble for sport and mischief, to the great annoyance of civil people; and while they are flourishing about with their crackers, pistols, and gunpowder plots, some who, at least, *think* themselves men, are employed alternately in gambling, drunkenness, blasphemy, vulgarity, personal insult, and "smiting with the fist of wickedness." The inconsistency of such conduct is surpassed only by that of the apology which is rendered for it; namely, it is *Christmas*—the anniversary of the advent of the Son of God, the Redeemer of the world. Indeed! And is it suitable to celebrate such an event by increased wickedness and rebellion in all their forms? Awful will be the account which such enemies of Christ must render, when he shall appear to judge the world.

This will be a high day in several respects. It will be variously regarded by different classes of society, but in all cases for the same reason. Those whose practices lead to opposite extremes, will still refer to the same circumstance for an explanation of their conduct. Though it is not Sabbath, congregations will appear in temples of worship, ministers will preach on the birth of Christ, and Christians will sing of his advent, and pray for the extension of his kingdom on earth, because it is *Christmas*. Friends and relations will pay visits, feast, and send portions—not to the suffering poor, but—to those alike prosperous with themselves, because it is *Christmas*. Old grandfathers and grandmothers will pass round the snuff-box and the pipe, and talk over the scenes of olden times, because it is *Christmas*. Little children will appear abroad in their best apparel, oft repeating to their friends the accustomed salute, "A Christmas gift," to secure the repast of nuts, fruits, and ginger-cakes, because it is *Christmas*. Students, apprentices, and servants, will have holiday, and "lots of fun," because it is *Christmas*. Rude boys will fling their crackers as thick as lightning bugs on a summer's evening, and with many mischievous consequences; they will collect in large groups, swear like sailors, scream like drunken savages, and fight like dogs, because it is *Christmas*. Young people will have their tea-parties, dancing-parties, and much foolish hilarity, because it is *Christmas*. Many statesmen will go from the halls of legislation to their wine-parties, and engage in the folly and dissipation of high life, because it is *Christmas*. While those of low life, in imitation of their pernicious customs—though at other times sober men—will drink, carouse, quarrel, and fight, because it is *Christmas*. Prodigals, sportsmen, drunkards, gamblers, pickpockets, and libertines of all sorts, will have a high time of it, because it is *Christmas*. After the day is past, the truly pious will remember with pleasure their acts of devotion and works of benevolence performed on *Christmas*. While all the workers of iniquity, who set apart this day to the service of the devil, and the destruction of their own souls, will wipe their mouths and say, "It was no harm, because it was done on *Christmas!*" But if they die without repentance, God will "rain snares, fire, and brimstone, and a horrible tempest: this shall be the portion of their cup," for the sins which they have committed on *Christmas*.

Such abuses render it very doubtful with some, whether

Christians ought to encourage the perpetuation of a festive day, instituted only by human wisdom and authority; for they think it is very questionable whether it does not afford more facilities to the enemies than to the friends of Christ; whether it does not contribute more to the works of darkness than those of righteousness. But if it must be observed, at least, by professors of religion, let it be done suitably. While the children of the world are collecting their forces to extend the reign of darkness, the children of God should record, with songs of gratitude, his tender mercies, and pray for the universal spread of that kingdom which is not of this world.

NEW-YEAR.

This is a suitable time to reflect a little on the *past*, the *future*, and the *present*.

The *past* year, like all the preceding ones of our lives, brought us a variety of pleasant and unpleasant things; but upon the whole, a vast amount of obligation to be thankful and obedient to our heavenly Father. While foreign lands have been blighted by famine, or threatened with blood and revolution, ours has been favored with general peace, and great plenty; and while the night of heathenism still covers its millions of our race, the light of Christianity shines on us, though a guilty nation, accompanied with the blessings of civil and religious liberty. Such are our national blessings; and those distributed among us and our families, have been without number. Amidst scenes of affliction, sorrow, and death, our lives and health, as individuals, have been preserved. Many strangers, some acquaintances, and a few friends, have fallen around each of us; but we still live, the witnesses of grace, possessed of opportunities to do good and receive good, preparatory to our final reckoning. All these blessings are received from above, and flow to us unworthy creatures through the mediation, advocacy, and intercession of our Lord Jesus Christ.

The *future* is covered with awful uncertainty. "Boast not thyself of to-morrow; for thou knowest not what a day may bring forth." Much less do we know what a year will disclose. But what has been, will, substantially, be again; and, judging of the future from the past, we may safely conclude that the toils, cares, recreations, pleasures, joys, griefs, gains, losses, revivals, and declensions of this will be very similar to those of other years; but the subjects of them will be continually changing, as fast as millions of births and deaths are recorded. One serious thought is, we shall not all live to witness these things. Nothing is more certain than that some of those we know will die before next year, and nothing is more uncertain than who they will be. The writer and reader of this article may be among them; yea, some now familiar with these pages, doubtless, will be numbered with the dead this year. Let each one, therefore, inquire, as the disciples of Christ did in another case, "Lord, is it I? Lord, is it I?" that must go so soon? It may be thou art the man, the woman. What, then, is thy prospect beyond the grave? Suppose the summons should come for that young man who is pursuing the road to worldly fame, reckless of the future; or that young lady whose heart is alive only to the things which perish, and who never yet prayed sincerely to God; suppose the messenger should come for the middle-aged man, so cumbered with much serving that God is not in all his thoughts; the irreligious one that has grown gray in the service of Satan; or a cold-hearted, backslidden professor of religion; what would be the consequence? Alas, all with them would be lost forever!

But now change sides a moment, and suppose those sent for to be the children of the Highest, called home to their "house, not made with hands, eternal in the heavens;" what ground of objection could they have to such a speedy release from earth and all its miseries, such promotion to glory, honor, and eternal life! Is he that has next to go a young convert? his early removal from the ranks of Zion will excuse him from the dangers and crosses of a long campaign. Is he an old pilgrim, who has passed through fiery trials, and borne the burden and heat of the day? how welcome his deliverance! Has he a family to leave? he can safely trust them in His hands who says, "Leave thy fatherless children, I will preserve them alive; and let thy widows trust in me." But is he a minister—for among so many of us bearing this title, some will doubtless have to give an account of their stewardship this year? to him it can be no misfortune, as an individual, if found faithful; and as it regards those he is related to, they can do very well without him. The Lord can provide for our families by means unknown to us. The world would scarcely observe the vacuum in society caused by the death of a few ministers of this age. And the Church will prosper without us after we are dead, as she did before we were called to her altars. Let none suppose that God is dependent on the best among us to forward his work, or that wisdom will die with us of this generation. When, where, or by what means we die, is of little consequence; all that is important to us in this matter, is a thorough preparation to meet it. This implies that God is now reconciled to us in Christ, and we to him; that we now love God supremely, and all men, for his sake; that we live, yet not we, but Christ liveth in us, the hope of glory, and that the life we now live is of the faith of the Son of God, who loved us, and gave himself for us. This is our privilege, and we need no more.

To attend to this preparation, the *present* time is all we have. The past will not return; to-morrow we may never see; the present alone is certain to us. "Behold, now is the accepted time: behold, now is the day of salvation." What we do must be done quickly. Yea, now or never. The night of death cometh, and is near, when no man can work. What are we *now* doing to please God, promote his cause on earth, obtain our own sanctification, and prepare to live forever? Let conscience answer, truly and understandingly.

WATCH MEETINGS.

Bishop Asbury once said to the preachers in conference, "When the ordinary means fail, use the extraordinary." (A good rule if always found in prudent hands.) Among these unusual means might be numbered our meetings on watch-nights, which are seldom held except on New-Year's eve. A well-conducted meeting of this sort commences at eight or nine o'clock in the evening, and continues till midnight. The exercises consist of preaching, exhortation, prayer, and praise, and usually ends with a renewal of the Christian's covenant to strive for "a closer walk with God;" which, after being distinctly stated and proposed by one of the ministers present, is generally entered into with great solemnity by spending five minutes in silent prayer. Nothing appears more solemn than to see a whole assembly kneeling in silent prayer at midnight, confessing the sins of the past year, returning thanks to God for the blessings of life and grace perpetuated to them, and engaging with the Lord, each for himself, to be for *Him* the ensuing year, whether called to live and labor, or die and go to eternity.

It is certainly a feast worth more than a few hours rest, to unite with the assembly of the saints, pleading with God for themselves and their friends, while others are asleep or at their revels. Very seldom do such worshipers fail to receive great blessings. Often revivals of religion are commenced at those meetings. Many in heaven will have cause of rejoicing that God ever put into the heart of Wesley to institute them in his societies.

If it be objected, that "such meetings are singular, and, therefore, improper," we answer, all true religion, when tried by the wisdom of this world, is singular. God's people are "a peculiar people;" they are different from others. And they who shun duty for fear of being thought singular, can never be decidedly pious. It was singular for Jacob to wrestle with the angel all night; for the brethren and sisters to hold a special prayer meeting at a late hour for Peter's deliverance from prison at the house of Mary; for Paul to "continue his speech all night," and for the Savior to go into a mountain and continue "a whole night in prayer to God;" but they all obtained satisfactory answers. In company with the prophets, Christ, and his apostles, let me be singular too, and enjoy singular blessings.

CURIOSITY.

THAT inquisitive disposition, or propensity for novel things, called curiosity, holds a prominent place in the heart of man. If the love of novelty be restrained within proper bounds, it may contribute to improvement, by the cultivation of useful knowledge; but if it be unrestrained, and encouraged by gratification, its tendency is to mischief; leading its votaries to interfere with the private business of families, or individuals, while they neglect their own. It often decoys them on to dangerous ground, that they may discover something new under the sun. Many a heedless youth could be made a strong witness in this case.

The indulgence of vain curiosity, also, tends to idleness; and is, therefore, ruinous to our business, property, morals, and peace of mind. Were this principle cultivated in childhood and encouraged in manhood, habitually, it would end in the abandonment of every useful employment, and reduce us to the degraded condition of the Athenians in the days of St. Paul, as described, Acts xvii, 21: They "spent their time in nothing else, but either to tell or to hear some new thing." The consequence was, they degenerated into such ignorance and superstition, that they erected an altar to an "unknown god, whom they ignorantly worshiped."

That the love of novelty already exerts too much influence on the American family for their good, there can be no doubt, from facts well authenticated. A Shaker attracts more attention than a consistent, devoted Christian; because he has more claim to novelty and less to piety. Joe Smith and Fanny Wright are successful proselyters; because one attracts notice by an unknown tongue, and the other deals in impudence as a female declaimer, in court-houses and theaters. It is owing to the same rage for novelties, that more people can be collected at a high pontifical Latin mass, for the repose of the soul of a deceased right reverend Roman dignitary, than usually assemble to worship God in the spirit.

But the evil is not peculiar to characters and transactions professedly religious. A philosopher conceives a notion that the earth is concave, and immediately embarks on search of a creep-hole at the poles, that he may enter and explore the interior; but after exhausting his fortune, time, and mental energies, dies in despair of accomplishing the object.

Now, if such things happen among the learned, what may be expected of the vulgar? "There was no mistake in Sam Patch," he said; and an idle, dissipated crowd of followers confirmed his vanity, as they witnessed his fearful leaps, which they hired him to make; but the next sad leap he landed in eternity. Recently an overgrown Kentuckian had his picture posted up with an advertisement to exhibit himself in sundry museums, east and west, and, in one instance, received more than twenty thousand visitors. Had his soul been large, in proportion to his body—which weighed five hundred and twenty-six pounds—he would have found better employment; and if the people had possessed more sound discretion, and less curiosity, they would have kept their cash, or applied it to some better purpose than paying to see his corporality.

Our love of novelty is becoming notorious among foreign nations, it would seem, from recent circumstances; and they are profiting by their knowledge of our weakness. This may account for some singular importations and extra arrivals, announced from time to time. Those children of misfortune, the Siam twins, should never have left the precincts of their mother's residence; but the love of gold, the root of all evil, caused their habitual exposure among strangers. Shame on those who made gain of their natural deformity! But even female delicacy vanishes before the love of revenue arising from the gratification of vain curiosity. A young lady, whose artificial deformity is a humiliating monument of the caprice of fashion and a nation's folly, has been imported from China, is now exhibiting herself in New York, and thousands run on a fool's errand to see her crippled feet.

It is time for every man of influence, especially Christians, ministers and editors, to set their faces, like flint, against every idle foolery, intended to collect large crowds of people, and feast their eyes with empty display, without any prospect of mental or moral improvement. And though I have not the vanity to suppose that I can turn the tide of popular feeling any more than I could arrest the torrent rushing over the cataract, yet I can and will keep out of the current—and advise others to do the same—by recording my vote in opposition to every species of dissipation, and thus throwing the responsibility where it belongs. I speak as unto wise men: judge ye what I say.

January, 1835.

THE AGE OF IMPROVEMENT.

(WRITTEN IN 1835.)

The spirit of improvement is good if well directed. To make it profitable, it must be brought to bear on proper objects, and regulated by sound principles. When rules of human action are just, well developed, and firmly established, they may be safely carried out and applied to an increased variety of purposes, but should not be abandoned through rage for improvement; for this would be giving up the benefit of all the labor, research, and experience of past ages, and throwing ourselves back entirely on our own resources. Among other rules of this sort, the following should be kept in view: 1. No discovery is valuable which can not be applied successfully to some good, practical purpose. 2. No important object can be accomplished by human agency without care and exertion. The first rule sets aside aerial voyages, phrenology, conjuration, the circus, and all that sort of things, which are of no important use to society, and seriously injure many people. They engender idle curiosity, and lead to the neglect of business and solid improvement. The second rule sweeps aside all those modern new-fangled schemes for improvement without study and labor. When we hear of boats to navigate the air without oars, sail, or machinery; of stoves that cook without fuel; corn that grows without culture; doctors that can cure without medicine; instructors that teach the sciences without requiring the learner to study; blacking which shines on our boots without applying the brush; religious reformers who convert people by the agency of water, or what is still more convenient, put people in the way to "born themselves again," by an act of volition; the application of the second rule may be of some service in forming a judgment in the case.

There appears to be, more or less, in almost every class of society, a sort of feverish excitement, urging them on to the accomplishment of something which is generally not well defined by its projectors, nor understood by their adherents, and, consequently, of doubtful utility in its practical results. The general idea is *improvement*, and there is a great uproar on the subject; but the greater part of the multitude seem not to know wherefore they are come together; for some cry one thing and some another, making much confusion and really accomplishing but little. It is true, this is a fruitful age, emphatically an age of invention, both as it regards new projects, and the means of accomplishing old ones. Before one scheme of improvement is fully tested, or even half matured, it is superseded in whole, or in part, by another, proposed by a different individual. The usual mode selected by the several reformers, or advocates of modern improvement, for introducing their favorite schemes, is to trumpet them with such unblushing confidence, as to keep the world gaping and running to find out some method of becoming wise without study, wealthy without industry and economy, honorable without justly asserting any sufficient claims to reputation, and to be happy without the trouble of being pious or virtuous. In this state of morbid excitement, and so far as the votaries of novelty are concerned, he who makes the largest pretensions to the discoveries of facilities for improvement, and gives the least proof of it by actual usefulness, seems to acquire the greatest applause.

That there have been some valuable discoveries made in modern times, respecting the mechanical arts, husbandry, the means of conveyance by land and water, etc., calculated to save labor, and facilitate business, is not denied; and possibly this circumstance has contributed to the desire of some to ascertain a plan for mental improvement without much mental exertion. They may reason thus: As the wants of the body are supplied by means of various machinery, at a great reduction of time, labor, and expense, why not those of the soul by certain improvements within our power? But if the latter object has been realized to any considerable extent, the judicious part of society do not appear to be apprised of it. It is true, some things are taught now in a shorter time than formerly, but it is believed that the knowledge obtained under the new modes is usually more superficial; and if there is a more general thirst for knowledge among the people, it is feared that, in a large number of cases, it is not the knowledge which will render us more holy on earth or happy in heaven, but which puffeth up. We will here give a few specimens of modern improvement to sustain the positions we have taken.

The art of penmanship used to be considered not only ornamental, but highly useful in the practical business of life. Young men, after leaving school or college, would, in some cases, employ a part of their time for years, as clerks in public offices, to acquire the habit of writing a fair, elegant, and rapid hand, as though this was a matter of some importance. But what folly to spend so much time to learn what is now professedly taught in ten short lessons of two hours each; and what imbecility to be making plain letters, when zigzag lines, hieroglyphics, and fanciful dashes, are—with a few honorable exceptions—all the learned care to make! What is a printer good for who can not *guess* at words, especially in the pure classic style, embellished with Latin quotations? Who that has the reputation of a distinguished scholar, troubles himself about the mechanical process of making his thoughts legible on paper?

The science of English grammar in the days of Murray filled a respectable volume; and a young man of ordinary mind, who mastered it in six months, connected with a few other branches, did well. But now it is by some reduced to a mere table, printed on a single sheet, and taught by twelve short lectures, in the same number of evenings. Is not this a vast improvement? And what appears to be a more important discovery is, that, in the present polished state of society, grammar is no longer strictly necessary except for the vulgar and mere novices in science. What distinguished statesman, doctor of law, or president of a theological college, pays any particular attention to syntax, either in speaking or writing? Such cases are believed to be comparatively few. Indeed, to do this would afford evidence that they had attended to little things, and, consequently, that they are not the great men the world takes them to be. What! a literary character speak and write grammatically? Away with such school-boy trifles in this age of improvement.

In the style of composition and book-making, the improvement is wonderful. The time was when such writers as the plain John Bunyan, the pious Baxter, the amiable

Bishop Watson, and the conscientious John Wesley—who said he did not dare to write in a fine style—passed pretty well even among men of reading; but who, of all the zealous advocates of modern improvement, cares for their simple, easy, graphic style? When books were comparatively scarce, the old-fashioned works of English reformers were read and could be sold; but who will buy and read them now, when the world is full of novels, plays, annuals, and other works adapted to the present refined state of society? They may be esteemed by some old-fashioned Christians, who still read their Bibles, and adhere to the principles of piety, truth, and common sense; but with the advocates for new-fashioned improvement, these principles appear to be out of fashion, and generally laid aside to make room for their heroes in the world of fiction.

Oratory has of course been remanufactured and rendered conformable to the refined taste of the people, in this age of wonders. In the rude state of society, at the commencement of this century, public speakers, to succeed well, had to seek out the truth according to the standards of their profession; arm themselves with facts and sound argument, and address them to the understanding and the heart. This was somewhat troublesome. It cost the orator some research and preparation, and the people were put to the trouble of thinking and feeling under the discourse. But since the world has felt the polishing hand of recent fashionable improvement, facts and logic are dull things, and none but ordinary speakers, who have no popularity to lose, can safely deal in them. The imagination of our novel-reading community is rendered so prominent by the light of fiction, that if they have any judgment and conscience left, they are thrown quite in the background; and to gain the reputation of a popular orator, you must aim higher than the heart. The fancy must be addressed by a tremendous display of uncommon words and phrases, imagery, compound figures, and double superlatives. And as the object is neither to convince nor persuade, but merely to gratify the taste of the hearers, and keep up the credit of the orator, the less he deals in simple truth, the less he understands himself or is understood by the people, the better; for this will confirm them in the belief that he is a very great man, too much so to be comprehended; and they will, as a matter of course, reward him liberally with unqualified praise.

It would be easy to multiply examples to show the character of some boasted improvements of this age, in support of our positions, but these are sufficient. I might also have treated the subject more gravely, had I thought it suitable. And, lest some should think me censurable for adopting a different style, I will just add two reasons in self-justification. 1. I doubt whether the specimens of modern improvement above named are proper subjects of grave discussion. 2. I am persuaded that the votaries of such improvement are too far advanced in the regions of fancy to be reached by sober, rational arguments, if I were capable of wielding them.

INFLUENCE OF FASHION.

Those who object to the restraints of a religious life, would do well to consider whether they are not in general the vassals of a system far less tolerable to an enlightened mind; namely, that of fashionable life. Much is said of late about negro slavery—of which I am no advocate—but who is a greater slave than the dupe of *fashion?* Has he any judgment, any will of his own? It appears not. Fashion dictates to him in all things, as rigidly as the master does to his servant. More particularly, it prescribes his manner of life, dress, and intercourse with society. The real wants and comforts of life are comparatively few, simple, and cheap; those regulated by fashion are numerous, complex, and costly. It renders a bill of articles for housekeeping, without regard to means and prospects; ordering judgment and conscience to stand aside, it prescribes the form of the table, figure of the mantle-piece, finish of the sideboard, and color of the carpet, while convenience, utility, and economy, all have to bow implicitly to its rules. When a suit of clothes is to be purchased, no authority is consulted, by many, but fashion; without regard to price or quality, it dictates the color of the cloth and cut of the garment. This drudgery becomes the more troublesome on account of continual changes invented by idle spendthrifts, who study nothing else but how to keep in the foremost ranks of fashionables, while others strive to follow hard after them. What is considered the very "tip of the mode," when the suit is made, may become obsolete before it is half worn; the consequence is, it must be laid aside, lest the owner be thought unfashionable.

Fashion regulates, by severe rules, the intercourse of its subjects with society, regardless of convenience or pleasure. If you have occasion to call on them, however important your business, or limited your time, it is only by a very tedious process that you can obtain an interview. The success, however, will depend much on observing the proper hours to suit the etiquette of high life. The fashionables usually start out to make their *morning calls* about half after twelve to one o'clock, P. M. From that till about half past two, they make and receive short visits, dodging in and out among their acquaintance, with the ordinary salutation, "Good morning." About three they return, and by four are ready to commence dinner, which, with all its ceremonies, they finish some time toward night, with much loquacity and fine glee, which is not at all lessened by the quantity of tea and wine consumed. From eight to nine o'clock—the time prudent people prepare for rest—they go out to "spend the evening." Supper may be expected to commence as early as eleven and end before one, so that they can be at home and in bed by two, or three at the farthest. People who keep such timely hours may be expected to rise next morning by nine or ten o'clock, which will be in time for what they esteem early breakfast; for which, however, they will have but little relish after the surfeit of the night and the nap of the morning. Such are the characters who are most addicted to complaints against the restraints of religion; they object to its duties and crosses, the simplicity of its ordinances, and the general seriousness of character it imposes. They are not willing to be bound by her silken cords of love, though they seem too well content to wear the galling chains of bondage imposed by a life of fashion, which is a life of sin and folly, and, consequently, of misery, without any hope of a better state hereafter.

If such folly as above described was confined to a few that have much wealth, and who promise no other good to society than that of putting it into circulation by foolishly squandering it, the subject would be less afflictive; but the evil is contagious. Those whose circumstances are limited and even embarrassing, are too often tempted to imitate the manners of the rich and fashionable; for such is the pride of man's heart, that even poor people are mortified if thought to be out of fashion. But before we yield to this temptation, let us pause and consider if this is the true road either to usefulness or felicity. Of what use to the world are any of the blind devotees of fashion? Who of them are distinguished as philanthropists, patriots, scholars, statesmen, or professional men?

Do men of dress, fashion, and pleasure, ever excel in any of these useful departments of society? We believe not. What fashionable lady, properly so called, is remarkable for relieving the sick, instructing the ignorant, educating the orphan, or encouraging, by her property and example, any humane efforts to better the condition of her suffering fellow-creatures? Alas! it is doubtful whether she either knows or cares any thing about the sufferings of the unfortunate, or the means of their relief. Why, then, such a proneness among us to imitate characters so unprofitable? Yet this exists to so great an extent that not a few families and individuals are ruined in their temporal circumstances, sometimes in their characters, and often in their enjoyments, by its influence. The vanity of the rich is no excuse for the vices of the poor; but the bondage of the former to the rules, or, rather, caprice of fashion, should reconcile the latter to their more humble condition.

There is another fact which adds to the mischief and mortification occasioned by the operation of this principle. Fashion extends its slavish dominion, to a great extent, over the borders of Zion. Many professed disciples of the meek Savior, are, in fact, only fashionable gentlemen and ladies, aiming to keep friends with both parties—the Church and the world—but enjoying the confidence of neither. To be a humble Christian requires true courage. He that possesses independence and virtue enough to be governed by his own judgment and conscience, in accordance with the Gospel, is charged with being singular; and though God calls all his children to be "a peculiar people," but few have the courage to obey. What a condescension it is for the children of the Most High to be under bondage to the elements of the world! How much more honorable and happy are they, who, like Paul, can say, "God forbid that I should glory, save in the cross of our Lord Jesus Christ, by whom the world is crucified unto me, and I unto the world!" My object is not to recommend singularity for its own sake, but to encourage professors of religion to do right, regardless of fashion and the reproach of being accounted singular. This is not only possible, but grace can make it easy and delightful. There are some worthy examples and living comments on this doctrine, both among the rich and poor.

Some of the former have been enabled, "through Christ strengthening them," to dismiss all their affected airs, vain and worldly-minded associates, fashionable parties, and other fooleries, and become sober-minded, happy Christians, devoting their time, talents, property, and influence, to the service of the Lord. On the other hand, some in the humbler walks of life have been effectually cured of a desire to be *thought* fashionable, and are well reconciled to their lot, having Christ for their portion, and viewing heaven as their final home. May the Lord increase the number of truly-pious souls among all classes of people!

LOQUACITY.

LOQUACITY, which, according to Walker, means "too much talk," is a fault as disagreeable as it is common. It is not restricted to either sex. The reader must not suppose that I judge women to be more faulty in this respect than men. In either it is unlovely, and when indulged to excess, becomes reprehensible in the estimation of all judicious people.

Loquacity is objectionable, because it savors of vanity. It indicates that the speaker wishes to bring himself into notice by a display of words; and, consequently, that he presumes much upon his own intelligence, and upon the ignorance of others, as if they knew nothing till he enlightened them. The talkative individual seems, also, to take it for granted, that his neighbors have leisure and patience to be lectured by the hour, on any subject which fancy, inclination, or accident may lead him to introduce. This is a great mistake in most cases. Such a character would do well to study the import of Solomon's maxim, "A fool's voice is known by multitude of words."

Again: loquacity is troublesome. It breaks in on the regular calling of all who have the misfortune to be assailed by it. Few things are more annoying to a man of business or a man of study, than to be frequently interrupted by the idle and loquacious. It embarrasses him in his necessary avocation, and, of course, chafes his feelings; and, unless he possesses uncommon forbearance, lays him under temptation to rudeness of manner. There are individuals in every extensive community who seem to have no employment but to talk. They are generally very willing souls to give direction concerning the business of others, while they neglect their own; for, as Solomon said, "every fool will be meddling." But they are as poor counselors as they are unpleasant companions. Let it not be supposed that talkative characters are peculiar to this age or country. Paul said, "There are many unruly and vain talkers, and deceivers, especially they of the circumcision, . . . whose mouths must be stopped;" and he instructed Titus to "rebuke them sharply."

It is frequently observed, that they who talk most do it to least purpose. Public speakers, of a loquacious disposition, are generally diffusive; they often lack point, and obscure their arguments by a superabundance of words. If they be members of deliberative bodies, they are apt to become troublesome, lose their influence, and, sometimes, secure to themselves an unenviable notoriety. Such orators might profit by the advice of St. James, "Let every man be swift to hear, slow to speak, slow to wrath."

A loquacious disposition leads to many indiscretions, of which some examples may here be furnished. It influences confidentials to divulge secrets, betray confidence, and produce open ruptures between neighbors. It leads families to discuss their private business in the presence of strangers, which is improper. It betrays many individuals into the very impertinent and annoying practice of catechising civil travelers as to their residence, destination, name, and business. This is an extremely rude practice. Loquacity interrupts the harmony of conversation; for a talkative individual will often break in upon another while speaking, which is embarrassing and uncourteous. It makes people appear self-important and unteachable. For example, when a minister of the Gospel calls on a talkative family, instead of being heard as their religious teacher, he is compelled to keep silence, and listen to their desultory harangues, perhaps all speaking at once, till his time and patience are exhausted, or retire abruptly. To visit such a family, except for the purpose of teaching them better manners, is a waste of time.

In some instances, loquacity is an infirmity of old age, and in others, of partial insanity, and in all such cases should be endured with patience. But in young and sane persons it is usually a defect of education, or of natural judgment, or both together. It leads some very young persons, like saucy children, to monopolize the time in conversation, to the exclusion of the aged and experienced. This is very indiscreet. Few things are more disgusting than the frivolous conversation of young people to each other in the presence of seniors. Well-educated and sensible young people, of both sexes, always pay respect to strangers and seniors, however inferior their accomplishments may be; but the ignorant and talkative respect no one, and, of course, no person respects them. They are radically defective in sound understanding, and in civility, and, therefore, introduce their uncalled-for questions and topics, without regard to circumstances.

A few individuals of loquacious habits, are sufficient to cause general confusion in a large social company; because no one of them is willing to be a hearer—they all speak at once, which produces sound without sense, very much resembling the gabble of a large flock of geese. Hence it is that social parties seldom afford any instructive or profitable conversation on subjects of general interest.

I have not the vanity to suppose that this short essay on loquacity will reform any confirmed talker; but it may possibly be the means of preventing some individuals from becoming such; and with that result I should not only be content, but feel amply rewarded for the labor of writing.

It is admitted that there is an opposite extreme to loquacity; that is, taciturnity, or habitual silence. This is also a fault to be guarded against. Very diffident and reserved persons are most liable to fall into this error. Often, when a few words might be spoken to the edification of some individual, or company, they keep silence, from timidity, or disinclination to talk, and thereby lose an opportunity of doing good. Man is a social being. It is wisdom in all to cultivate social habits and feelings; and one of the best means of doing so, is a familiar, friendly conversation. When we engage in social converse, it should be to instruct, impress, amuse, or gain information; and as some one of these objects may be effected with any civil companion, there is no necessity of confining our conversation to a few select friends. Extreme taciturnity is not profitable or commendable. Still, I am of the opinion, that to say too little is a less fault than to say too much, and, indeed, that it is better to say nothing than to speak unadvisedly.

There is, between the two extremes of loquacity and taciturnity, a happy medium; that of speaking on a suitable subject, at the right time, and in a proper manner, so as to accomplish some good purpose. If all would endeavor to speak thus, much idle and unprofitable talk would be dispensed with. Fine colloquial powers are among the choicest accomplishments of human life. If properly employed, they may be rendered exceedingly entertaining and instructive. They afford their possessor ready and easy access to society, and great facilities in accomplishing any object for which he is dependent on the co-operation of others; provided, always, that they be not used too freely. To be able to say enough on all occasions, without saying too much, is a rare attainment. It is the perfection of human converse, which every individual should aim to approximate as far as practicable.

THE TONGUE.

The term, tongue, is used not only to signify the organ of speech, but likewise good or evil conversation. The tongue is designed to render social intercourse convenient and agreeable, to communicate intelligence from man to man, and to celebrate the praise of God; but it is too frequently employed for evil purposes. It is a good or evil member, according to the use or abuse made of it. Who has not been entertained with the soft, broken accents of the babe, in his first efforts to imitate language, or profited by the conversation of an intelligent friend, or moved to pity by the plaintive cries of distress, or fired by the tongue of the orator, or charmed by the rich melody of song? And who has not been pained by the tongue of slander, shocked with the demoralizing tones of blasphemy, or disgusted with the insolence of self-conceited ignorance? Each individual is responsible for the use he makes of his own tongue, and should, therefore, learn to speak discreetly. Every word spoken contributes to the weal or woe of its author, if not to that of others. How solemn are the words of Christ, "But I say unto you, That every idle word that men shall speak, they shall give account thereof in the day of judgment. For by thy words thou shalt be justified, and by thy words thou shalt be condemned!" This awful truth needs no comment. Conscience approves, and warns us to prepare for its fulfillment. What, then, will be the final doom of thoughtless millions, who deal only in "the filthy conversation of the wicked!" Nay, what will become of thousands of the professed followers of the lowly Savior! Many who, in other respects, appear to be pious, are given to "evil-speaking;" that is, relating the faults of absent persons, which is as plainly forbidden as any other sin. While James says, "Speak not evil of one another, brethren," Paul requires Titus to "put them in mind" of what he had previously taught the brethren; namely, "To speak evil of no man, to be no brawlers, but gentle, showing all meekness unto all men," whether friends or foes. To expose the faults of one who is not present to answer for himself, betrays a want of moral courage, and is called, by the inspired writers, "backbiting;" and he who perpetrates it, is designated a "backbiter," because he acts like a dog that creeps after and seizes you unawares. When evil-speaking is carried on confidentially, in a low, soft tone, it is called "whispering;" and when the evil report is received and carried on to another, it is called "tale-bearing." But whatever form it assumes, it is condemned as sinful. Evil-speaking is productive of discord and strife. It hardens the heart of the speaker, prejudices the mind of the hearer, and injures the victim of it, with all concerned. It alienates friends, and frequently ends in Church trials, lawsuits, or acts of violence. Well might an inspired apostle say, "Behold, how great a matter a little fire kindleth! And the tongue is a fire, a world of iniquity; . . . and setteth on fire the course of nature; and is set on fire of hell." The same apostle testifies, "If any man among you seem to be religious, and bridleth not his tongue, but deceiveth his own heart, this man's religion is vain." Yes, such a man's religion is worthless, however long his face, or loud his profession. The only hope for him, and all other evil-speakers, is in sincere repentance for the past, and full confidence in the blood of Christ, which alone can wash out the deep stains of their guilt. Also, they would do well, for the future, to adopt the resolution of David: "I said, I will take heed to my ways, that I sin not with my tongue: I will keep my mouth with a bridle, while the wicked is before me." Most people are pleased with the idea of a long and prosperous life. The means of securing it is clearly pointed out in the following beautiful words of the Psalmist: "What man is he that desireth life, and loveth many days, that he may see good? Keep thy tongue from evil, and thy lips from speaking guile. Depart from evil, and do good; seek peace, and pursue it."

DANCING.

The reader of this article will scarcely suspect me of being influenced by the love of popularity, in selecting this topic. I am fully persuaded, however, that the signs of the times suggest it as an appropriate one; and I have as much right to claim the blessing of persecution for introducing it as any other person.

Various opinions appear to prevail respecting the practice of dancing. Some profess to regard it as a useful exercise, for the promotion of health. Whether any regular-bred physician, of good reputation, ever gives this prescription, is doubtful. Perhaps the process by which operatives in the business arrive at this conclusion has more to do with the heart, "which is deceitful above all things," than with enlightened reason. No intelligent individual, whose single aim is to promote health, it is presumed, would ever think of accomplishing that object by spending his or her nights amidst the revelry of a ball-room, in preference to quiet slumber at home. That exercise, taken in moderation, is good for health, is readily admitted; but it can be always had in a much more rational and profitable manner than dancing.

There are others who seem to view dancing, if not as a necessary recreation, at least as an innocent amusement. But how can any amusement be innocent which consumes a large amount of time, attention, and means, without imparting any good whatever? No one will seriously contend that dancing confers any useful knowledge, any love of mental improvement, any means of support, any lasting pleasure, or any weight of character in respectable society: on the contrary, it tends to idleness, frivolity, prodigality, the neglect of domestic duties, and lowers its devotee in the estimation of all serious and sensible people.

The inquiry is occasionally heard, is it not advisable to teach young people the art of dancing, in order to give them a graceful carriage? I have yet to learn that any affected carriage is either graceful or becoming. It may pamper the pride of the young heart, and call forth the empty applause of deceitful admirers; but the natural gait and appearance of any individual will always be preferred by the judicious of every community. The good opinion of those whose admiration of a lady could be excited by seeing her leaping and stepping to the sound of a violin, is of no real value. What sensible young man would choose a companion for life, who was celebrated only for the dissipating amusements of the merry dance? He would very naturally conclude, that those who are good for dancing, are seldom good for any thing else. But if the art of waltzing, with its kindred fooleries, be unworthy the attention of an intelligent lady, it is certainly more contemptible in the view of any sensible man.

Of what real use to mankind is a French dancing-master? What respectable man or woman in America envies him on account of all the influence he acquires in society, by teaching little misses to walk on tiptoe, and caper about like imitative monkeys? The children, of course, are not to be blamed; but what estimate will be placed upon the judgment of the parents, who commit the responsible duty of forming the principles and manners of their juvenile daughters to such a fashionable trifler, newly imported from a country famous for its libertinism? The tendency of all dancing schools among us, is to rear up a generation of dancing Americans, and even to impart the spirit of the thing to those who can not practically participate therein; so that when any foreigner of doubtful morals comes along, dancing for pay, they can readily get clear of hundreds and thousands of dollars, without receiving any, the least, benefit in lieu thereof.

The most inconsistent of all people, however, on the subject of dancing, are those professors of religion who show it any countenance. A member of any Church who attends masquerades, or balls, or allows his children to attend them, or sends his children to cotillon parties, or dancing schools, publicly contradicts his own profession of religion, and thereby notifies all men, that he has only a name to live, while he is spiritually dead. "Ye can not serve God and mammon." Praying and dancing never can be carried on to advantage at once, led by the same individual; nor can parents ever succeed in giving their children a religious education, who teach or have them taught to dance, any more than they could teach them to practice the principles of temperance, while giving them bitters in the morning, grog at noon, and wine in the evening. The idea of dedicating children to the service of God, with an expressed or implied pledge to train them up to a life of piety, and then sending them to a dancing school, is too absurd to be entertained for one moment.

I know that many professors of religion entertain the opinion that, though it is wrong to dance in public, it is proper to dance in private; and ask, how can young people enjoy this harmless recreation at home, or at a friend's house, unless they learn it at school, in their childhood? This notion is as dangerous as it is absurd. Children who are taught to dance at school, and encouraged to practice with their young companions at home, or at a friend's house, will have strong temptations to go to the public assemblies, and show with what skill they can "trip the light, fantastic toe." If your son be taught to play cards at home, first for amusement, then for apples, then in the social party for half-dimes, to keep up the interest, and then for something to drink, you may next expect to find him among blacklegs, staking his money, reputation, and happiness, at once, on the uncertain game of hazard. Vice is progressive, and in no cases more so than in drinking, gambling, and dancing.

All the truly pious, of every Church, regard dancing to be foolish in itself, and sinful in its tendency. The time and money wasted in preparations—the needless ornaments and costly decorations supposed to be requisite for appearing at the "splendid ball"—the chaffy conversation indulged in about beaux, belles, and parties, and the public performance itself, are all foolish in the extreme, and unbecoming rational beings; but how much more unsuitable do they appear, when those rational beings are viewed as candidates for an eternal state of retribution! God has often rebuked such folly in a signal manner, by the sudden affliction and death of some one of the party. In all such cases, the ball is at an end; but if dancing, with its appurtenances, be right in the sight of Heaven, why not dance on amidst affliction and death? The devotion of religious people is not checked, but rather increased by those solemn dispensations. The fact is, their own conscience reproves the votaries of the ball-room. They not only feel that all its professed pleasure is hollow-hearted and unsatisfying, but that the whole affair is one of sin and condemnation; and when the shafts of death begin to fall around them, they have not the courage to proceed, but acknowledge with some of old, "The joy of our heart is ceased: our dance is turned into mourning." What young lady would feel prepared to exchange the habiliments of the ball-room for a shroud? What young gentleman would be willing to be summoned from that scene of folly and rebellion to the judgment-seat of Christ? And how inconsistent it is to indulge in that course of conduct for which we know we must repent sorely, or be undone forever!

The appeal which some make to the Bible, in justification of this fashionable vice, is unfortunate for their cause. What was seriously performed, as a religious act of praise to God, though under a dispensation of comparative darkness, affords no excuse for those who dance for worldly amusement. David danced before the Lord, in a religious procession after the ark, thus performing his part of a religious ceremony, which would be a questionable mode of public worship under the Gospel dispensation. When our modern pleasure-takers dance in the fear of God, and in the conscious enjoyment of his love, as David did, we will let them pass.

There are other cases, quite different from this, on sacred record. Some of the Israelites in the wilderness forsook the God that made them, and had miraculously delivered them, and danced round a golden calf, the work of their own hands, for which their names were blotted out of the book of life. In this matter they acted about as wisely as do those of our day, who dance round the imaginary idol of worldly pleasure. Another case is recorded for our admonition in the New Testament. King Herod's birthday was celebrated with feasting and dancing. At the time referred to, his "august majesty" was living with his sister-in-law, Herodias, in an unlawful manner, for which John the Baptist had reproved them sharply. She had a daughter by her lawful husband, Miss Salome, who figured largely at the ball; for she danced before the king, and pleased him well, so that he rashly bound himself with an oath, in presence of witnesses, to give her whatsoever she would ask, to the half of his kingdom. Instructed by her infamous and revengeful mother, she said, "Give me, by and by, in a charger, [or dish,] the head of John the Baptist," which was done. This cruel and outrageous murder of a faithful minister of God was one of the fruits of dancing, and its kindred vices. It is to be hoped that American patriots may never disgrace the memory of Washington, by celebrating his birthday in a similar manner.

Dancing, like other sinful amusements, has had its ebbs and flows of popularity; has been sometimes in more, and then in less repute among us. It is a barbarian practice. There is much more dancing in heathen nations than in Christian nations. The lower people are degraded by ignorance and sin, the more they are devoted to this sort of dissipation. It flourishes most in this country when religion prospers least, and then declines again as vital piety prevails. The extraordinary revivals in the United States, some years ago, nearly drove dancing out of the country; but during the religious declension of the past few years, it has again reappeared more generally. This is easily accounted for: the more people pray, the less they feel like dancing; and the more they dance, the less they pray, or love praying. It was said by Solomon, "The heart of the wise is in the house of mourning; but the heart of fools is in the house of mirth."

I will close this article with an extract from Mr. Wesley's sermon on The More Excellent Way: "I can not say quite so much for balls or assemblies, which, though more reputable than masquerades, yet must be allowed, by all impartial persons, to have exactly the same tendency. So, undoubtedly, have all public dancings. And the same tendency they must have, unless the same caution obtain among modern Christians which was observed among ancient heathens. With them, men and women never danced together; but always in separate rooms. This was always observed in ancient Greece, and for several ages at Rome, where a woman dancing in company with men, would have at once been set down for a ——."

OBJECTIONS TO PROFANE SWEARING.

It is ungrammatical. Murray says, "The first rule for promoting the strength of a sentence, is, to prune it of all redundant words and members. It is a general maxim, that any words which do not add some importance to the meaning of a sentence, always injure it." Now, profane words never add importance to the meaning of a sentence, but are always redundant, and therefore ungrammatical. No profane swearer is a good practical grammarian. This abuse of language is found, mostly, among the ignorant and illiterate part of the community.

It is uncivil. A civil or polite man never wantonly insults any company into which he may be incidentally thrown, however he may differ from them in opinion on religious subjects, or respecting his general manner of life; but the profane man outrages the feelings of every serious, orderly company in which he appears. This is insufferable. Children who have been kindly and genteelly brought up, are sorely grieved to hear their parents slandered and abused, or even lightly spoken of; but not more so than Christians are, to hear the name of their heavenly Father profaned, or blasphemed. This is known to all intelligent men: hence, he who swears profanely, is not only no gentleman; he is a ruffian, unfit for civil society, and should be expelled from it, if he can not be reformed.

It is immoral. Legislation on the subject has so defined it, making it a penal offense, which subjects the offender to a fine in all cases; and public sentiment is in favor of this law, and would sustain magistrates in the enforcement thereof, otherwise it would not continue a part of our civil code in a free, elective government. Moreover, the offender's own conscience confirms this truth, unless it be "seared as with a hot iron." How awful he feels, when he thinks of facing the Judge of all the earth, whom he habitually insults, by a language more like the dialect of devils, than that of a rational man!

It is impious. A profane use of the name of God is characteristic of extreme wickedness, and is expressly forbidden by the divine law, under penalty of endless death. The following are a few of the many prohibitions and threats in the case: "Thou shalt not take the name of the

Lord thy God in vain: for the Lord will not hold him guiltless that taketh his name in vain." "Swear not, neither by heaven, neither by earth, neither by any other oath." "Because of swearing the land mourneth." "By swearing, and lying, and killing, and stealing, and committing adultery, they break out, and blood toucheth blood." "Every one that sweareth shall be cut off." "But he that shall blaspheme against the Holy Ghost hath never forgiveness, but is in danger of eternal damnation." These denunciations of the divine law are too awful for comment; let those who violate, read them, and tremble.

From this rapid view of the whole subject, I think the following inferences are legitimate: Profane swearing is unprofitable; it adds nothing to a man's fortune, reputation, or personal happiness; it does not secure for him the good opinion of others, nor a belief in the truth of his declarations, but the contrary; for it is generally admitted, that "he who will swear, will lie;" this is obvious from his daily practice, because the less truth there is in his words, and the more they are disputed, the harder he swears to confirm the belief of them.

It is a heinous offense against society, being a palpable and inexcusable violation of the laws of God and man; those who indulge in it are abominably wicked, and should receive no countenance from decent society, till they leave it off entirely.

Magistrates should so execute the duties of their office, as to be a terror to all such evil-doers. They are bound not only by their honorable and responsible relation to society, but also by the oath of office, to enforce the law for the suppression of vice, and can not, consistently with that oath, suffer men to swear with impunity under their jurisdiction, from any consideration of fear or favor. He who does so, betrays his trust, and is not worthy of the place he fills.

Lastly: all good men should co-operate with civil officers to put down this desolating vice. Ministers should preach pointedly against it; private Christians should reprove it; and all parents should positively prohibit and prevent it among their children, teaching them the fearful consequence of such evil; and to this end, keep them from all swearing company, for "evil communications corrupt good manners."

FALSEHOODS.

The propensity of our fallen nature to falsehood, or to utter what is known not to be true in fact, for deception, is not new. When David's mind was much affected, not only with sore trouble, from which no human power could deliver him, but with an awful sense of man's universal depravity, "he said in his haste, all men are liars." The sin of falsehood was prominent in the days of Christ and his apostles, as appears from their frequent and public reproofs of it. Indeed it appears to be one characteristic of our native depravity. Of the wicked, David says, "They go astray as soon as they be born, speaking lies." If this vice were to prevail universally, as it now does with some, all the confidence that men now have in each other would be lost: every useful organization in society, whether civil, religious, social, or benevolent, would be prostrated; the world would become one great scene of disorder, and universal despair would reign throughout the whole. With this view of the subject, and believing that the "spirit of lying" is abroad in the land, I make no apology for writing a few plain, but well-meant things on the subject. I will just premise, however, that these remarks are intended for general purposes; therefore, those who feel clear in these matters, will have no occasion to receive the reproof; those who may feel guilty, are requested not to transfer to their neighbors what belongs to themselves; and if they suit no one's case, then let this article go for lost labor.

Falsehoods are of various kinds, involving different degrees of criminality, according to the intent of him who commits them, and the evil they are calculated to produce. Some things, spoken or written, are untrue, but not known to be so by the speaker or writer at the time they are put forth; these are rather mistakes and infirmities, than sins, and, therefore, excusable. Yet they who commit such errors should embrace the first opportunity of correcting them, for the sake of truth, justice, and mutual confidence. But falsehoods, properly speaking, are numerous and various. Of these, I will here name a few.

LIES OF CEREMONY, OR FASHIONABLE LIES. Of this description are most of the compliments paid to men high in office, the puffs bestowed on play-actors, and the fashionable ceremonies of social life. In this country we have nothing to do with his Imperial Majesty, King of ——, his Holiness, the P——, or his Lordship, Bp. of ——. We sometimes hear of an intellectual feast, presented, with inimitable grace, by the highly-accomplished and justly-admired Mrs. ——, who appears on the stage for the entertainment of the *rabble;* enough to sicken any man of sense, not to say of religion. But the same spirit of "lying vanity" appears more or less in the daily intercourse of men. When two strangers are introduced, it is common to hear it said, "I am very happy to be acquainted with you," though, in most cases, no such happiness is felt. One individual, wishing to be thought hospitable, or to accomplish some other selfish object, will say to another, in conformity to the rules of politeness, "I should be highly delighted to see you at my house," while, in his heart, he hopes the invitation may not be accepted, or, rather, that the visit may not be paid. Again: a man will write a letter filled with abuse, that betrays prejudice and hatred, and finish with these words: "I am, dear sir, yours, respectfully." This short compliment, in every such case, contains two lies; for the person addressed is neither *dear* to, nor *respected* by the writer. Another will subscribe himself, "Your obedient, humble servant," who could not be more highly incensed, by any insult, than to be called the "servant" of any man.

Marvelous lies. These are often told by those who are addicted to relating wondrous stories, and who, for the sake of the tale, or blowing the trumpet of their own fame the louder, will magnify a little occurrence into a large one; changing or supplying facts so as to set off the story to the best advantage. Can a man tell what he knows to be false, in whole or in part, to excite admiration or wonder, even though the story, in other respects, be harmless, and yet remain innocent? "I trow not." Again: many individuals, perhaps without designing any evil at first, contract a foolish habit of indulging in extravagant sayings and comparisons, such as these: "I am as cold as ice;" "I thought I should have died laughing;" "I am wearied to death;" "This bread is as hot as fire;" "I would ten thousand times rather live in the country than in the city," etc. This impropriety is found occasionally among people who, in other respects, appear to be harmless and even pious, which shows that, in such cases, it is more the result of habit than evil intention. Some years since, a brother in the Church given to this fault, was reproved by a venerable minister, and advised to be more guarded in future; he received it kindly, and promptly acknowledged he was sorry for his numerous offenses of the sort; adding, "Brother C., I have shed *barrels* of tears on that very account!"

Selfish lies. These are often told by trading men, from considerations of interest, to impose on others for the sake of "a good bargain." If "salesmen," "horse-swappers," and "land-mongers," are clear of the charges, so much the better. Some men involve themselves in the charge of falsehood by want of punctuality in business. A mechanic advertises to execute work with neatness and dispatch, and invites custom. A bill is handed in for work, and accepted. The work is promised at a certain day, and called for, but not obtained. The customer is put off with some trifling apology, and a renewal of the promise that his work shall *certainly* be done by a given time; but he is again disappointed. After going from three to six times after a hat—I did not say bonnet—coat, pair of shoes, watch, or some implement of husbandry, or mechanism, of which he has the promise, and hearing twice that number of lies told by the master of the shop, it may possibly be obtained for the full value of it, beside the disappointment and loss of time. The sin of the disappointing party does not consist in failing to perform what is impracticable, but in promising what he knows to be so, rather than lose a job by letting the customer go elsewhere. And how much better is the farmer that engages to bring your breadstuff, fuel, or provender, and fails; the debtor who secures your property on an obligation to pay at a certain time, which he knows he can not do, or does not intend to perform; the minister who calls out the people by the promise of a sermon, and then, for a trivial difficulty, or from want of inclination, fails to meet them; or, in a word, any individual of any calling, who is in the habit of making voluntary engagements, and willfully breaking them, which is no more or less than habitual *lying?* If such people could be convinced that "honesty is the best policy," and persuaded to act accordingly, it would add much to their interest, by an increase of public confidence and patronage, and much to the comfort of all concerned. One point more should be noticed here. Not unfrequently, men having committed faults, will deny them, or tell lies to conceal them; thus adding sin to sin, instead of seeking pardon for those already committed, by suitable acknowledgment. O, human nature, how art thou fallen!

PROFESSIONAL LIES. The charge of falsehood no more lies against all professional men, than it does against all mechanics, farmers, or traders. But is it not too just in reference to some of each profession? What think you of the doctor who, to get employ, will tell the patient he is very ill, when he knows but little ails him; or, what is worse, that the patient is in a curable condition, when he knows the contrary? Are there not just such doctors in the world? Again: what think ye of that "limb of the law," who encourages his client to bring suit, by assuring him of success, while he believes that success is doubtful; and who represents the said client as a worthy citizen, while he knows him to be a scoundrel; and awards a fair reputation to the perjured witness that is used to swear him clear, and stamps with infamy the character of every honest man who dares to tell the truth against him? He may be a shrewd lawyer, but he is not a respectable one, nor a man of truth. Of just such characters, there are too many. Once more: what think ye of the pretended minister of Christ, who preaches what he knows to be false as certainly as he knows the Bible to be true; as, for instance, that there is no general judgment in a future state, no punishment to the wicked after death? Is he not a "lying prophet?" Every man must admit this, or deny the truth of the following texts: "It is appointed unto men once to die, but after this the judgment;" "I saw the dead, small and great, stand before God;" "For we must all appear before the judgment-seat of Christ:

that every one may receive the things *done* in *his* body, according to that he hath done, whether *it be* good or bad;" "Then shall he say to them on his left hand, Depart from me, ye cursed, into everlasting fire, prepared for the devil and his angels."

Malicious lies. Of all falsehoods, these are the most criminal, being uttered not only to deceive those to whom they are told, but purposely to injure the characters against whom they are directed, and to gratify the spirit of malice in the propagator of them. Of all the principles of our fallen nature, this is one of the most degrading. The victim of slander may be one whose only crime or offense is, that of an amiable character, forming such a contrast with that of the slanderer, as to become an object of hatred; for the carnal mind, which is enmity against God, is also opposed to his image, formed on the hearts, and exhibited in the lives of his children. Hence, "all that will live godly in Christ Jesus, shall suffer persecution"—will be pursued with malice and intent to injure. Or the pretext for slander may be some personal offense, real or supposed, for which revenge is sought without regard to truth; or it may originate in envy, on account of rivalship; but no matter what, the principle of slander is the same.

Now, as lies are more or less criminal, and as men are to be judged according to their deeds, some of those who deal in falsehood may be punished more than others; but fearful will be the doom of them all. He that is to judge the world in righteousness, has said, "All liars shall have their part in the lake which burneth with fire and brimstone; which is the second death."

Lies of misrepresentation. One of the most successful methods of propagating falsehood, is to mix some appearance of truth with it, to render it less suspicious to those who at first are not prepared to enter entirely into the views of the propagator. A compound of truth and falsehood, is more dangerous than simple falsehood, because it is more difficult to understand, disprove, and counteract. Open infidelity is less to be feared than semi-infidelity. But our business is with practice rather than opinion. When the Jews demanded of Jesus a sign, he meekly replied, "Destroy this temple, [meaning his body,] and in three days I will raise it up." Whereupon they charged him with affirming, that he could rebuild the Jewish temple in three days, which cost their fathers forty-six years labor. Thus they perverted his words. This case forcibly illustrates a principle of our nature as old as the fall of man; one which is characteristic of his children who is the *father of lies*. When prejudice is formed in the mind against an individual, his enemies, instead of interpreting his conduct by the rules of fairness, catch at every word that can be wrested from the true design of the author, and use it to his disadvantage. This is not doing as they would be done by. Simple lies are easily detected, in most cases, and therefore comparatively harmless, except to the authors of them; but dark insinuations and lies, mixed with some truth to make them current, require a nice investigation to separate the good and evil, and are, consequently, more mischievous in their tendency. This principle of misrepresentation is too common among violent partisans, both in politics and religion, whether expressed through the press, in legislative halls, or from the pulpit. Desperate, indeed, must be that cause, which requires slander to support its claims on public opinion.

COMMONPLACE LIES. Let any candid man make his observations on men and things as he pursues his ordinary business in any populous place, and then say whether there be any just ground for this charge, we do not say against all, but against too many. Let him take a few lessons, as an observer, where he will see human nature acted out in little things. Examples:

Wherever I turn my eyes, they are frequently met with the word GROCERY. In some cases, it is a fair index to the shop which bears the inscription; as such, it is convenient and right. But when the grocery is in fact a "drunkery," and, instead of sugar, coffee, etc., contains barrels, kegs, and bottles full of rum, gin, brandy, and whisky, it has a *lie* inscribed, in large letters, without, and bears the strong marks of pollution and crime within. Another word made very conspicuous among us, of late, is, COFFEE-HOUSE. Where the term is truly applied, it means a house of entertainment. But when a house is set apart for retailing strong drink, drunkenness, gambling, swindling, and swearing, all days and nights of the week—Sunday not excepted—no man can nail up his sign over his door, with the title coffee-house, without publicly recording a falsehood. Enough of this for the present.

LIES IN HIGH PLACES. The Bible says, "Men of high degree are a lie." In most cases their pretended patriotism is empty show. What they profess to do for the love of their country, is too often done for self-aggrandizement; and what they pretend to do from principle, is frequently done for party purposes. I speak not of any party exclusively, but of individuals in all parties. The unrenewed heart is deceitful above all things, and desperately wicked.

If falsehood and deceit existed only without the pales of the visible Church, the consequence would be less evil. But this is not the fact. Suppose a man should profess belief in the doctrine and government of some branch of the Christian Church, in order to gain admission to her privileges, or obtain ordination among her ministers, and then spend most of his time in writing, preaching, or speaking against the same things to which he had subscribed in a public and formal manner; with what would he be justly chargeable? If, in such case, he be sincere and speak the truth when he makes his formal profession of belief, which should be done with all the solemnity of an oath, he is not sincere and does not speak truly, when he opposes that belief; and if true and honest in his opposition, then he is not so in his profession. If it be said, he might change his belief after joining a Church, or being ordained a minister; I answer, then let him proclaim that change, and peaceably retire like an honest man, unite with those of the same opinion, and he will be both believed and respected. But he who remains in any Church, and so opposes her doctrines and his own former creed as to disturb her quiet, and break the peace of her members, is not entitled to much credit for his honesty or veracity. "Their deceit is falsehood," Psalm cxix, 118. All hypocrisy is falsehood. Every hypocrite is a liar. His profession, his prayers, songs, alms, and acts of public devotion, are all lies. He may deceive himself by aiming to deceive others; but God can not be deceived, and will not be mocked. He can not look upon sin with allowance, but he abhors *lying* in all its forms, especially in those who "depart from the faith, giving heed to seducing spirits, and doctrines of devils; speaking lies in hypocrisy, having their conscience seared with a hot iron, forbidding to marry, and commanding to abstain from meats," etc. For further proof of the Divine displeasure against this sin, I refer to the fearful end of Annanias and Sapphira, who having "lied to the Holy Ghost," suddenly fell down, and were carried out to their burial. See Acts v, 1–11.

HOW TO PREPARE SUBJECTS FOR THE PENITENTIARY.

As the state is mostly dependent on parents for the raw material, I would suggest a few things to those parents who live in cities and large towns, and who wish to propose their sons as candidates for penitentiary distinction, which, if they attend to, will probably prove successful.

If young children cry for what they want, be sure to give it to them, that they may be encouraged to cry again.

When the mother bids her little son to do her any service, let his father put these words in his mouth for answer: "I won't." And if his mother undertake to correct him for a fault, let his father take the rod from her and throw it in the fire: this will greatly confirm him in his rebellion.

As soon as boys are large enough, let them run at large in the street, selecting their own company. If they want candy or toys, give them money to go and buy at will, to encourage their extravagance. Furnish them also with marbles, and send them out with larger and worse boys, that they may not only learn the game, but also the art of profane swearing: but do not send them to school; it is too confining. As they advance in years, let them know that Sunday is a day intended for strolling, fishing, and swimming, and not for Church and Sabbath school. Send them to all shows and public occasions, but more especially to the circus and theater.

Instead of training them to labor and habits of industry, let them race all day through the market-house, throwing stones at each other, and at night go the rounds wherever inclination leads, sport with squibs, and halloo without restraint.

It will not be necessary for parents to be at the trouble of continuing this course long; boys at ten or twelve years of age, under such training, will have such a fine start, as to be able to proceed with success in the school of vice; many of them will graduate before they are eighteen; be turned loose on society well prepared to act their part in villainy, and obtain an honorable seat in the penitentiary before they are eligible for one in the legislature. There is a large and promising lot of them coming on in Cincinnati, and some smaller classes of them in the less populous places of the west.

BEECH-LOG SCHOOL-HOUSE.

To ONE who was born in, and has ever hailed from the west, it is matter of interest to compare the present state of society in the Mississippi Valley, as it regards the knowledge of letters, with what it was at the beginning of the nineteenth century. The contrast is striking. Well do I remember the first school I ever attended in the days of my childhood, the latter part of the year 1800, which may serve as a specimen of the literary institutions of that period, and in that part of the country. I was but little more than six years old, but had the advantage of going in company with two older brothers and a sister. To receive the benefits of that school, we had daily to cross and recross the Big Kanawha river in a canoe. Our temple of science was a small hut, built of round logs and covered with clapboards, having no floor but the naked earth. During the forenoon of the first day the school opened, the teacher and large boys were employed in repairing the house, while the smaller children were scraping up an outdoor acquaintance. Amid those scenes, to me perfectly novel, one of the teacher's sons, older than I, took from my hand Dilworth's Spelling-Book, and examining it, asked questions and received answers as follows: "Are you in baker?" No. "Are you in a-b ab's?" No. "Are you in a b c's?" No. "What then?" In nothing yet; I have just come to begin. In the afternoon we heard the call, "Come to books." I began with the alphabet, and before night could read it all correctly, and felt encouraged, especially so when allowed to "turn a leaf" next day.

Our school-house was situated in a beech grove on the bank of the river, a few miles above Charleston, Va., on the present site of the celebrated Kanawha Saline, where, in those days, our slumbers were often disturbed by the howling of wolves, or an uproar among the swine, occasioned by the attack of a wild bear, which was always promptly repelled by the hardy settlers, with their dogs and rifles, and generally attended with a total defeat on the part of the ferocious enemy.

The teacher—Mr. Clayton—was little more than a dwarf in stature, but decidedly a gentleman in his manners, and a very popular schoolmaster of that day. It is true his scientific attainments were very limited, but that was not then objectionable, as the standard of education was very moderate. Indeed, many of those born and reared in the west, among the early settlers, had none at all, nor did they generally feel much concern on the subject. Those who did pretend to afford their children a knowledge of letters, had many difficulties to contend with, especially the want of competent teachers. The custom in country places then was, for some one of the farmers best qualified for the task, to spend a few weeks, or months, of the most leisure season of the year, in teaching the children of the neighborhood, whose parents might choose to send them, at a small expense, say $1.25

a quarter, payable in work or provisions. In this way some of them succeeded in obtaining such an education as was then thought to be necessary among the common people; for the course was very short and superficial. Girls learned to spell and read imperfectly—the art of writing being a rare attainment among the native daughters of the west of that day, except in the larger towns, and a few favored spots in the older settlements. The education of a boy was then considered sufficient among us if he could spell, read, write, and had "ciphered to the rule of three;" and if by any superior privilege was added to these a knowledge of grammar and geography, he was considered quite learned. The following were the principal items in the bill of expense for the entire course of studies: one child's book, one spelling-book, one reader, one New Testament—which should never be excluded—one quire of foolscap, one arithmetic, one slate, and the tuition fees of a few quarters—the pupil gathered his pencil from the brook, and plucked his quills from the wing of a raven, or wild goose, killed by the father's rifle.

Great simplicity of manners then prevailed. The teacher and children ate their dinners from their school-baskets, and frequently united, on a common level, in the sports of "play-time," as they called the recess at noon. The amusements consisted of athletic exercises, such as foot-racing, leaping, catch-ball, corner-pen, etc. Those of the girls, who were always required to occupy different ground, were milder and more simple. The scholars were, generally, disposed to conform to the rules of the preceptor, except once a year, when they would deliberately enter into a plot to "turn out the master," that they might enjoy a Christmas frolic without restraint. The manner of conducting on such occasions was sufficiently ludicrous. When the appointed time arrived, which they took good care to keep concealed from the master, they met early in the morning in the school-house, and secured the door with bars, logs, etc., shutting themselves in and him out. They also took care to arm themselves with clubs, sharp-pointed sticks, and shovels for throwing ashes, should he attempt to descend the chimney. When he came and demanded entrance, it was refused; but they presented him with written terms of compromise, securing to themselves as much holiday as they desired. If he complied, the door was unbarred; if not, they put him at defiance. In some instances he obtained a reinforcement, and attempted to storm their fort, when a general engagement would ensue; but knowing what would be the consequence if overcome, they fought like little heroes and heroines, and generally maintained their ground too; for their cause was popular with the citizens, and but few would join to oppose the little rebels. Strange as it may seem, this custom prevailed with the knowledge and consent of the parents and patrons of the school, who frequently took more delight in feats of strength and activity among their children, than in literary acquirements.

Since that I have had occasion to travel considerably through the west, and from the information obtained in this way, I am satisfied that the same state of things that existed in our own neighborhood at the beginning of the nineteenth century, in reference to learning, very generally prevailed in the western states and territories; from which the reader can judge of the opportunity we had of becoming scholars.

A few years subsequently, however, a brighter day began to dawn upon us.

In 1811 Mr. Paine, a native of England, who was a member of the Methodist Church, came to the west, and taught the first grammar class ever formed in Cabell county, where we then lived. He had been employed about forty years as a teacher in different parts of America, raised a large family, and given them a good English education, but had little else as the proceeds of his toils to leave them. He died a few years after, a poor, but pious and highly-respectable man. Such were the encouragements of teachers among us in those days, who were competent, for he was eminently so. Of his first grammar class in that part of the country, several became professional men, and have since been useful to society as physicians, jurists, and divines. Mr. Paine's school was a mile and a half from the clerk's office, in which I was then employed; and after completing my day's work, I walked that distance every afternoon to recite my grammar lesson, prepared at home in the evening, and reviewed on my way to school. Still I kept up and graduated with the class, and never since regretted my extra effort to secure that little stock of knowledge.

BURNING CANE.

Pioneers of the south-west often settle in the midst of extensive cane-brakes, and occupy camps for temporary habitations, till they can erect houses. To prepare the ground for cultivation, they first cut down the cane, which is from fifteen to twenty-five feet high, from a half an inch to an inch and a half in diameter, and so close together in places, that it can be passed with great difficulty by man or beast. The main stalks are straight, hollow, and jointed; these put forth small branches toward the top, covered with a foliage of evergreen. Among these beautiful reeds, an experienced hand, with his crooked cleaver, makes great havoc, taking the forest in throughs, like the reapers do the field of corn, and laying the cut cane with some degree of regularity behind him, that he may have room to work. When all is laid waste, the whole ground is covered with a layer some two feet thick, which, when properly dried, is set on fire, and creates a flame sufficient to clear the ground of underbrush and all light combustible matter. Burning the cane also kills the standing trees, which are generally few and large on such ground; for it not only produces an immense heat about the trunks, but also communicates flame to the long moss which is attached in large quantities to the boughs, till the whole area seems to be enveloped in a general conflagration, rising above the tops of the tallest sweet gums and elms. What adds greatly to the interest of the occasion, is the terrible sound caused by the action of the fire on the cane stalks, all the joints of which, unless previously fractured by accident, burst with steam pressure, making reports similar to those of fire-arms. In a very dry time the fire will run through standing cane, where there is enough of the dead article to set the green on fire; and in such case the reports are louder, though less rapid, for the green cane produces more steam than the dry. Perhaps there is no noise which so much resembles that of a fearful battle between two extensive armies of enraged soldiers, as the noise of a cane-brake on fire. As the fire passes through the thinner places, the explosions of the small, the medium, and the large joints, resemble the reports of numerous pistols, rifles, and muskets, all distinctly heard in quick succession; but when the fire gets properly under way in the stiff cane-brake, whether cut or standing, the explosions are like a heavy volley simultaneously poured from the whole length of the opposing lines in battle array. The effects, however, on the feelings are very different; while the noise of the battle thrills the soul with horror, that of the burning cane forest imparts emotions at once sublime and pleasant.

ZOOLOGY—ALLIGATOR.

THE American crocodile, or alligator, has been justly styled "the king of reptiles." Those of the south-west, when fully grown, are usually from nine to twelve feet long, rather larger round the middle than a common-sized man, and weigh from two to three hundred pounds. In their general form they resemble the lizard. The mouth is of fearful dimension, especially when extended; for, unlike other animals, they have power to move, not only the lower, but also the upper jaw, by reason of a joint on the back of the head where it joins on to the neck, which gives the head a singular and frightful appearance. The upper and lower parts of the alligator are shielded by scales, or connected, bony substances, as large as silver dollars, a quarter of an inch thick, and nearly as impenetrable as iron. These scales are overlaid with a thin membranous substance, which gives them rather a smooth, spotted appearance. Immediately over the spine there is a row of scales with horns, or knobs, projecting upward, which causes the animal's back to appear scolloped or indented. His sides are covered only with thick, tough hide, which will answer for tug-strings, or coarse leather. His legs are short, resembling those of the tortoise, and better adapted to swimming than traveling on land, the hind feet being much larger than the fore ones. The tail is flat, and finned at the end, like that of a fish, and is used in the same way for swimming. The alligator is amphibious. On land he is inactive, and moves slowly, as a quadruped; in water more rapidly, by the double motion of feet and tail. The oil of this animal is valuable for dressing leather; the flesh is inferior, similar in appearance and taste to the flesh of a monstrous cat-fish.* His tusks are very large, and sometimes they are manufactured into chargers, to measure powder for the woodman's rifle. The strength of alligators is thought to be immense; and they are known to be very destructive to swine and other stock, which resort to the edge of their native rivers and bayous. The manner in which this creature usually takes his prey deserves a passing notice. Where he expects stock or wild animals, he lies concealed near the shore, as still as a log, with only one eye and the tip of his nose above water; or, if he discovers his prey near the water's edge when he is distant, he will approach so slowly and slyly, as not to be discovered till he gets within striking distance; then making a sudden, powerful sweep with the tail, knocks down the animal, and at the same time throwing the head round, and snapping with the mouth, by which he forms himself into a circle, seizes his victim, and instantly disappears under water till it is drowned, when he brings it to shore, or to a log that appears above the water, where he soon devours the carcass. When they are on land, they will strike at whatever comes in their way, though they are not there so dangerous; because being exceedingly clumsy, it is easy to keep out of their way. It is said they will bite nothing while it is under water, but will seize any animal on the surface, from a duck to a horse, and draw it under with great force, always seizing that part of the animal which is above the water. The female alligator deposits her eggs on dry land, where they are hatched by the heat of the sun; they are white, about the size of turkey eggs, and are

*My information respecting the taste was derived from a gentleman, who stated that he and a few others, when employed as soldiers in Florida, some years ago, being in a starving condition, had made a repast on an alligator's tail. But if we may judge of the taste from the smell, it was not a very delicious meal—the animal puts forth a perfume resembling musk.

numerous—from forty to sixty in one nest. The nest is usually formed of sticks and leaves near the water, and is often found by the alligator's slide, or smooth path up the bank of the river, which she makes by traveling to and from her nest. The bellow of the male alligator, which is often heard in the spring of the year, is hideous, reminding one of distant thunder. On the Black river, in Louisiana, and the neighboring lakes and bayous, where they have not been so frequently alarmed by steamboats, nor the sportsman's gun, alligators are quite tame, and may be easily killed with a well-charged rifle, or a strong spear, as they lie half torpid on the shore, sunning themselves during the first warm spring days along the water's edge. In 1837 I saw a very large one receive, on the side of his head, a deadly shot of a rifle, fired from the hurricane deck of a steamboat, as she ascended Black river. On receiving the shot, he suddenly turned on his side, quivered a few seconds, and commenced his death-struggle, like any other animal shot through the brain.

A HAPPY COLONY.

Good news; glad tidings of great joy unto all people! A colony has been formed, calculated to meet the views and promote the happiness of all concerned. Let the north give up, and the south keep not back. Let the friends of abolition and of colonization cease their strife, and unitedly go into the highways and hedges to bring in colonists. There is ample territory provided for all. Multitudes are willing to go, and only wait to learn by what means they can get there. About this, there need be no failure, for exhaustless treasures are pledged for the success of the enterprise. The colony is located in the best climate, and on the best soil in the universe, where there is no war, no lawless tumult, no poverty, no toil or peril, disease or famine. Though the colony is remote, the voyage to it is soon made; and with perfect safety, if you take a passage in the colony's daily packet, which plies constantly between it and all the ports of the known world. The benefits of this colony are not limited to the colored race; but extend to all of every nation, whether black, red, white, or tawny, who were in bondage, but have been redeemed by an incalculable price. The ransom was paid by a most benevolent King, who proposes now, with their consent, to knock off their manacles, "make them free indeed," and colonize them in the choicest part of his dominions. Very many are already there, who find prepared for them a city more splendid, with mansions more spacious and beautiful than any described by ancient or modern historians; and this colony is finally to become the permanent home of all the truly wise, virtuous, and pious, among all nations, but of none others. None possessed of intemperate habits, vicious principles, or malevolent feelings, can ever be admitted to that peaceful country. It is situated in the regions of IMMORTALITY, and is called THE PROMISED LAND; the name of the chief city is NEW JERUSALEM; and the King of the country is styled, THE DESIRE OF ALL NATIONS. His throne resembles a mountain of ivory environed with evergreens, from the foot of which issues a crystal stream, deep and broad, called the River of Life. The habiliments of the King are flowing robes, extending to the feet, as bright as the morning light, and fastened with a golden girdle; a rainbow encircles his head; his face outshines the sun; and on his breastplate of righteousness is written, "KING OF KINGS, AND LORD OF LORDS." Immediately around HIM, are the myriads of his redeemed subjects, who "have washed their robes, and made them white in the blood of the Lamb," singing the new song, which none can sing but those redeemed from the earth by the King. These are the colonists proper. Next to them, but a little further from the throne, are the natives of the country, called "the sons of God;" they are the same who shouted when the foundations of the earth were laid. These natives, though they can not sing the new song, appear to be much delighted with it. They stand the ready and willing messengers of the King on all errands of mercy and love, especially in reference to all those who are candidates for the promised land. The number of these is increasing every day. The population of the colony is already immense; our informant—Revelation, 7th chapter—says he saw "a hundred and forty and four thousand of all the tribes of the children of Israel" there; and adds, "After this I beheld, and lo, a great multitude which no man could number, of all nations, and kindreds, and people, and tongues, stood before the throne, and before the Lamb, clothed with white robes, and palms in their hands; and cried with a loud voice, saying, Salvation to our God, which sitteth upon the throne, and unto the Lamb!" Who will go and join this happy colony? All who accede to the King's terms, can have an inheritance among their brethren, for the King says, "Look unto me, and be ye saved, all the ends of the earth; for I am God, and there is none else."

MORAL CONFLICT.

There is a revolt in one of the provinces of the King of kings, and a terrible war in progress. The whole world is more or less interested in and affected by it. The things in dispute are the souls of men—deathless spirits, destined to endless bliss, or endless woe. The value of an immortal spirit may be inferred from the vast expenditure of blood and treasure for its recovery from the ruins of the fall; also from the fact, that the energies of both worlds are engaged in the conflict over it. God and his angels are for it, the devil and his angels are against it, and men and women are divided on the subject. At first view, the prospect looks gloomy; especially when the soul itself is so intoxicated by sin as to be bewildered, and apparently indifferent as to whose hands it may fall into, or what destiny awaits it hereafter. The immediate scene of action is this earth we inhabit; and in no part of the earth is the conflict more signal than in these United States. Here the enemy is intrenching himself; struggling to get and keep possession of the strongholds, especially about the large cities and great thoroughfares of travel. A very brief survey of the ground is sufficient to observe the inroads the enemy is making. Those public lines of Sunday travel are prostituted highways for the transportation of the devil's troops and military stores; gaming-houses are the devil's military academies; tippling-houses are the devil's outposts, where he enlists his raw recruits; dancing-masters and fiddlers are his fuglemen to train them in his infernal tactics; infidel papers are the devil's banners, on whose vile folds is inscribed, "I believe in all unbelief;" distributors of novels and all sorts of infidel publications are the devil's colporteurs; infidel orators, whether called lecturers or preachers, are the devil's embassadors; race-grounds are the devil's muster-fields, where he reviews his troops and numbers his forces; theaters and circuses are the devil's chapels, where his worshipers shout his praise; houses of debauchery are favorite places of resort, where the devil and his personal friends hold their night revels; but that place of general resort and fashionable dissipation on the Lord's day, wherever it may be selected, is the devil's headquarters, where he holds councils of war with his subalterns, and plans his general onslaughts. Thus the enemy covers a broad surface.

This array of opposition looks fearful; but "He that is for us is greater than all that can be against us; and, though he works by means and second causes, he will go before us, and fight our battles for us. Our thirty thousand churches, like so many fortifications, well supplied with heavenly munitions, are weekly filled with some millions of soldiers of the cross, armed with the shield of faith and the sword of the Spirit. These, like patriot soldiers, defending their own just rights, are nerved with courage more than mortal—knowing that truth is mighty, and must prevail. Our colleges and seminaries are preparing many minds to act a distinguished part in this glorious cause. Our Bible houses and religious book concerns, are armories, preparing abundance of ordnance. Religious tract societies are throwing incessant showers of bird-shot into the faces of the invading foe; the religious press continually pours a galling fire of grape-shot through all the ranks of the enemy; Bible societies are driving a million of battering-rams against the bowing walls of the devil's kingdom, and shaking them to their sandy foundations; while missionary societies are hurling Gospel bombs into all his strongholds, and blowing up his magazines. In the mean time, thirty thousand pulpits are filled with embassadors of heaven, exhorting millions to yield to the scepter of mercy, and render obedience to the King of Zion. Many wounded in spirit are brought into the Gospel hospital, and healed by the heavenly Physician; while others, convinced that they are waging an unequal and inglorious warfare against their rightful Sovereign, make a Gospel surrender at the altar of prayer, and become the willing subjects of the Prince of life. By our own division of the Christian army, during the past year, more than thirty-two thousand souls were made joyful prisoners of hope. Our German missions are extending the victories of the cross of Christ even among the legions of the Pope's invincibles, which were sent over to invade our happy land. Thus, by fire and sword, does God plead with all flesh; but they are the fire of love, and the sword of the Spirit. Triumphantly does the peaceful banner of the Gospel wave over thousands of places, once the strongholds of Satan. "The Captain of our salvation," made perfect through suffering, never loses a battle. He is "mighty to save, and strong to redeem." In his service, the race is not to the swift, nor the battle to the strong. His strength is made perfect in our weakness; so that one shall chase a thousand, and two put ten thousand to flight.

If it be asked what is the prospect before us, let the reports of the Sabbath school unions answer. In all the American Churches the number of children trained in Sabbath schools is about two millions—enough to fill a field containing a hundred acres. By these the Churches will be filled with spiritual worshipers, new colonies formed, and the Gospel carried to heathen lands. Now, suppose all these were assembled in one place, and they should all at once begin to sing,

> "Praise God, from whom all blessings flow;
> Praise him all creatures here below," etc.;

or suppose that, like the children who saw Jesus descending from the Mount of Olives, they should wave their palm-leaf banners, and shout, "Hosanna to Him that cometh in the name of the Lord! hosanna in the highest!" would it not send a thrill of joy to the hearts of millions of Christians, and spread dismay and terror through all the ranks of the enemy? But, distributed, as they are, over these United States, they are doing a thousand times more for the cause of Christ than they could, if all were assembled in one solid square. And when they reach maturity, and become fully imbued with the spirit of piety, as most of them will, what shall stand before them? The sight of them would be sufficient to make the stoutest infidel hearts quail; and when they raise the torches of salvation, and shout, "The sword of the Lord and of Gideon," the ranks of the devil must give way, and break into general confusion; for "one shall become a thousand, and a small one a strong nation: I the Lord will hasten it in his time."

Part Second.

BIOGRAPHICAL SKETCHES.

Biographical Sketches.

REV. VALENTINE COOK.

Among the fathers of American Methodism, but few, if any, were more distinguished in the work than the Rev. V. Cook. Though no regular biographical sketch of his life and labors should ever be published, his name would be handed down by tradition from father to son, and from mother to daughter, to the third and fourth generations. His monument is in the affections of the people. I am pleased, however, to learn that some of his lineal descendants are collecting materials for such a work, and wish them great success. The Church of Christ has already suffered much loss by its being deferred so long.

While Mr. Cook was a student in one of the colleges of Pennsylvania, if I am correctly informed, he gave indications of deep piety, and of talents which promised extensive usefulness in the work of the ministry, to which he was evidently called of God. And such was the demand for laborers in that day, that Bishop Asbury made a call for him to go out into the vineyard of the Lord before he was ready to graduate; and feeling himself moved thereto by the Holy Spirit, he left all and followed Christ. He was admitted as a traveling preacher in 1788. His first appointment was to Calvert, in the Baltimore conference; but most of his life was spent in the western country, especially Kentucky.

Mr. Cook's person was peculiar. He was very tall, but somewhat stooping in the shoulders; had a giant frame, without any surplus flesh. His small, dark eyes were set far back in his large head: his mouth was unusually large; the general features of his face were coarse, his complexion somber, and his beard heavy. Still, when he was preaching, and his countenance lighted up with intelligence, and his features softened with a glow of benevolence, and smoothed over with heavenly serenity, his appearance was not only striking, but, upon the whole, rather agreeable. No doubt one simple-hearted, pious woman thought so, when, having received a great blessing under his preaching, she looked up to him in the pulpit and said, "Father Cook, God bless your big mouth!"

In his manners, brother Cook was a pattern of Christian simplicity; so much so, that children felt unembarrassed in his presence. His colloquial powers were of a high order; and to all pious people he was at once an instructive and agreeable companion. Though capable of discussing any subject, his standing theme was religion. Whatever topic of conversation was introduced, he, in the end, turned it to the account of godly edification. He was considered, by all who knew him, a good fireside preacher, and, of course, was always a welcome guest.

Brother Cook, as a preacher, was altogether above the medium grade. His pulpit performances were marked for appropriateness, variety, fluency, and extraordinary force. Though possessed of a pacific spirit, he soon became distinguished as a defender of the faith against the various antichristian systems of the age and country in which he lived and labored; for in that day our fathers had numerous opponents, and had to contend with the sword of the Spirit, which is the word of God, for every inch of ground they occupied. But he became much more distinguished on account of his wonderful success in winning souls to Christ. Though he was a man of science and letters, he placed no dependence in either when preaching; but dealt only in the article of Gospel truth, presented in the most simple form, but in demonstration of the Spirit and of power. This he did, apparently, with a firm confidence that God would bless his own truth to the present salvation of his hearers; and he was but seldom disappointed. Thousands received the word of life from his lips, who never heard it to profit before, and became the humble and happy subjects of the saving grace of God.

After being employed some twelve years as a regular itinerant preacher, want of health, or some other circumstance, induced him to take a local relation. Subsequently he was, for some years, principal of an academy in Kentucky, and otherwise employed in teaching. But he was one of the few located brethren who never lost the spirit of their Gospel mission. So soon as he got his large family situated on a farm, so as to get along without him, without changing his relation, he became an itinerant in fact, and gave himself wholly to the work of the ministry. His service was in great demand. Invitations from places far and near—more than he was able to fill—poured in upon him.

He was emphatically a man of prayer and faith, and—like Enoch—walked with God. Perhaps no man of modern times was more deeply imbued with the spirit of grace, had more experience in "the deep things of God," or felt more deadness to the world, than V. Cook. One consequence was, he sometimes betrayed absence of mind in commonplace matters. Indeed, when he retired for secret devotion, just before public service, his friends had to watch him, or he would pray till after the time appointed for him to commence preaching. In the winter of 1811–12, a succession of earthquakes caused such a shaking of the earth, that many people were greatly alarmed. The most violent concussion was felt on a certain dark night, at an untimely hour, when men were wrapped in slumber. It was enough to make the stoutest heart tremble. Brother Cook, suddenly roused from sleep, made for the door, exclaiming, "I believe Jesus is coming." His wife was alarmed, and said, "Will you not wait for me?" Said he, "If my Jesus is coming, I will wait for nobody." Of course, he felt both ready and anxious to meet his Lord and Savior.

While brother Cook was remarkable for solemnity, both of appearance and deportment, there was, in his natural composition, a spice of eccentricity, sufficient to attract attention, but not to destroy his ministerial influence. On one occasion he commenced his public discourse—in a country place—thus: "As I was riding along the road to-day, I saw a man walk out into his field with a yoke under his arm; by the motion of the stick, he brought up two bullocks, and placed the yoke upon them. At another place I saw an ass standing by a corn-crib, waiting for his daily provender." Then he read for his text, "The ox knoweth his owner, and the ass his master's crib; but Israel doth not know, my people doth not consider," Isa. i, 3. He was a ready man, had a fruitful mind, and, no doubt, what he had seen on the way suggested the subject of his discourse. Another instance of his well-meant eccentricity occurred at the Shaker village in Logan county, not far from his residence. Believing the Shakers were deluded, and feeling deeply concerned for their souls, he sought an interview with their head men, and, as he understood it, obtained leave to address their people on a certain Sabbath, at the close of their regular exercise. However, at the time agreed on, the Shaker preacher dismissed the congregation, and urged them to retire from the chapel immediately. But brother C. was not to be so easily defeated; and running before the people, mounted upon a hen-house, and called on them to stop and hear the word of the Lord. Some of them did so, and he preached to them from the words of Paul: "Now as Jannes and Jambres withstood Moses, so do these also resist the truth," 2 Tim. iii, 8. This novel movement arose from his ardent desire for the salvation of all men. But, so far as the result was known, it was lost labor.

My personal acquaintance with brother Cook commenced in his own house, near Russellville, Ky., in the summer of 1815, and was renewed when I became a member of the Kentucky conference, by transfer, in 1821. From that time till his death, my fields of labor being somewhat contiguous to his residence, I saw something of his movements, and heard much more. He was then an old man, and honored as a father in the Church, but still possessed of strong physical and mental powers. His aid was anxiously sought after on all important occasions in the west part of the state; and wherever he appeared in a religious assembly, he was hailed as a harbinger of mercy. Whole multitudes of people, on popular occasions, were moved by the Spirit of grace under his preaching, as the trees of the forest were moved by the winds of heaven. His last public effort, as I was informed by some who were present, made at Yellow Creek camp meeting, in Dixon county, Tenn., was a signal triumph. While preaching on the Sabbath, such a power came down on the people, and produced such excitement, that he was obliged to desist, till order was partially restored. Shortly after he resumed speaking he was stopped from the same cause. A third attempt produced the same result. He then sat down amidst a glorious shower of grace, and wept, saying, "If the Lord sends rain, we will stop the plow, and let it rain."

When he returned home from this meeting, early in the week, he received a message requesting him to visit Major Moor, in Russellville, who was dangerously sick of a fever; and he went immediately. The incidents of that visit were related to me by Mrs. Russell, of Greenville, who was mother-in-law of the sick man, and was present on the occasion. Her word was good authority in all that region of country. After a short conversation with Major Moor, the aged minister kneeled down and prayed most fervently for him several times, as if he did not intend to cease pleading till his petition was granted. At length the physicians ordered the room to be cleared, the effect, if not the design, of which was to exclude the praying minister. They, however, could not stop his praying. As Mrs. Russell stood in the back yard, after nightfall, she heard his voice amidst the shrubbery of the garden, still pleading, in most plaintive strains, for the dying man. Subsequently, as he walked slowly toward the house, bringing his hands softly together, she heard him say, in a subdued tone, to himself, "He will not die to-night, nor to-morrow, nor to-morrow night, for so far the Lord has made known to me; but beyond that I have as yet no answer." So it turned out; he did not die within the time specified, but he died the day following. Before he expired, however, brother Cook went home sick, and died himself in a very few days—I think on the next Sabbath. But he died as he had lived, a man of God, and was lamented by the whole community, which had been so often moved and profited by his powerful ministrations. This was perhaps in 1823, though I am not quite certain.

A year or two after his decease I attended a camp meeting near the farm on which he died, and where his family still resided. During all the public prayer meetings in the altar, I observed a small boy exceedingly active among the penitents. His fine, shrill voice, was distinctly heard on every such occasion, cheering them on by his exhortations and prayers. Finally, I asked a friend with whom I was conversing, whose little son he was. He replied, "That is the youngest son of father Cook, whose remains lie interred just behind that meeting-house"—pointing to a plain building in sight. He then proceeded to relate the following incident, which I give as nearly in his own way as I can remember it: "Sister Cook's four younger sons were one day working together in the field. This youngest one, that you see, had for some time been seeking religion. That day he absented himself for a time, and while praying in the woods, alone, the Lord converted him. When he returned to the field, and told his brothers what the Lord had done for him, they were deeply affected, especially the next youngest brother, whom he exhorted and prayed for till he was converted. The two young converts, strong in faith, then commenced praying for the next youngest brother, and prayed alternately till he was converted. Immediately all three commenced exhorting and praying for the oldest brother, and hung on till he was converted. Having made a clean sweep, they all returned together to their widowed mother, rejoicing in their first love, and told her what great things the Lord had done for them." This remarkable instance of saving grace reminded me of God's method of working, "from the least even unto the greatest;" and also of the promise, "Leave thy fatherless children, I will preserve them alive; and let thy widows trust in me," Jeremiah xlix, 11.

JESSE WALKER.

The name of Jesse Walker will secure a careful reading of this article, however imperfectly it may reflect his person and character. Among the people of the west, where he was a noted pioneer, it will awaken the memory of thousands to incidents not only of stirring interest, but occasionally bordering upon moral sublimity. Having emigrated, with his family, from North Carolina to Tennessee, about the close of the last, or beginning of the present century, he was for some time employed in dressing deer-leather, an article then in great demand, being much used for gloves, moccasins, pants, vests, hunting-shirts, etc. No substitute for this early staple of the west has ever been imported from England or France, nor manufactured in America, to excel it in durability or comfort. Of course, the business of the "skin-dresser," as he was sometimes familiarly called, placed him upon ground, in his day, similar to that now occupied by respectable manufacturers of woolen and cotton goods.

That readers may form some faint idea of the personal appearance of our hero, let them suppose a man about five feet six or seven inches high, of rather slender form, with a sallow complexion, light hair, small blue eyes, prominent cheek-bones, and pleasant countenance, dressed in drab-colored clothes, made in the plain style peculiar to the early Methodist preachers, his neck secured with a white cravat, and his head covered with a light-colored beaver, nearly as large as a lady's parasol, and they will see Jesse Walker as if spread out on canvas before them.

As to his mental endowments, he was without education, except the elementary branches of English imperfectly acquired, but favored with a good share of common sense, cultivated some by reading, but much more by practical intercourse with society, and enriched with a vast fund of incidents, peculiar to a frontier life, which he communicated with much ease and force. His conversational talent, his tact in narrative, his spicy manner, and almost endless variety of religious anecdotes, rendered him an object of attraction in social life. Unaccustomed to expressing his thoughts on paper, he kept his journal in his mind, by which means his memory, naturally retentive, was much strengthened, and his resources for the entertainment of friends increased. He introduced himself among strangers with much facility, and so soon as they became acquainted with him, his social habits, good temper, unaffected simplicity, and great suavity of manners, for a backwoodsman, made them his fast friends. As a pulpit orator he was certainly not above mediocrity, if up to it; but his zeal was ardent, his moral courage firm, his piety exemplary, and his perseverance in whatever he undertook was indefatigable. Consequently, by the blessing of God upon his labors, he was enabled, in the third of a century, to accomplish incalculable good as a traveling preacher.

My object, in this article, is not to write a journal of Jesse Walker's ministerial life, but to rescue from oblivion a few incidents thereof, which he narrated to me as we journeyed together on horseback to the General conference in Baltimore, in 1824, he being then a delegate from Missouri conference, and I a delegate from Kentucky. Those incidents made a strong impression upon my mind as he recited them. Subsequently, I heard him repeat them to others; and having related them occasionally myself, I believe I can write them out substantially as he told them. It is possible that some of those events, in part, may have been published through other channels, but I shall follow my own recollection of them, as they came fresh from the original source.

It appears, from the printed Minutes, that Jesse Walker was admitted as a traveling preacher in the Western conference in 1802, and appointed alone to the Red river circuit, in Tennessee, and that the next three years he was on Livingston and Hartford circuits, in Kentucky. In 1806 he was appointed to Illinois. The work had no designation on the Minutes but Illinois. Of course, it was a mission, embracing the entire population of that territory, and it was under the superintendence of Rev. William M'Kendree, afterward bishop, but then presiding elder of Cumberland district. Between Kentucky and the interior of Illinois was then a wilderness, and to reach the mission was difficult. The enterprising M'Kendree determined to accompany the missionary through the wilderness, and aid him in forming his plan and commencing the work. They put off together on horseback, camped in the wild woods every night, roasted their own meat, and slept on their saddle-blankets under the open canopy of heaven. Their chief difficulty was in crossing the swollen streams. It was a time of much rain; the channels were full to overflowing, and no less than seven times their horses swam the rapid streams with their riders and baggage; but the passengers, by carrying their saddle-bags on their shoulders, kept their Bibles and part of their clothes above the water. This was truly a perilous business. At night they had opportunity, not only of drying off and resting, but of prayer and Christian converse. In due time they reached their destination safely. Mr. M'Kendree remained a few weeks, visited the principal neighborhoods, aided in forming a plan of appointments for the mission; and the new settlers received them both with much favor. After preaching near a place called Turkey hill, a gentleman said to Mr. M'Kendree, "Sir, I am convinced there is a divine influence in your religion; for though I have resided here some years, and have done all within my power to gain the confidence and good-will of my neighbors, you have already many more friends here than I have." It is presumed that the presiding elder went next to Missouri, to visit a mission there.

Jesse Walker, though left alone in his new field of labor, was not discouraged. After pursuing the regular plan of appointments till the winter closed in severely upon him, he suspended that plan from necessity, and commenced operating from house to house, or, rather, from cabin to cabin, passing none without calling and delivering his Gospel message. He went by the openings of Providence, and took shelter for the night wherever he could obtain it, so as to resume his labor early next day; and continued this course of toil till the winter broke. The result of this movement was a general revival with the opening spring, when the people were able to reassemble, and he resumed his regular plan. Shortly after this, a young preacher was sent to his relief; and being thus reinforced, Jesse determined to include, in the plan of the summer's campaign, a camp meeting, which was the more proper, because the people had no convenient place of worship but the shady forest. The site selected was near a beautiful spring of pure water. All friends of the enterprise were invited to meet upon the spot on a certain day, with axes, saws, augers, hammers, etc., for the work of preparation. The ground was cleared off and dedicated by prayer, as a place of public worship. Jesse took the lead as boss of the work; and tents, seats, and pulpit were all arranged before the congregation assembled. It was the first experiment of the kind in that country; but it worked well, admirably well. After the public services commenced, there was no dispute among preachers or people as to the choice of pulpit orators. The senior preached and the junior exhorted, then the junior preached and the senior exhorted, and so on through the meeting of several days and nights; the intervals between sermons being occupied with prayer and praise. They had no need of night-guards, or even managers, to keep order. The congregation, gathered from a sparse population, was of course limited; no populous city was near to disgorge its rabble upon them; and there was a divine power resting upon the people, which bore down all opposition, and awed every soul into reverence. Early in the meeting, a young lady of influence, sister-in-law of the territorial judge sent out by the General Government, was so powerfully converted, that her shouts of joy and triumph broke the silence of all the surrounding forest, and sent a thrilling sensation through every heart in the encampment. This example of the power of saving grace cheered on the soldiers of the cross, and inspired all with confidence of success. After operating till, as Jesse Walker expressed it, "the last stick of timber was used up"—that is, till the last sinner left on the ground was converted—the meeting adjourned.

The impulse which the work received from that camp meeting was such, that it extended through most of the settlements embraced in the mission, which was constantly extending its borders as the people moved into the territory. Jesse visited one neighborhood, near the Illinois river, containing some sixty or seventy souls. They all came to hear him, and having preached three successive days, he read the General Rules, and proposed that as many of them as desired to unite to serve God according to the Bible, as expressed in those rules, should come forward and make it known. The most prominent man among them rose to his feet and said, "Sir, I trust we will all unite with you to serve God here;" then walked forward, and all the rest followed. As the result of his first year's experiment in Illinois, two hundred and eighteen Church members were reported in the printed Minutes.

Jesse Walker's next field of labor was Missouri, which, as may be supposed, was similar to that of Illinois. From that time forward he operated alternately in the two territories, till 1812, when he was appointed presiding elder of the Illinois district, which, however, included all the ground then occupied both in Illinois and Missouri. That was an ample field for the exercise of all his zeal. The old Western conference having been divided, in 1812, into Ohio and Tennessee conferences, the Illinois and Missouri work pertained to the latter. He was continued on districts in the two territories, till 1819, when he was appointed conference missionary, to form new fields of labor among the destitute, or, as they used to say, "to break up new ground;" a work to which he was peculiarly adapted, both by nature and grace, and in which he continued to be employed for many years.

In 1820 our veteran pioneer formed the purpose, at once bold and benevolent, of planting the standard of Methodism in St. Louis, Missouri, where, previously, Methodist preachers had found no rest for the soles of their feet; the early inhabitants, from Spain and France, being utterly opposed to our Protestant principles, and especially to Methodism. He commenced laying the train at conference, appointed a time to open the campaign and begin the siege, and engaged two young preachers, of undoubted zeal and courage, such as he believed would stand by him "to the bitter end," to meet him at a given time and place, and to aid him in the difficult enterprise. Punctual to their engagement, they all met, and proceeded to the city together. When they reached St. Louis, the territorial legislature was there in session; and every public place appeared to be full. The missionaries preferred private lodgings, but could obtain none. When they announced their profession, and the object of their visit, no one appeared to show the slightest sympathy with them. Some laughed at, and others cursed them to their face. Thus embarrassed at every point, they rode into the public square, and held a consultation on their horses. The prospect was gloomy; no open door could be found; every avenue seemed to be closed against them. The young preachers expressed strong doubts as to their being in the order of Providence. Their leader tried to rally and encourage them, but in vain. They thought the Lord had no work there for them to do, or there would be some way to get to it. Instead of a kind reception, such as they had been accustomed to elsewhere, they were not only denied all courtesy, but turned off, at every point, with insult. As might be expected, under these circumstances, they thought it best to return whence they came immediately; and though their elder brother entreated them not to leave him, they deliberately brushed off the dust of their feet, for a testimony against the wicked city, as the Savior had directed his disciples to do in similar cases, and, taking leave of father Walker, rode off, and left him sitting on his horse. These were excellent young ministers, and, in view of the treatment they had met with, no blame was attached to them for leaving. Perhaps that hour brought with it more of the feeling of despondency to the veteran pioneer than he ever experienced in any other hour of his eventful life; and, stung with disappointment, he said, in his haste, "I will go to the state of Mississippi, and hunt up the lost sheep of the house of Israel," reined his horse in that direction, and with a sorrowful heart rode off alone.

Having proceeded about eighteen miles, constantly ruminating, with anguish of spirit, upon his unexpected failure, and lifting his heart to God in prayer for help and direction, he came to a halt, and entered into a soliloquy on this wise, "Was I ever defeated before in this blessed work? Never. Did any one ever trust in the Lord Jesus Christ and get confounded? No; and, by the grace of God, I will go back and take St. Louis." Then, reversing his course, without seeking either rest or refreshment for man or beast, he immediately, and with all convenient haste, retraced his steps to the city, and, with some difficulty, obtained lodging in an indifferent tavern, where he paid at the highest rate for every thing. Next morning he commenced a survey of the city and its inhabitants; it being his first object to ascertain whether any Methodist, from distant parts, had been attracted there by a prospect of business, who might be of service to him. Finally, he heard of one man, who, by rumor, was said to be a Methodist, and went directly to his shop, inquired for him by name, there being several persons present, and he was pointed out, when the following conversation was held: "Sir, my name is Walker; I am a Methodist preacher; and being told that you were a Methodist, I have taken the liberty to call on you." The man blushed, and, with evident confusion, called the preacher one side, and said: "I was a Methodist once, before I came here; but finding no brethren in St. Louis, I never reported myself, and do not now consider myself a member; nor do I wish such a report to get out, lest it injure me in my business." The missionary, finding him ashamed of his name, concluded he was worthless, and left him.

While passing about the city, he met with some members of the territorial legislature, who knew him, and said, "Why, father Walker, what has brought you here?" His answer was, "I have come to take St. Louis." They thought it a hopeless undertaking, and, to convince him, remarked, that the inhabitants were mostly Catholics and infidels, very dissipated and wicked, and there was no probability that a Methodist preacher could obtain any access to them, and seriously advised him to abandon the enterprise, and return to his family, then residing in Illinois. But to all such suggestions and dissuasions, Jesse returned one answer: "I have come, in the name of Christ, to take St. Louis, and, by the grace of God, I will do it."

His first public experiment was in a temporary place of worship occupied by a few Baptists. There were, however, but few present. Nothing special occurred, and he obtained leave to preach again. During the second effort there were strong indications of religious excitement; and the Baptists, fearing their craft was in danger, closed their doors against him. He next found a large but unfinished dwelling-house, inquired for the proprietor, and succeeded in renting it, as it was, for ten dollars a month. Passing by the public square, he saw some old benches stacked away by the end of the court-house, it having been recently refitted with new ones. These he obtained from the commissioner, had them put on a dray and removed to his hired house; borrowed tools, and repaired, with his own hands, such as were broken, and fitted up his largest room for a place of worship. After completing his arrangements, he commenced preaching regularly twice on the Sabbath, and occasionally in the evenings between the Sabbaths. At the same time, he gave notice, that, if there were any poor parents who wished their children taught to spell and read, he would teach them five days in a week, without fee or reward; and if there were any who wished their servants to learn, he would teach them, on the same terms, in the evenings. In order to be always on the spot, and to curtail his heavy expenses, which he had no certain means of meeting, he took up his abode and kept bachelor's hall in his own hired house. The chapel-room was soon filled with hearers, and the school with children. Some of the better class of citizens insisted on sending their children to encourage the school, and paying for the privilege; and to accommodate them, and render the school more useful, he hired a young man, more competent than himself, to assist in teaching. In the mean time he went to visit his family, and returned with a horse-load of provisions and bedding, determined to remain there and push the work till something was accomplished. Very soon a work of grace commenced, first among the colored people, then among the poorer class of whites, and gradually ascended in its course till it reached the more intelligent and influential, and the prospect became truly encouraging.

About this time an event transpired, which seemed, at first, to be against the success of his mission, but which eventuated in its favor. The work of death caused the hired house to change hands; and he was notified to vacate it in a short time. Immediately, he conceived a plan for building a small frame chapel; and, without knowing where the funds were to come from, but trusting in Providence, put the work under contract. Jesse was to furnish the materials, and the carpenter to have a given sum for the work. A citizen owning land across the Mississippi gave him leave to take the lumber from his forest as a donation, and when he started with his choppers and hewers, followed them to the boat, and had them ferried over, from time to time, at his expense. Soon the chapel was raised and covered; the ladies paid the expense of building a pulpit; and the vestry-men of a small Episcopal church, then without a minister, made him a present of their old Bible and cushion. They also gave him their slips, which he accepted, on condition of their being free; and having unscrewed the shutters, and laid them by, he lost no time in transferring the open slips to his new chapel. New friends came to his relief in meeting his contracts; the chapel was finished, and opened for public worship, and was well filled; the revival received a fresh impulse; and, as the result of the first year's experiment, he reported to conference a snug little chapel erected and paid for, a flourishing school, and seventy Church members in St. Louis. Of course he was next year regularly appointed to that mission station, but without any missionary appropriation, and considered it an honorable appointment. Thus "father Walker," as every one about the city called him, succeeded in taking St. Louis, which, as he expressed it, had been "the very fountain-head of devilism." Some idea of the change there had been effected for the better, may be inferred from the fact, that Missouri conference held its session in the city, October 24, 1822, when our most excellent and lamented brother—William Beauchamp—was appointed successor of the indefatigable Walker. St. Louis is now a large and flourishing city, well supplied with churches and a church-going people.

Jesse Walker was continued conference missionary, and in 1823 began to turn his special attention to the Indian tribes up the Mississippi. When he reached their villages, he learned that most of them had gone a great distance to make their fall's hunt. Not a whit discouraged by this disappointment, he procured a bag of corn and an interpreter, and set off in pursuit of them, crossing the Mississippi in a canoe, and swimming his horse by the side of it. After a difficult and wearisome journey, they reached one cluster of camps, on the bank of a small stream, about the dusk of evening. When they first rode up, an Indian—who knew the interpreter—said, "Who is with you, a Quaker?" "No." "A minister?" "Yes." Word was conveyed to the chief, a tall, dignified man, who came out and gave them a welcome reception, secured their horses, with ropes, to the trees, with his own hands, and then showed them into his own camp, which was a temporary hut, with flat logs laid round inside for seats, and a fire in the center, and, in his own Indian style, introduced them to his wife, who received them kindly, and entertained them cheerfully.

The chief, learning that his white guest wished to hold a talk with him and his people, sent notice to the neighboring camps of a council to be held in his lodge that evening. In the mean time, the chief's wife prepared a repast for the occasion, consisting of broth, enriched with venison and opossum, served up in wooden bowls. After the council convened, and each member was seated, with his dog lying under his knees, the chief's wife handed the first bowl of meat and broth to her husband, the second to the missionary, and then went round according to seniority till all were served. Each man having picked his bone, gave it to his own dog to crack, which knew the rules of the council better than to leave his place behind his master's feet before the feast was ended. Next the tomahawk pipe of peace passed round, each taking his whiff in turn. This ceremony over, the chief struck the blade of the instrument into the ground, and inquired what was the object of the meeting. Jesse informed him that he had come a long journey to bring them the book which the Great Spirit had sent to all his children, both white and red, and to ascertain whether they would allow him to establish a school among them, and teach their children to read it. So saying, he handed a Bible to the chief, who examined it deliberately and carefully, as a great curiosity, and then passed it round till every member of the council, in his proper place, had done the same. After examining the Bible, the chief rose and replied as follows: "The white children's Father had given them a book, and they would do well to mind what it told them; but they doubted whether it was intended for his red children. However, as some of their older men were absent, they could not then decide the matter; but, in a few days, they would hold a larger council, and then give him an answer." The result of the second council was leave to establish a mission school. Having settled this matter to his mind, Jesse returned to make preparation for the mission, and to attend the General conference next spring, at Baltimore, leaving a pledge that he would visit them next summer, and commence operation in their villages. After he had proceeded nearly a day's journey from the camps, a messenger came galloping after him, and said, "The chiefs have sent me to tell you to be sure to come back next summer," which he again promised to do. While on his way to Baltimore, he called on the Secretary of War, at Washington City, and obtained his sanction to go on with the mission.

Here his verbal narrative ceased. The Minutes of the Missouri conference, for 1824, contain this entry: "Jesse Walker, missionary to the Missouri conference, whose attention is particularly directed to the Indians within the bounds of said conference." But few men, even of his day, performed more hard labor, or endured more privations, than Jesse Walker, and certainly no one performed his part with more cheerfulness or perseverance. While his ashes quietly sleep in the north part of Illinois, his spirit is with Christ above.

WILLIAM B. CHRISTIE.

Rev. William B. Christie was born at Williamsburg, Clermont county, Ohio, September 2, 1803. Of his early history but little is known to us of much importance to the public. He embraced religion and joined the Methodist Episcopal Church when a youth; and so far as we are informed ever after adorned his Christian profession. Subsequently he was for some time a student at Augusta College, when the Rev. John P. Finley, of precious memory, was president of that institution, where he made rapid progress in his literary studies; and where he laid the foundation on which he, in after life, erected a superstructure of knowledge, creditable to himself and useful to his fellow-men. Having commended himself to the confidence of his brethren as a member of the Church, and as an exhorter, and as one called of God to the work of the ministry, they licensed him to preach, and recommended him to the Ohio conference for a traveling preacher. He was admitted on trial in 1825; received into full connection, and ordained deacon in 1827, and graduated to the office of elder in 1829. In all these relations he was not only acceptable, but highly esteemed for his work's sake, and also on account of his personal virtues and consistent piety. He was a man of regular habits, even temper, easy manners, and great self-possession; and though possessed of a high sense of honor, and of that dignity of character which becomes the Christian minister, he was influenced by a "meek and quiet spirit," which so chastened his conduct and conversation, that he seldom had the misfortune to offend any one. He has been heard to say, that naturally he was as ambitious as Cæsar, but this only prompted him as a preacher to excel in the acquisition of useful knowledge and in doing good, so that he enjoyed the confidence of his brethren generally in the ministry and membership, and was highly respected by the entire community wherever he was known.

For some years after brother Christie entered the itinerant ministry, he applied himself with uncommon assiduity and perseverance to close, hard study, which, together with his abundant pulpit labors, materially injured his health and superinduced such bodily afflictions as ever after embarrassed him more or less in the prosecution of his ministerial work. If, during the latter years of his life, he studied less and made less rapid progress in knowledge, it was because his constitution was broken and his mental labor thereby restricted. His particular friends need not to be informed that he was a man of much affliction; and when some individuals occasionally complained that he commenced his public discourses in too low a tone of voice, they should have known that it was not for want of zeal, but want of physical strength. We trust that young brethren in the ministry will learn by the things which he suffered, to regard their health for the good of the cause; and that unreasonable hearers will learn to make some allowance for such of them as labor under bodily infirmities, lest they die in the midst of their usefulness.

Notwithstanding brother Christie's difficulty, arising from the want of good health, he attained to an eminent position in the Church, and for a series of years filled some of the most important stations and districts in the Ohio conference, acceptably and usefully. Thrice his brethren elected him as one of their delegates to General conference, where he filled his place with dignity and usefulness. He was a man of general information. Few individuals of any profession were more familiar with the history of our country, its institutions and leading men, than he was. His literary attainments were respectable, especially such as were most intimately connected with his profession as a preacher; but his greatest proficiency was in the study of theology. He was an acute theologian, an accomplished divine. There are but few men in our connection of his age that equaled, and perhaps none that surpassed him, in a critical knowledge of the doctrines of the Gospel, or that can explain and defend them with more clearness and force than he could. Rich in figure, fluent in speech, chaste in language, strong in argument, and mighty in the Scriptures, he seldom failed to enchain the attention and affect the hearts of the multitudes that thronged his ministry. He could reason like a wise master-builder on a controverted point of doctrine, divest it of every needless appendage, present it in its proper form, and then test its truth by "the law and the testimony," with as much ease as any other man of my acquaintance. But his favorite topic was Christ crucified. It was his delight to offer every son and daughter of Adam a present, full, and free salvation, through simple faith in the blood of Christ. And when he had shown the necessity, nature, consistency, fullness, and freeness of the atonement, he was not satisfied with merely arriving at triumphant conclusions in the argument, but added powerful appeals to the heart and conscience, urging the people to accept offered mercy, and secure everlasting life. Of course his preaching was attended by the Spirit of all grace to the hearts of many, and was frequently followed by salutary consequences. Many sons and daughters in the Gospel, from his different fields of labor, will rise up at the last day and call him blessed.

Brother Christie's acknowledged ability to preach was not the only qualification he possessed for the work of the ministry. He was, for one of his age, exceedingly well versed in all questions of ecclesiastical law, all rules of discipline connected with the Church of which he was a minister, and united becoming firmness and moderation in the administration of it, so far as it was committed to his hands. His mind was adapted to the discussion and comprehension of such subjects; and he did not bury this talent, but used it diligently in accomplishing the great objects of his ministry. Taken altogether, he was justly regarded as an able minister of the New Testament. What he taught publicly, was enforced by private example. He enjoyed not only the communion of saints, but the fellowship of the Spirit. The Lord sealed his ministry with the conversion of souls, which are his living epistles known and read by all; and while he rests in the grave, the effect of his labor tells favorably on the interests of the Church. He lived a bright luminary in the Church on earth; and, we doubt not, will "shine forth as the sun in the kingdom of his Father" forever.

In the morning of his existence, this man of God, in obedience to the Spirit's call, had devoted himself, his time and talents, lite and reputation, soul and body, to the work of the itinerant ministry; but before he reached the meridian of life, his constitution began to give way, and with it his hope of extensive usefulness. For many years his health had been precarious and declining, and his complicated diseases finally resulted in pulmonary consumption, with which he died. His brethren and friends saw that his strength was failing two or three years, and rather encouraged him to desist from regular service, and seek relief in rest and retirement; but he could not feel reconciled to leave the work, and continued to receive regular appointments from year to year, and do what he could. And while his extraordinary resoluteness induced him to continue in the field longer than was expedient, zeal for the cause of his Master frequently carried him beyond what his strength would bear. Some months later, however, he was compelled by bodily weakness to desist from preaching entirely. After lingering through the winter, he concluded to visit his friends in Cincinnati, and avail himself of such means of recovery as could there be afforded. When about to leave Urbana—his regular field of labor—the brethren kindly offered to convey him to the city, but he declined the favor; and with a courage, peculiarly his own, drove the carriage which conveyed himself and family to Cincinnati, only about eleven days previous to his decease. On the way he appeared to be revived, so that he attended public service at Ridgeville, where he rested on the Sabbath, and heard preaching. But when he reached Dr. Wright's, in Cincinnati, on Tuesday evening, he was much prostrated, took his bed, and declined more rapidly than before. The next morning after he arrived, two of us called to see him; his face was flushed with fever, and his system wasted almost to a shadow. He was much affected at the interview, and said his nerves were shattered, but his confidence in God was unshaken: he knew in whom he had believed: he had not preached an unknown, or unfelt

Savior, and the Gospel which he had long preached to others, was then his consolation. The calls of his numerous friends so taxed his sympathy and his strength, that his physicians found it requisite to lay some restriction on them, or suffer him to be much hastened in his departure; and with all the care that could be taken by physicians and friends, he did not last long.

Among the numerous incidents indicating the state of his mind during the last hours of his earthly existence, I will recite only a few.

Saturday morning, a little after midnight, he requested a brother who was sitting with him, to call Dr. Wright, who came in and found him rapidly sinking. He asked brother C. if he felt worse? His reply was that he had great difficulty of breathing. After some means of temporary relief had been administered, he asked the Doctor, "What does this mean?" In reply, the Doctor inquired if he would like to see some of his friends? Brother C. then said, "Why do you ask the question? Do you think I am pretty near home?" On being informed that he was undoubtedly worse, he looked round upon his wife and friends, calm and collected, and said, "I am not alarmed. I am not afraid to die." Extending and looking at his hands, he remarked, "Jesus, with his bleeding hands, will not thrust me away." Next, he took his two little sons, embraced and commended them to God. Soon after this, brother Sehon—having been sent for—entered his room, to whom he extended his hand, and with a countenance bright with hope, said, "Brother Sehon, I am almost home." After exchanging a few words, he requested brother S. to pray; and, during the prayer, he appeared to be perfectly happy. This over, he beckoned brother S. to his bed, and by him sent the following message: "Tell my brethren at the conference, if they think my name worthy of being mentioned, that I have not preached an unknown and unfelt Christ. Tell them that though unworthy and unfaithful, that Gospel which I have preached to others now sustains me. Tell the preachers to preach Christ and him crucified. Tell them my only hope, my only foundation is in the blood of sprinkling. Precious blood! O the fullness, the sweetness, the richness of that fountain!" After praising God for some time, he turned his eyes on his weeping companion, and made some reference to his temporalities, but instantly observed they were small matters, little things, assuring her that God would provide for her and his little children. About two o'clock I arrived, and found him bolstered up in his bed, covered with the sweat of death, and much exhausted by the efforts he had made to speak, as above described. He, however, reached out his hand, and said distinctly, "I am almost home. I feel that God is good to me, and that Jesus Christ is my salvation." No question being asked him, and exhausted, he desisted from speaking for awhile, and then looking at his distressed wife, I understood him to say, "Jesus is precious." When unable to articulate, he often lifted his cold hand in token of victory; and again, as though anxious to make us understand his meaning, he raised his hand high above his head and waved it in triumph. After some time, he raised both his hands at once, and extended them before him, as if just rising on "the wings of love and arms of faith;" and then, in an animating manner, brought his hands together, triumphing over death, his last enemy. At that time, I supposed he would speak no more; for when his companion desired to hear his voice once more on earth, he could only look at her and point his finger toward heaven. However, not long before his exit, he raised his hand high, and brother S. asked him if he wanted any thing? He shook his head. Brother S. then asked him if it was power and glory? His countenance brightened up, while he nodded his head affirmatively, and his strength returning to him, he shouted aloud, clapping his hands and giving glory to God. The same peculiarity of manner, form of expression, and even gesture, which marked his pulpit and altar performances, were strikingly exhibited in his closing scene. To the last, he seemed to be conscious and triumphant. About seven o'clock, Saturday morning, March 26, 1842, without a sigh or groan, his deathless spirit passed in peace and triumph from earth to appear before the presence of God with exceeding joy.

Most of my early associates in the ministry, and many of my junior brethren, have disappeared from these scenes of earthly toil and sorrow, while I am still lingering on the stage of life. How pleasant to recall to mind the names, the religious conversation, the Gospel labors of those loved ones now sleeping in Jesus!

Among the departed, there are few, if any, of whom I think more frequently or pleasantly, than the lamented William B. Christie. My impressions of his personal appearance, voice, action, social habits, and manner in the pulpit and in the altar, are as vivid now as when he lived, mingled, and talked with us. His person, of medium hight, was always delicate, but erect, and of manly bearing; head unusually large, and covered with a beautiful suit of fine dark hair; eyes black, sparkling, glowing with intelligence, and softened with benevolence. In his social habits, he observed a proper medium between levity and melancholy; he was cheerful but not trifling, religious but not sad. In action he was easy, graceful, and dignified, and neat in his apparel; but nothing in his dress or address indicated any *hauteur*. He was, in the best sense of the phrase, a Christian gentleman; always displayed independence and firmness in maintaining his own views of every important subject, but never contradicted any one, or betrayed rudeness of any sort.

As a preacher he excelled, greatly, in three particulars; namely, beauty of language, strength of argument, and power of application. By the first he secured the attention of all; by the second he convinced the judgment, pouring floods of light upon the understanding; and by the last he overpowered the feelings of his audience. While his profound knowledge of theology and his logical acumen deeply interested the most learned, his religious ardor and fervid eloquence arrested and led captive the most careless, and made the most simple-hearted joyful. Perhaps his only fault in the pulpit was occasionally preaching a long sermon, which, however, was but little complained of, because his superior intellectual strength, and an unction from the Holy One, enabled him to enchain multitudes to the last moment of his longest effort. Nor was he satisfied merely because many hearts were subdued under his powerful discourses, and retired with tearful eyes and throbbing bosoms: he followed such to their homes, led them to the altar of prayer, and pointed them to the Savior, till he could rejoice over them as happy converts to Christ. The character given to the amiable Barnabas would, in some degree, be applicable to brother Christie; "For he was a good man, and full of the Holy Ghost, and of faith: and much people was added unto the Lord."

It is to be lamented, that such a mind as his left so few traces of itself upon paper. He had no ambition whatever to figure as a writer; otherwise, it would not now be necessary to tell those who never saw or heard him, that, when he died, "there was a prince and a great man fallen that day in Israel."

The closing scene of his earthly pilgrimage was all that could have been expected, or even desired by his most partial friends. Though I have often seen happy Christians die, never did I witness a more signal victory than that of brother Christie. It was enough to inspire confidence in the most timid believer, and enable him to sing,

"When death o'er nature shall prevail,
And all the powers of language fail,
Joy through my swimming eyes shall break,
And mean the thanks I can not speak."

The immense concourse of people that attended his funeral, at Wesley Chapel, filling it to overflowing, while multitudes retired for want of room, was ample proof of the influence which he had exerted in Cincinnati. In that assembly distinguished individuals appeared who were never seen in that church before, nor since. All was solemn as death, and silent as the grave, except the voice of the minister, and the sighs of the weeping multitude, while he attempted to draw a brief outline of the Christian and ministerial character of the deceased, under the appropriate motto, taken from Daniel xii, 3, "And they that be wise shall shine as the brightness of the firmament; and they that turn many to righteousness, as the stars forever and ever."

MRS. JANE B. RUST.

Mrs. Rust, my only daughter, was born at Spicewood Cottage, Cabell county, Va., February 27, 1815, and was baptized the same year by Rev. David Young, of the Ohio conference. Her constitution was naturally feeble, and her health delicate all her life; but that did not materially injure her mild and amiable disposition. Neither her parents nor teachers ever had any difficulty in governing her. She was as steady and thoughtful in childhood and youth as most persons are at mature age. The most striking features of her character were meekness and kindness; the former appearing in every thing pertaining to herself, and the latter in whatever respected others. As a member of the family she was always attentive to her duties, and as a student, to her studies. When only five years old, she read fluently and gracefully. She learned her lessons with great facility, especially such as were committed to memory, and being always diligent in preparing to recite them, seldom failed to stand first in her class; but was never known to take any credit or praise to herself on that account. On the contrary, kindness to her classmates frequently led her to extra exertions in learning the dullest and most negligent of them, to keep them out of difficulty with their teachers.

When Jane left Science Hill Academy, at Shelbyville, Kentucky, in the fifteenth year of her age, she had acquired all the essential elements of a sound and useful education, and some of the ornamental branches, and bid fair to excel in literary attainments. The state of her health, however, about that time, rendered it necessary that she should exchange her sedentary habits and mental exertions for an active life in the domestic business of the family, then residing in Lebanon, Ohio. But subsequently, by reviewing and extending her studies, she improved her education, so that, when seventeen years old, she read her French Bible nearly as well as the English. Her books were then all the recreation from domestic business that she desired. No place was so pleasant to her as home, however humble its appearance. She strictly regarded the rules of Christian courtesy toward all classes of society, which to her was an easy task, but had no relish whatever for fashionable amusements or gay company. She never wore a particle of jewelry or any superfluous article of dress in her life, but always appeared plain and neat at home and abroad. When she made calls out of the immediate circle of the family, they were generally made at the chamber of affliction, and accompanied with some supplies, or other tokens of kindness toward the distressed. The Sabbaths of her youthful years were taken up with her Bible, attending Church, and Sabbath school, first in the capacity of a scholar, and subsequently that of a teacher, where she was both diligent and useful, till broken off by family engagements.

At the age of twenty-one years, she was happily united in marriage to Mr. Joseph G. Rust, of Cincinnati, who was an only child, had been pious from his youth, and whose natural disposition and moral habits were congenial to her own. She became the mother of three children, two of whom are still living. As she had been a most affectionate and dutiful child to her parents, so she proved herself to be a faithful wife, and tender-hearted but judicious mother.

Mrs. Rust never abandoned the principles of her early religious education. From the time she was first able to repeat the Lord's Prayer at her mother's side, she never omitted prayer one day during life. But the form of religion did not satisfy her mind. She commenced seeking a change of heart very earnestly, as near as I can recollect, in her ninth year, and for seven years missed no opportunity of going forward to be prayed for when circumstances were such as to allow it. She became a member of the Methodist Episcopal Church in her fourteenth year, but did not obtain a satisfactory evidence of the desired change of heart till about two years after. From the time she made a profession of religion, she attended all the means of grace regularly, but ever spoke of her experience with diffidence and humility, regarding herself as one of the least and most unworthy of God's children. Though her piety was uniform, and her life highly exemplary, she never dealt much in professions of assurance till after the commencement of her last illness but then her confidence in God seemed to gather strength in proportion to the increase of her affliction and prospect of death.

Her health began, perceptibly, to decline, in the spring of 1842. Much sympathy was felt for her on the part of her family and friends generally, and every possible precaution was taken to prevent disease from fixing itself on her lungs; but in vain. Her health continued, regularly, to decline. The protracted illness and ultimate death of her mother, and the mental anxiety consequent thereon, seemed to lessen her own prospect of recovery; for never did mother and daughter love more ardently and constantly than they did. The language of inspired David, respecting Saul and Jonathan, might well be applied in their case; they "were lovely and pleasant in their lives, and in their death they were not divided."

Another circumstance which tended to weigh down her spirit, and tax her sympathies severely, was the loss of her interesting little son, Joseph Guest, who, after suffering much for four months, died July 31, 1842, aged fifteen months and eight days. When she returned from his funeral, on the first of August, she took a severe chill, and was subsequently confined to her bed most of the time, as she had been partially for months previous. These successive bereavements, which fell so heavily upon the family, were too much for her tender sensibilities in a feeble state of health, and no doubt hastened her own dissolution.

The last letter which my daughter ever wrote was dated August 26, 1842, and addressed to myself at Delaware, Ohio, and was received during the session of the North Ohio conference, from which the following is an extract:

"My hand shakes so that it is with great difficulty I can hold my pen. I am very glad to hear you are well, and are sustained under your arduous labors. I thank you kindly for all your letters, and especially for the first one. . . . I have read it many times over, and still it always interests me. I have been very deeply afflicted since you left home, as you know. The loss of our dear little babe was a great trial to me, and for several days after, I felt as if I could not give him up; but since that I feel a sweet resignation to the will of the Lord, and would not have him back for asking."

When in ordinary health, she wrote an excellent hand; but the trembling debility apparent on the face of that letter fixed a deep and painful impression on the father's already sorrowful heart, because it indicated too clearly that her feeble constitution was giving way under the influence of fatal disease.

Returning home September 12th, my worst fears were fully confirmed. I found her prostrated, and far gone in pulmonary consumption, but patient and resigned. She said to me, "I have never felt like murmuring during my affliction. The Lord has been good to me all my life. He blessed me wonderfully at the late camp meeting. I there enjoyed the preaching much as I heard it while lying in my chamber. And such singing I never heard before." In a conversation with me a few days after, she remarked, "I neither look back nor forward, but live a day at a time. I am in the hands of the Lord, and am willing that he should dispose of my case. If I get better I shall be thankful on account of my family; but if not, the Lord will support me to the end."

On the following Sabbath she was exceedingly happy, and rejoiced aloud, and exhorted her brother not to be discouraged seeking religion, for he had a kind, all-sufficient, and willing Savior to come to, who was ever ready to hear the cries of the penitent. The next day she told her physician she never expected to be much better, but she was resigned; for the Lord supported her. She said it would be a trial to part with her family, but she trusted the Lord would give her grace to resign them all up cheerfully into his hands, and it would be no misfortune for her to go to heaven at any time. When I returned from the Ohio conference, the first week in October, I found her still failing under the wasting influence of cough, chills, fevers, and night sweats, and fully apprised of her certain approach toward the point of dissolution, but strong in faith, and joyful through hope in our Lord Jesus Christ.

Monday, 17th, she said to me, "I am determined to trust in the Lord, come what will; not that I feel fully prepared for heaven, but God is able to perfect that which is lacking, and I believe he will—bless his holy name!" As I had to leave next morning in the stage, at three o'clock, for the Indiana conference, I went to her room, at two o'clock, that I might spend an hour with her. At her request I prayed with her once more: she was deeply affected, but rejoiced in spirit. In my absence, the property of her father-in-law and husband was destroyed by fire; and while the fearful conflagration shed a glare of light on her chamber window, she thanked God that she had a more enduring substance beyond the ravages of the destructive element, "an inheritance which is incorruptible, undefiled, and that fadeth not away;" and exhorted those near her to lay up their treasure in heaven.

When I returned from Indiana on the 27th, I found her disease greatly increased, and her strength so much reduced that she was never after able to sit up any; but she was still patient and resigned, professing to feel assured that the Lord cared for her, and that he could and would sustain her. When her affliction was extremely painful, she was willing to suffer all the will of God, and would not dare to ask her sufferings less, and prayed only for patience to endure, and grace to support her under them; and when they were mitigated, she would express much gratitude to her heavenly Father for a little relief.

The first week in November she finished the distribution of some small presents among us, which we will ever regard sacredly as mementos of her affection. In this affair we were struck with the appropriateness of the selection for her children. To her little daughter she presented a small Polyglot Bible, which she had been in the habit of reading from the days of her youth; and to her little son, the younger of the two, she gave the pocket Testament, handsomely bound in morocco, with a tuck, which she had received as a gift from her father when she was a child, still in a good state of preservation. These presents were attended with suitable advice to the children. May they be thereby influenced to follow their mother as she followed Christ!

Sabbath afternoon, November 13, when I returned from Church, she said to me, "Pa, this has been a blessed Sabbath to me; I have enjoyed a sweet foretaste of that Sabbath which never ends. I was in a struggle all night and all morning for a blessing, and got rather discouraged, but it occurred to me, the Lord could bless me here on a sick bed as well as if I was in the church: I prayed earnestly, and he did bless me in a wonderful manner. I never felt so happy in all my life. I felt that I could endure all my sufferings cheerfully, and that I should be a conqueror in death, through the blood of the Lamb. I used to feel so unworthy I scarcely dared to call myself a follower of Christ, but he has forgiven me all, and I think I shall never again be tempted to distrust him. He will support me to the end."

Thursday, 17th, being just six months from the day her mother died, she made this remark to me in the evening: "Pa, I have been thinking, to-day, what a happy meeting

I should soon have with Ma, where we shall rănge the blest fields together, and on the banks of the river shout halleluiah forever and ever. O what a blessed thing to be free from all suffering and sorrow! and, best of all, to see Jesus as he is, and praise him as we ought!"

Wednesday, 23d, she spoke of feeling discouraged, lest, under affliction so severe and protracted, she might become impatient and lose her fortitude, though we saw no indication of it, and if we had, knowing how much she endured, it would not have surprised us at all; but next evening, while a pious and favorite sister conversed and prayed with her, she felt relieved in mind, and spoke to this effect: "I feel now somewhat encouraged. Thank the Lord for a little reviving! Jesus is the sinner's friend. He was made perfect through suffering. He has supported me in my affliction, and he can support me to the end. All I ask is triumph in death, and trust he will give it to me. I can give up the world; yea, and my family, for though they will feel lonely after I leave them, the Lord can provide for and comfort them. I should rejoice to be released at any moment, even this night, if it is the will of God; but I will try to wait patiently his time, and then O the heaven of rest where there is no more suffering!"

The next Saturday evening she said to us, "I rest in the hands of God. I should be thankful to him if he would release me, but I wait his time." She then prayed most fervently, for some two minutes, sufficiently loud to be distinctly heard by all in the room. In that prayer, the blood of Christ was made the sole ground of her confidence in the mercy of God; and the tenor of the petition was for full sanctification, and supporting grace to the end.

Sabbath morning, 27th, there appeared to be a general inflammation of the interior of the chest, attended with extreme pain, and such a diseased state of the throat as to prevent her receiving any nourishment, or even cold water, and threatened speedy dissolution. In this extremity, she exclaimed, "Bless the Lord! I feel that I have nothing to fear; if I die this day all will be well with me, and I can cheerfully give up my family into his hands." During the day she said to her mother-in-law, "This is the last Sabbath I shall spend on earth, but I shall soon enjoy a Sabbath that never ends. Yes, mother, and I am not going to a land of strangers;" and then named many of her departed friends whom she expected to meet, including her own mother and infant son. Most of the day she was under the influence of languor and drowsiness; but when a particular friend called to see her, in the afternoon, she roused up a little, and said to her, "Sweet heaven, my happy home, I shall soon be there." A pleasant smile came over her emaciated countenance; she raised her hand and exclaimed, "Then I shall be free!"

On Monday, she had several paroxysms of strangulation, in which we thought her in immediate danger of dying. While we were silently waiting the next paroxysm to come and hurry her into eternity, she calmly remarked, "I know not that I shall be allowed the privilege of speaking in my last moments, but I wish it understood that I am perfectly safe; that God does and will accept me, not for any worthiness of my own, but for Christ's sake, and will save me with an everlasting salvation in heaven." She then called her husband to her, and with many expressions of love and gratitude for his uniform kindness, and especially for waiting on her so faithfully and cheerfully in her sickness, took leave of him, adding her blessing upon and commending him to God. Next she called her father, and spoke to him in like manner. Then her mother-in-law, pouring out a full heart of grateful affection upon her, and then another sister whom she loved much, giving to each such blessings and words of encouragement as suited our respective cases. Amid the sobs and tears of that solemn and moving occasion, the sufferer was the only one who appeared to be perfectly self-possessed, requesting us, several times, not to weep for her, as we should soon meet again, where all tears are wiped away. She then proceeded to name her little children, and all the absent members of the two families, prayed for and pronounced a blessing upon them severally; and added, "Give my love to all my friends, and tell them I am gone to heaven." Next she spoke of her funeral with great composure and deep humility, and said, "I wish no display, only a plain little funeral here at the house; and let brother Young [her own pastor] make a few remarks, as he may think proper." She then subjoined, "My work is done; I have nothing more but to wait the will of God. 'Lord Jesus, receive my spirit.'" But after a short pause, she again recollected her absent brother, and made his a special case. Addressing herself to me, she said, "Be sure to send a great deal of love to my dear brother, and tell him his sister is gone to heaven, and hopes to meet him there. Tell him I know there is a blest reality in religion, for it has sustained me under all my sufferings, and now cheers me in death. I should be glad to see him once more in the flesh, but trust I shall see him in a better world."

About five o'clock that evening she passed through another extreme paroxysm of coughing and strangling, in which we fully expected she would expire; but at last she revived so as to speak, and said, "Jesus is with me! Jesus is with me! Jesus is with me! Death has no sting; the grave has no victory! I have the victory through Jesus Christ, and I view the grave as a sweet resting-place for my body, while my blood-washed soul will rest in paradise!" After she was composed, she addressed her husband, of whose class she was a member, and said, "Don't forget to tell my classmates farewell! and tell them, though I can not be permitted to meet with them again in this world, I hope to meet them all in a better!"

Her ill turns continued, at irregular intervals, through that night and the next day. In an unusually-severe paroxysm, which occurred on Tuesday evening, about five o'clock, she appeared to be beyond all hope of living through it, and the family were called in to witness her departure. She, however, revived again, after a very long and painful struggle; and the first words she uttered were a recital of the beautiful verse,

"Yonder's my house and portion fair,
My treasure and my heart are there,
And my abiding home:
For me my elder brethren stay,
And angels beckon me away,
And Jesus bids me come."

The longest and hardest struggle of the kind occurred the same evening, at half-past six o'clock, and continued till we really believed her spirit was in the act of departing, insomuch that, when she finally recovered, it appeared similar to a resurrection from the dead. If it were in my power to give the reader a just idea of that agonizing and heart-rending scene, I would not inflict it upon him; and if it were practicable, would obliterate the recollection of it from my own mind. At the commencement of each of these attacks, she expected her release, and with much apparent reluctance returned again to life, praying most earnestly to be set free. Indeed, her disappointment in not obtaining her final deliverance when expected, was the most difficult thing to be reconciled to that occurred during her whole affliction; but grace was afforded to secure the victory even over this. At one time she remarked, "You thought I should have got home before now; but I feared the news was too good to be true.

However, I must wait patiently the Lord's time." Again she referred to the subject in these words, "I will not calculate as to the time of my departure, but wait the days of my appointed time. I would be the Lord's every minute, living or dying."

The last-named paroxysm so prostrated her strength, and was followed by such languor, that she was never after able to hold a regular conversation, though she lingered till next morning, Wednesday, November 30th, at a quarter past eight o'clock, speaking a few words occasionally of her friends and of the goodness of God, and frequently repeating the prayer, "Lord Jesus, receive my spirit!" but the bitterness of death was passed. Though she had suffered long and much, God, in great mercy, granted her oft-repeated request at last, for a quick and easy passage over the Jordan of death. Less than two minutes before her exit, she spoke rationally and distinctly; and then, without a single groan, or any distortion of the features, or any struggle whatever, calmly and sweetly slept in Jesus.

BISHOP ROBERTS.

The late Bishop Roberts was a man whose memory deserves to be perpetuated: "the righteous shall be in everlasting remembrance." That he bore the infirmities of fallen human nature is admitted; and with all my confessed partiality for his character, it is not pretended that he had no faults; but I am safe in saying, they were as few and harmless as those of any other minister of Christ with whose acquaintance I have ever been favored. For more than fifty years he was a consistent professor of religion, during which time he exerted an extensive and salutary influence, by precept and example, in favor of experimental and practical godliness. His name is still precious in the memory of many who knew his various personal excellences, and the value of his protracted public service as a minister of the Gospel; so that he being dead yet speaketh.

In contemplating the history of his life, one is forcibly reminded of the wisdom and goodness of God in the selection and training of human instruments to execute the benevolent purposes of his providence and grace. Considering the age and country in which he lived, and the peculiar work in which he was called to act so distinguished a part, there was not a man in a million that could have filled his place as he filled it. The enterprise in which he was unceasingly engaged for more than forty years was, "to spread Scripture holiness over these lands." The means employed to accomplish that object were various, such as circulating Bibles and religious works; but the most prominent of means in that labor of love was the Christian ministry of itinerants, interchanging pastors, acting on aggressive missionary principles, who, instead of waiting to be called by the people, went out into the highways of sin, and called the people to repentance, faith, and Gospel obedience, with a confidence and force of authority that almost compelled them to come to the Gospel supper. This work, of course, subjected Methodist ministers in early times to much toil and peril, much privation and hardship, not only in following the emigrant to his retreat in the western wilderness, without the advantage of roads or bridges, or any suitable accommodation, but also in carrying the Gospel to neglected districts in older sections of the country, and the suburbs of cities, to seek the lost, and bring them to the saving knowledge of the truth. For such a work Bishop Roberts and his early coadjutors received a training which was of more importance to them than that which could have been acquired in the shade of a college. They had the advantage of being hardy pioneers, plain, matter-of-fact, common-sense men, not easily discouraged, because they knew their cause was good, and especially because they had confidence in Him who had sent them into all the world to preach the Gospel to every creature, with the promise that he would be with them and bless his own truth.

As to himself, Bishop Roberts was the son of a plain farmer in very limited circumstances, who taught him from childhood the wholesome lessons of industry and economy. His father's family observed the simple modes of life common to people in new countries the latter part of the last century. They resided in Ligonier Valley, Penn., to which place they removed from Frederick county, Md., when the subject of this notice was yet a child. He had no early literary advantages beyond those of common-school education; but his pious mother not only taught him religious duty, but excited in him ardent desires for useful knowledge; and being naturally possessed of a vigorous mind, and apt to learn, he obtained a respectable knowledge of books, as well as of men and things in practical life generally. His habits, formed in clearing up forests and cultivating the soil, first in Ligonier and subsequently in Chenango—a still newer part of the country—where he acquired the elements of a pioneer and hunter, were of great use to him in after life. They secured to him a firm constitution, which evinced much power of endurance, and such principles of economy and independence, that the real wants of life with him were few and simple, while its luxuries were lost sight of, or dispensed with altogether without serious inconvenience.

He appeared to be piously disposed from his childhood, but became decidedly religious in his fourteenth year, being then Scripturally converted. About the same time he was appointed by the minister whose circuit included his father's residence, to catechise the children of the neighborhood: such was the confidence which his pastor had in his sincerity and discretion. From that time forward young Roberts was justly regarded as an example for the youth of the country where he was known. In early life he was strongly impressed that a dispensation of the Gospel would be committed to him; but his uncommon diffidence and fearful sense of responsibility, were ample security against any danger of entering the ministry prematurely. The time which intervened between his first conviction of duty to preach and his actively engaging in the ministry was not lost, as he applied himself to the study of theology and other necessary means of preparation; so that when he began, his pulpit performances were from the first both popular and useful. He possessed by nature the elements of an orator—an imposing person, a clear, methodical mind, a ready utterance, a full-toned, melodious voice; and when to all these were added an ardent love of souls and an unction from heaven, he, of course, became a powerful preacher. He did not aim, however, at display, but at usefulness; and, therefore, commanded the more respect and confidence as an able minister of the New Testament.

The first years of his ministry were spent on circuits in the west; but his worth became known to the Church, and he was removed to the eastern cities, where he soon acquired a reputation which rendered his name familiar to thousands who had never seen him. After filling his regular terms of service in Baltimore and Philadelphia, he was appointed presiding elder on Schuylkill district, embracing the latter city, which brought him into constant intercourse with numerous ministers and their congregations on popular occasions, thus affording him a broad surface over which to exert his salutary influence. At the next session of the Philadelphia conference, there being no bishop present, the rule required the conference to elect by ballot a President *pro tempore* from among the presiding elders; and though the youngest of the board, he was chosen. While performing the duties of President, delegates from the northern conferences, on their way to General conference in Baltimore, called in; and, after witnessing the dignity, discretion, and promptness with which he presided, they concurred with the delegates of his own conference, that he was one of the men they needed in the Episcopal office; and he was accordingly elected and set apart for that responsible work, in May, 1816. Thus, in about sixteen years, he rose from the obscurity of a western circuit preacher, on trial, to the highest office in the gift of the General conference, and became one of the joint general superintendents of the whole connection throughout the United States and territories. In this office of high trust and hard labor he continued twenty-seven years—then ceased at once to work and live.

During his superintendency, he peregrinated the entire country, from Michigan to Florida, and from Maine to Louisiana, and even the Indian countries west of Missouri and Arkansas; and though unwieldy in person, most of his journeying was performed on horseback, as very little of it could then be accomplished by any other mode of conveyance. The last twenty-four years of his life he hailed from South Indiana, a tolerably-central position to the whole field. From that point he diverged in all directions, "every-where preaching the word," and superintending the general work. In the performance of his official duties he seemed to take no account of toil or fatigue, poverty or hunger, suffering or peril; always patient and pleasant, he moved as a burning and shining light amid thousands of ministers and hundreds of thousands of Church members in the spirit of a true evangelist, regarded by all as an affectionate father in Christ, and a wise ruler in the Churches. Among his official duties were, presiding in the conferences, ordaining deacons and elders, arranging districts and circuits, and, last, though not least, stationing the effective traveling ministers, than which nothing requires more care, more discretion, or more independence; and yet it is believed that no one ever performed those various and responsible duties with more judgment and propriety, or less censure, than did Bishop Roberts.

In person he was not above ordinary hight, but broad set, and of corpulent habit; so that in the full vigor of life, his weight was probably not far from two hundred and fifty pounds. The features of his face were large and manly rather than elegant, and its general expression was frank and agreeable. That his commanding person and forcible utterance were of service to him as a presiding officer, must be admitted; yet he possessed other qualifications still more essential. His well-developed faculty of common sense, tempered by mildness of disposition, and uniformly regulated in its exercise by Christian courtesy, gave him uncommon influence over deliberative bodies. He was not careful about technical niceties; his usual manner in the chair, as well as out of it, indicated more of the patriarch than the prelate, more of the fraternal friend than of the officer. Still he never failed to magnify his office when it became necessary to maintain order. In several instances, when the members of conference were strongly excited, and the floods of passion began to lift up themselves, he has been known to assume as much authority as would suffice to command a British war-ship engaged in battle, till order was restored, and then to ease the conference off from its agitation by a few gentle remarks, illustrated by reciting an amusing incident, so as to turn all into pleasantry in a few moments.

His manners were unexceptionable, combining the ease and gracefulness of a finished gentleman with the simplicity of a plain, Christian farmer. He was apparently as much at ease while dining with the Governor, as when surrounding the simple board of his pious friends in a log-cabin. The Christian simplicity which pervaded his early home, was never corrupted by ecclesiastical honors. In 1837 the writer, then the junior colleague of Bishop Roberts, had the pleasure of sojourning a few days at his unpretending residence in Indiana, where, free from all needless ceremonies, I enjoyed the substantials of life, served up by the hands of his consort, and mingled with much social pleasure. Indeed, the intellectual repast furnished by his godly conversation, spiced with numerous incidents connected with the introduction and progress of Methodism in this country, and especially in the west, would scarcely allow one to bestow a thought on his apartments or table. As a religious friend and social companion, no one excelled him. One thing observed with approval was, whoever else was present to enjoy his society, his wife always shared in his attentions, never failing to address parts of his conversation to her. He called her Betsy, and she called him Robert; and thus, by the plainness of their habitation and conversation, their guest was frequently reminded of the history of Abraham and Sarah, dwelling in tents with the heirs of promise. Now, certainly, he who could feel alike at home in the pulpit of an eastern city, and in the open stand at a western camp meeting, in the chair of General conference, deciding questions of order, and in an Indian's camp, talking about Jesus and heaven, and who could render himself both pleasant and useful to others in each of those positions, must have been a man combining in himself the most desirable elements of character. Such was the case of Bishop Roberts. When his earthly pilgrimage terminated, what King David said of Abner might have been truly applied to him, though in a higher and better sense: "Know ye not that there is a prince and a great man fallen this day in Israel?" 2 Sam. iii, 38.

The most prominently-developed trait in his character, however, was meekness. Nothing is risked in saying he was the most unpretending man I ever knew of his importance in society. No official authority, no personal popularity, ever induced him for a moment to think more highly of himself than he should have done. On the contrary, all his movements indicated, without any voluntary humility, that he undervalued his real worth. Every one by him was preferred to himself. He ever looked to the accommodation of others, at the expense of his own. Nothing but grace imparting to him a lively sense of responsibility, in view of the claims of God and souls, it is believed, could ever have overcome his excessive modesty and diffidence in the performance of his various public duties. One-fourth of the well-authenticated incidents of his life, bearing on this point of his history, would abundantly establish its truth. Only one need be recited. In 1836, when he had been bishop twenty years, and was the senior in that office, he deliberately, and in good faith, tendered his resignation to the General conference, simply because, in his own estimate of himself, his qualifications for the office, small at best, would soon be so diminished by the infirmities of age, that he could not be safely intrusted with it. No member of that vast body, however, entertained the same opinion of him that he did of himself; and, to his great mortification and disappointment, no one moved to accept his resignation, and he bore his official honors as a cross to the end of life, which was calm and peaceful. His dust slumbers beneath a plain monument near the Indiana Asbury University at Greencastle, where the surviving, but now infirm partner of his earthly joys and sorrows still lingers on the shores of time.

REV. NOAH LEVINGS, D. D.,

FINANCIAL SECRETARY OF THE AMERICAN BIBLE SOCIETY.

By request of the New York conference, at its session in Poughkeepsie, May, 1849, I preached before that body a funeral sermon on the death of Dr. Levings, which, by subsequent request of the conference, was published in pamphlet form. At the close of that discourse I read the following sketch:

Of the early history of this distinguished brother we have no knowledge. It appears, from the official Minutes, that he was received, as a traveling preacher, in the New York conference in the year 1818, and had been, at the time of his death, a traveling preacher nearly thirty-one years. His ministerial labors were extensive, and highly appreciated. With his brethren he soon became a favorite. He was generally and favorably known in the east. Subsequently his position in General conference enabled him to form an acquaintance with our leading men in most or all of the conferences in our extended connection, all of whom became his friends. He was also much esteemed by other Churches. When Bishop Janes was elected general superintendent, in 1844, and, consequently, had to resign his office as Financial Secretary of the American Bible Society, Dr. Levings was immediately chosen by the Society as his successor, in which office he continued serving the Society acceptably till his decease. In his office as Bible Secretary, he sustained the same relation to all the evangelical Churches, and, indeed, to all true friends of that noble institution, the American Bible Society, and its auxiliaries. Of course his duties called him much from home, and required very extensive travel; but he cheerfully made the sacrifice for the cause he loved so dearly.

Dr. Levings left his home, in New York, October 11, 1848, solemnly impressed he should return no more. So deep was that impression, as he informed a friend, that he rode to the boat weeping, and continued to weep till he felt embarrassed. Still duty called, and he felt bound to go. He passed through Baltimore, Pittsburg, and Cincinnati, every-where preaching the word. The Sabbath he spent in Cincinnati he preached at Morris Chapel, in the morning, the most moving sermon I ever heard him deliver; and it is believed the discourse he delivered in Wesley Chapel that evening will not be soon forgotten. On Monday he left for Clarksville, Tennessee, the seat of the Tennessee conference, where he arrived October 26th; thence to Memphis conference at Aberdeen, which place he reached November 17th, after a most fatiguing journey. On the 28th he had a distressing attack of asthma, and on the 29th was very ill with palpitation of the heart. December 4th he left for Jackson, Mississippi, and arrived there on the 8th, after traveling over rough roads and dismal swamps; thence to Vicksburg, the seat of the Mississippi conference, where he was indisposed, took medicine, and was cupped; but, notwithstanding his feeble condition, he delivered an address the same evening, and next day, being Sabbath, he preached. Thus was he constantly engaged—journeying, addressing conferences, Bible meetings, and public assemblies. It appears, from his diary, that on his last tour he preached eighteen sermons, delivered nine public addresses, and traveled, I presume, not less than four thousand miles, partly in stages, over difficult roads. Such exertions and exposures, amid the heavy rains of the south-west, during the months of November and December, were too great for his enfeebled constitution to endure. From Vicksburg he proceeded to Natchez, where he preached his last sermon, in the Presbyterian church, probably on Sabbath, December 24th. His entry on the 25th was in these words: "A day of great feebleness of body. Wrote a melancholy letter home, but wrote as I felt; it will give some pain to my dear family." That letter probably communicated his dying charge to his now sorrowful widow and orphan sons. On the 26th he wrote in his day-book, "Still weak, but more cheerful." Having despaired of accomplishing the balance of his intended tour southward, he turned his thoughts toward home, and left Natchez December 27th, in the steamboat Memphis, bound upward, on board of which several deaths occurred by cholera, two the first night after he went aboard. His entry of 28th was, "On the Mississippi, in much feebleness of body, but in peace of mind. Thank the Lord, have hope of seeing home." On the 29th he wrote thus: "On the river. One more poor fellow, an Englishman, found a grave on the bank last night." This was his last entry, and, probably, the last he wrote, except to sign his last will and testament. He remained on that boat till she reached Cincinnati, in all eight days, with declining health. The boat was much crowded, had many sick, and some dying; so that a lone stranger, in his prostrated condition, and unable to help himself, had poor prospect of much comfort under such circumstances; though we are informed that some fellow-passengers rendered him what aid they could.

Dr. Levings arrived in Cincinnati on the third of January, and was conveyed to the residence of Mr. S. H. Burton, one of the Doctor's devoted personal friends, with whom he usually made his home while in the city, and where he received every possible attention, day and night, from Mr. Burton and his family, from two respectable physicians, Drs. Mendenhall and Woodward, and from our Bible agent, the Rev. W. P. Strickland, and other brethren, till his sufferings terminated. But neither kind attentions, medical skill, nor the prayers of his numerous friends, could stay the work of death. He expired Tuesday evening, January 9th, seventeen minutes past nine o'clock, aged about fifty-two years.

Though there is sadness in the thought of dying in a strange city, far removed from one's family and home, yet in the case before us there is much to relieve that sadness. Doctor Levings complained of nothing much but debility and labored respiration. Though he had some diarrhea, his disease was chiefly congestion of the lungs. He suffered no extreme pain, had no convulsive agony, nor severe paroxysm of any kind; but gradually sunk away without any struggle, till the weary wheels of life stood still. He also had communion with Christian friends, who felt deeply interested in his welfare, and attended faithfully to his spiritual wants. They likewise cheerfully aided him in adjusting, to his satisfaction, all temporal matters which rested with any weight on his mind, both as regarded his domestic affairs and his official business, which being done, his mind was perfectly at rest.

The best of all, however, was, his religious preparation for death appeared to be complete, so that he was perfectly resigned to the will of God, and cheerfully yielded up all into his hands. No expression of dissatisfaction with being afflicted, or separated from his family, or dying from home, escaped his lips. Though fully apprised of his real condition, as understood by physicians and friends, he remained cheerful and happy to the last hour, patiently waiting his final release. His was a triumph indeed; not of human philosophy, but of grace. As might be expected of one who had devoted most of his life to the service of God, that he would be peaceful and happy in his last hours, so it was, in an eminent degree, with our beloved brother deceased. Most beautifully and thrillingly did he discourse to his friends of the love of God in Christ, of sustaining grace, of Christian triumph, and of bright and cheering hopes that animated him while entering "the valley of the shadow of death." Most of the particulars of his last hours were reported by Rev. W. P. Strickland, a brother who, being intimately associated with Dr. Levings, both by official relation and personal friendship, remained with him after he reached the city, day and night, to the closing scene.

On Saturday night and Sabbath morning, when, perhaps, passing the crisis of disease, the Doctor experienced great restlessness; but subsequently, when informed that his request for the prayers of the congregations at Ninth-street and Wesley had been attended to, and that numerous friends were interested for him, he replied, "To that I attribute my present composure and peace." Being asked if he realized strong faith in Christ, his answer was, "O yes, the Lord Jesus Christ is the strength of my heart, and my portion forever. I die in no other faith than the faith of the Gospel, and that as taught by the Methodist Episcopal Church." On one occasion, while sitting up and leaning against the bed, Mr. Burton placed a large Bible to support his head, that he might breathe easily, when, fixing his eye on the title, as printed on the back of the cover, he exclaimed, "O thou blessed book, thou lamp to my feet and light to my path, thou guide of my youth, directory of my manhood, and support of my declining years, how cheerless would this world be were it not for thy divine revelations and Christian experience!" At another time he said, "Pray for me, my dear brethren, that I may have strong faith for the hour of trial.

My religious states have been adjusted to a life of health more than one of sickness, but God my Redeemer will order all things well." Soon after he observed, "I have been sifting the motives of my entire life down to the very bottom, and can not discover any thing there that, dying, I would wish otherwise; but imperfections, O my imperfections! I have nothing whereon to rely but the merits of my Lord and Savior Jesus Christ. I feel he died for me." On Monday his will was written, as dictated by himself, and after signing it he exclaimed, "Thank God, one foot is in Jordan, and I shall soon cross over." Monday night his symptoms became worse, and he continued to fail rapidly from that time to the last moment.

On Tuesday afternoon, about seven hours before his death, your speaker, having just returned from the country, obtained an interview with him. After receiving a tonic, which temporarily revived him, he said to me, "Thank God that I am permitted to see your face in the flesh once more! I am not able to converse much, but I can still say, Glory to God!" My first inquiry was, whether he felt his way clear before him, to which he answered, "All clear; I have a clear sky." The second and last question proposed by me was, "If I live to meet the New York conference next spring, when your name is called, what shall I say to the brethren?" He replied, with perfect self-possession, and with a serene and peaceful countenance, "Tell them I die in Christ; I die in the hope of the Gospel: tell them I have a firm, unshaken confidence in the atoning sacrifice of our Lord Jesus Christ as the foundation, and only foundation, of my hope of eternal life; and, relying on that foundation, all before me is light, and joyful, and glorious." At the close of a short prayer then offered, as we kneeled round his bed, that he might be favored with a safe and easy passage to the promised rest in heaven, he responded, "Amen, amen, amen; glory to God!" Subsequently he conversed but little. Being asked if he wanted any thing, he replied, "The will of the Lord be done!" When brother Strickland asked him, in the evening, if he wished to say any thing to him, he only said, "Live for God!" His last words, uttered when Mr. Burton's little children came in to see him, before they retired for the night, were, "God bless the little children, and make them holy!" Thus he died, as Jesus lived, blessing little children, and thereby evinced that he retained the spirit of his Gospel mission to the latest moment of life.

On the morning of Thursday, 11th of January, the corpse was conveyed into Wesley Chapel, where a solemn funeral service was performed; thence to the public vault of the old Methodist burying-ground in the city, attended by his ministerial brethren, Christian friends, and fellow-citizens, where he was deposited in safety, to await the order of his family. After the arrival of his son, his remains were interred in the new Wesleyan cemetery, four miles north of Cincinnati. The body was inclosed in a handsome coffin, with a silver breastplate, on which his name was engraved. The Young Men's Bible Society of Cincinnati have resolved to erect over him a suitable monument, which shall designate to his surviving friends, in coming years, the last resting-place on earth of our deceased brother. We name these items for the satisfaction of his personal friends remote from the scene of his death.

Dr. Levings was an agreeable man, of fine personal appearance, excellent social habits, superior conversational powers, and sterling moral worth. He possessed a vigorous mind, well trained in the principles of theology and duties of the ministerial office, and a heart richly endued with heavenly grace. His elocution was at once easy and forcible; his pulpit discourses abounded with appropriate Scripture authorities, and were attended with an unction from the Holy One, rendering him an able and successful minister of the new covenant. As such, he filled many important positions in the Church, with credit to himself and usefulness among the people. He rests from his labors, and his works do follow him.

The news of his death spread a gloom over Cincinnati; how much more over his own adopted city, New York! When the telegraph dispatch announced the sad tidings of his decease, who could imagine the sensation produced in his desolated home; in the Bible-House, the scene of his late official action; in the numerous churches where he had so impressively held forth the word of life; and, indeed, throughout our extended Zion! But, on the other hand, who could conceive the joy which filled the minds of angels, as they witnessed the triumph of his faith over the last enemy, or the holy rejoicing of "the spirits of just men made perfect" in heaven, as the chariot of love bore his redeemed spirit over the everlasting hills, and neared the innumerable company above!

"And hadst thou seen him when the vail withdrew,
And his blest spirit from its prison flew,
What scenes of glory burst upon his sight!
What sounds melodious rang through worlds of light!
While heavenly friends throng thick the shining road,
And hail'd him welcome to the mount of God!"

COUNTRY FUNERAL.

How impressive is a funeral in the country, unembarrassed by haste, or needless ceremony, affording full opportunity for calm reflection! In crowded cities, the frequency of death measurably destroys its effect on the minds of the living, excepting those of intimate friends;

but in the country, the death of a prominent individual produces sadness in a whole community; worldly business is suspended, and the funeral becomes an occasion of general interest. The assembled multitude, the religious service, the extended procession, the death-like silence, and placing the mortal remains in their darkness and solitude, all leave a deep and solemn impression upon the memory and heart of those present. Such a funeral I recently attended.

The immediate scene of solemnity was a beautiful farm-house of white brick, in cottage form, on the Lebanon pike, Butler county, Ohio, fifteen miles from Cincinnati. The entire scenery was pleasant and airy. Recently that abode was as cheerful and happy, as its exterior is tasty and inviting; but it has been visited by the pale horse and his rider, leaving mournful desolation in their train. The subject of the funeral was one who had filled the important and endearing relations of wife and mother; was ardently loved by her large family and numerous relatives, and universally respected by her neighbors and friends. The hospitality and cheerfulness with which she had, for a long time, entertained the ministers of Christ, and other religious friends, had greatly extended her acquaintance and influence. Many a toil-worn itinerant had visited that rural scene of loveliness weary and hungry, but, after enjoying a comfortable repast, and a season of religious conversation and prayer, left refreshed and happy. By this and other means, one, who regarded herself as little and unknown, had contributed largely in promoting the best of causes while living; and the testimony which she bore to the power and efficacy of saving grace in the closing scene of her earthly existence, confirmed the faith of many; and it is hoped that this brief report of it may strengthen the confidence of some who never saw her.

Mrs. Anna Conrey was the daughter of a pious Baptist minister, Rev. David Laman, who still lingers on the shore of time, and was at her funeral. She was born August 14, 1799, in the neighborhood of her late residence, having never resided in any other. The state of Ohio, of which she was a native, was admitted into the Union when she was an infant. Of course, she acquired that fortitude and energy of character which the circumstances of a new country so generally and fully develop. New countries are generally settled by enterprising spirits, and the children of those hardy pioneers usually become the leading characters in Church and state, and the most useful members of community, not because they learn more of books, but more of practical life and common sense, than those of older and more refined countries.

Miss Laman was married to Mr.—now Rev.—James Conrey, November 21, 1816, and thus became the mistress of a family at a little over seventeen years of age. The Bible says, "Lo, children are a heritage of the Lord!" Their long and happy union was crowned with nine children, six of whom are still living, and three are not; for the Lord took them to himself in early life, two in infancy, and one son, a youth of piety and great promise, at sixteen years of age. No doubt but those departed children, and their now departed mother, had a joyful meeting in their heavenly Father's house above. "Blessed are the dead which die in the Lord."

Mrs. Conrey was favored with religious parents, and realized the benefit thereof in after life. In the twenty-eighth year of her life, being somewhat afflicted in body, and more so in mind, on account of her lost condition, some of her relatives urged her husband to go for a physician, and he went; but, differing in judgment from them as to her real condition, instead of bringing the doctor, he brought two Methodist brethren to converse with and pray for her; the very kind of help she most needed. While they sang that moving hymn,

"Awake, my soul, in joyful lays," etc.,

light, joy, and peace from heaven broke into her disconsolate heart, and she was soon well enough to leave her bed, and resume domestic business. Shortly afterward, she and her husband united with the Methodist Episcopal Church. Mrs. C. possessed much stability of character, as well as amiableness of disposition. Her piety was of the uniform kind, giving a steady and increasing light, which shone more and more unto the perfect day. In her feelings she seldom, if ever, rose so high, or sank so low as many others; but she was favored with a firm, unwavering confidence in God, attended with emotions deep and abiding, though scarcely ever with great ecstasy. Her professions of Christian experience were rational and prudent, saying but little of raptures on one hand, or of trials on the other; but walking in newness of life, her conversation was such as becometh the Gospel. In all her domestic affliction and sorrow, her religion sustained her, and enabled her to comfort her family in the day of adversity. The testimony of her pastor, Rev. Mr. Keely, in substance was, that, in the numerous interviews he had with her during her various seasons of affliction the past year, she was always calm and resigned, as one who appeared to be more under the influence of principle and settled confidence, than any excitement of passion, not now elevated, and then depressed beyond measure, but uniformly collected and peaceful, professing a firm trust in Christ, that she would make a safe crossing and joyful landing over the Jordan of death.

Her health was much interrupted, and declining for fourteen months previous to her decease. At different times she suffered severely, and was, apparently, brought near to the gate of death, so near that all her family were twice collected home to witness her departure; but she still survived. Subsequently, there appeared to be some improvement in her condition, and hope of her recovery revived for a time, but was soon withered. Her last illness, in its severity, was protracted some three weeks, during which period she suffered much, suffered constantly; her disease, most of the time, being wholly unmanageable. At different periods it was apprehended she was about to depart, but temporarily revived. On Tuesday her friends began to lose all hope, and on Thursday death appeared to be very nigh, and was expected hourly; but she lingered till Sabbath morning, November 26, 1848, at three o'clock, when she left her friends below to join her friends above.

As to her religious prospects, it was observed by those about her during her last sickness, that she was much engaged in prayer. To the last, she felt great solicitude for the welfare and salvation of her family, and on the Sabbath previous to her death, held a conversation with her husband on that subject. That concern for her family, however, was nothing new; she was only carrying out to the end what had been her constant aim all the time. The rule of her Christian life was, to do unto others as she would they should do unto her. This rule she taught her children, and what she thus taught she enforced by her personal example.

Amidst her protracted and painful affliction, she enjoyed singing, and other religious exercises, in her room, often repeating, herself, parts of hymns, especially the lines,

"Jesus, the name to sinners dear,
The name to sinners given;
It scatters all their guilty fear;
It turns their hell to heaven."

While Rev. Z. Connell spoke of her peace being made with God, she said that matter was all settled and arranged long ago, and she felt that her peace was made with God. When he reminded her that the promises of God to the believer were exceeding great and precious, she replied that she felt that they were verified in her. To all her religious friends who conversed with her on the subject of her future prospect, her uniform testimony was expressive of firm trust and hope in the Lord.

She frequently spoke of exchanging her suffering body for a new body—the resurrection body—especially after a night of weariness and pain; but was fully resigned to the will of God, and desired her family not to grieve for her. There were paroxysms of distress, during which she could not possibly speak. In one of these, on Tuesday, when she was presumed to be entering upon her last struggle, one of her daughters asked her if she felt Jesus precious. She nodded an affirmative answer several times. On Thursday morning, when apparently near her end, she desired to see her family alone, and they gathered round her bed; she spoke a few words to each, and desired them all to meet her in heaven. Having finished her dying counsel, and distributed some mĕmentos of her affection, her strength was much exhausted; and feeling that her work was done, she repeated the words of dying Simeon, "Now, Lord, lettest thou thy servant depart in peace." To a friend she said, at another time, "I am almost over Jordan, and feel that I shall have a safe landing."

Her son, who is a minister, said to her, "Mother, if you must be taken from us, you feel all is well?" She answered, "O yes; all I need is patience. If these are my dying words, I want you all to meet me in heaven. As for you, my son, I want you to be a burning and a shining light on the walls of Zion. Don't let the world too much engross you." Again, on Thursday afternoon, when it was thought she was just going, he said, "Mother, do you feel that you have the victory through the Savior?" She assented, and tried to raise her hands; one assisted her to do so, when she waved her right hand several times in token of victory. She was perfectly conscious, and to the last recognized her friends.

About twelve o'clock Saturday night, and some three hours before her exit, at her own request, she was removed from her bed to an armed chair; and being propped up nearly erect, she requested her friends to sing one of her favorite hymns:

"I have sought round the verdant earth for unfading joys," etc.

While they sang, she raised both hands, as if triumphing over her last enemy, and praised God in broken accents, till her strength failed, and she was replaced on her dying pillow. Some time during the last struggle, her son suggested that her end was nigh, and trusted she was not alarmed. She said, "No." Again, he said, "You have the same confidence?" She responded, "Yes." After she was unable to converse, her husband inquired if she still felt the Savior precious?—to which she distinctly nodded assent. Again, at a later period, he asked, "Do you still feel the sustaining grace of God?" and she again assented as before. Finally, he exclaimed, "Victory in death!" and she returned the same signal. Among her last words, turning her eyes upward, she said, "Who is that?" Soon after, she distinctly articulated, "A book! a book!"

When dying saints are losing sight of this world, it is presumed that eternity begins to break upon their mental vision. When Mrs. C. exclaimed, "Who is that?" perhaps she saw the pilot-angel sent to convey her happy spirit home; and when she exclaimed, "A book! a book!" who knows but she saw the "Book of Life," containing the names of all the saints, and hers among them? May we all follow her as she followed the Savior!

Part Third.

NOTES OF TRAVEL.

Notes of Travel.

ITINERANT WORK REVIEWED IN 1839.

OUR FATHERS.

HITHERTO I have been providentially hindered from attending any meeting of the Methodist Historical Society, but have not been indifferent toward that noble enterprise. The work which it proposes to accomplish is praiseworthy, and I have read its proceedings with much pleasure. Such an association is the most certain means, within our reach, of keeping future generations correctly advised of the character of our fathers in the Gospel, and the labor of love performed by them in the latter part of the eighteenth and commencement of the nineteenth century, in this western country. And what could be more interesting to our children and children's children, after we shall be numbered with the dead, than a correct history of the introduction and spread of Methodism, or, what is the same thing, Scripture holiness, over these western valleys? Of the commencement of this work, it does not become me, who am of yesterday, to speak. I leave that for a Burke, Kobler, Wilkerson, Lakin, Roberts, Quinn, Young, and their cotemporaries in the kingdom and patience of Jesus. And on this part of the subject I will only express the convictions of my mind respecting the general character of the pioneers of Methodism in the United States and territories.

As often as I have referred to the old Minutes, read the names of our fathers in the Gospel, and traced out their history by the best lights I had, so often have I received the impression, that they were a body of Methodist preachers vastly superior to those of this generation, both in the western country and elsewhere. In saying this, I do not mean to disparage our preachers of this day; in doing so, I should reproach myself also, for I am one of them; nor will it offend me if others differ in judgment; but I can not obey the clearest conviction of my own mind, in rendering honor to whom honor is due, without offering this tribute of respect to our fathers in Christ. That there are exceptions is admitted; but in making my comparison, I speak of primitive and modern Methodist preachers generally; and I do this not in reference to any one qualification, but to their entire qualifications for the work of the ministry. And the fact here assumed, that our fathers excelled us, may be admitted without involving any absurdity; for it is easily accounted for, in view of the work assigned them, and the circumstances under which it was performed.

In the first efforts to introduce and carry on that work of God called Methodism, such were the prejudices of the people against, and their ignorance of it, such the oppositions to be encountered and obstacles to be overcome by the teachers of it, that common men were not suitable instruments for its accomplishment. The ordinary blessing of God on such instruments, would not have rendered their labor successful; it would have required miracles. It is, therefore, reasonable to suppose, that, under such circumstances, most of those called of God to the work of the ministry, were men of more than common moral courage, as well as intellectual and physical strength. Dwarfs and shadows, without force or courage, were not the heroes for field-preaching, contending with mobs and savages, and sleeping in the woods without guard or shelter. And who does not know that a large proportion of the first American Methodist preachers were men, not only of vigorous and well-disciplined minds, but likewise of iron constitutions and tremendous muscular force? As examples in the east, we might refer to Joseph Everett, Jesse Lee, and S. G. Roszel; and in the west, to V. Cook, John Page, R. R. Roberts, and others.

It required more religion to enable our fathers in the Gospel to engage in and prosecute the work assigned them, than most of us have in this day, though not more than we might and should possess, if we sought as earnestly and perseveringly as they did. Time was when to be called a Methodist preacher, was, in the estimation of the great mass of the people, to be virtually charged with being every thing vile and despicable, and consequently only worthy of insult and personal violence, which he often received in abundance. That was a day that tried men's souls. And in view of the odium and insult, fatigue and peril, poverty, nakedness, and starvation, to be expected consequent upon such a calling, no one was prepared to engage in it, till he was crucified to the world, and the world crucified to him—till the love of God and man filled his heart, and constrained him to turn out into the highways and hedges, and exhort sinners to come to the Gospel supper—and till he had the clearest evidence that God called him to that work, and pronounced woe upon him if he preached not the Gospel; so that when our fathers agreed to enter the list of traveling preachers, they literally left all to follow Christ, gave themselves wholly to the work of saving their own souls and the souls of the people, and consequently received and continued to enjoy present and full salvation, and saw their labors crowned with glorious success among the people.

Beside their natural and spiritual advantages, they were prompted, by the force of circumstances, to more diligence, and made greater improvement of their time and talents. The doctrines, ordinances, and usages of Methodism were not then so well understood as at present. Those denominations that now compliment us with the appellative *evangelical*, treated our fathers, though more worthy than we, as heretics, fanatics, and impostors, and thus set the dogs of the people on them. Methodism was grossly misrepresented in public and private by those of different creeds, partly through ignorance and partly through malice; while the world and Satan directed their heaviest artillery against it, because it waged a potent and successful warfare against sin. Methodism being thus assaulted on every side, its first public teachers were continually thrown on the defense of truth; and to answer all objections, and stop the mouths of gainsayers, excited them to constant diligence in research and reflection; while daily practice in public, and extemporaneous speaking, rendered them more perfect; and knowing their cause was good, they fearlessly advocated it on all occasions. God blessed them in it, and they became able ministers of the New Testament. Beside, they were strong in faith, felt their awful responsibility as embassadors of Christ, spoke as in sight of his judgment-seat, and their word was attended with power and the Holy Ghost, and much assurance.

Such are briefly my views of the character of our early ministers, and the cause of their excelling. What remains for us but to follow them as they followed Christ, according to the ability given us, that both they who sowed, and we that reap, may rejoice together forever?

OUR TRAVELS.

Leaving the history of early Methodism in the west to those who understand it better, I beg leave to notice briefly a few things of which I have more personal knowledge. Great changes have appeared in our western fields of labor, even since I entered it in the fall of 1815, under the direction of Rev. D. Young, presiding elder; and such changes, too, as have some bearing on our work as traveling preachers. Among these changes none are more palpable than such as relate to the facilities for traveling. Where we used to convey our salt, venison, and bear meat on pack-horses, we now see canal-boats gliding along, richly laden with flour and all the essentials of good living. Where we once followed the dim path, guided by the blazes on the saplings, made with the woodman's ax, we now hear the coach wheels gently rumbling on the smooth M'Adamized turnpike. In the same place where we formerly swam our horses beside the little canoe, plies the steam ferry-boat, crossing and recrossing every five minutes, crowded with passengers; and where we used to plunge in on horseback at a venture, through flood and bog, current and quicksand, now rests the arched bridge on piers of granite. From these hints may be inferred some of the difficulties of traveling preachers in the west, only twenty years ago, or even less in some places.

In 1825 my district embraced that part of Kentucky west of the Tennessee river, which was then all in one circuit, called Clarke's River, of which John S. Barger was preacher in charge. We were not the first on that ground after the Indians left. Brothers Crouch and Parker had been there forming a circuit the year previous; and if they would speak out they could relate scenes of suffering sufficient to cause the ears of some readers to tingle. Still, when we went, the settlements were "few and far between," and frequently without any road, or even path, from one to the other. When we wished to visit a neighborhood fifteen or twenty miles distant, we ascertained as near as we could the general course, and struck off through the woods without road or guide. If the sun was visible, we steered by him, and if not, by a pocket compass; and if a creek—too deep to ford—obstructed our course, we had our choice to swim

21

or stay on our own side, having neither boat, bridge, nor canoe. Of the manner of overcoming these obstructions, I will here furnish an example or two.

At the close of a camp quarterly meeting in Clark's River circuit, July, 1826, the small streams were much swollen by reason of heavy rains. Soon after leaving the camp, we had to encounter a small stream, which was usually some three rods wide, but at that time spread over the banks and much of the adjoining low ground. However, we were told that by going to the Shallow Ford above the forks, we could probably ride across without losing bottom; but where we expected a shallow ford, we found a sheet of water about a hundred yards wide, it having overflowed its banks, with a rapid current in the middle. Our company consisted of Geo. Richardson, John S. Barger, Alexander H. Stemmons, another young preacher, whose name I have forgotten, and the writer. We were all sound except myself. I was sick—had been so for five or six days, and was much more fit to be in bed than on horseback. In consequence of this circumstance, the company objected to my swimming, lest the wetting, after taking medicine, might prove injurious. But by riding in mid-sides to the horse, I gained the large end of a great tree, which had been cut down so as to fall across the main channel just above the ford, for a temporary foot bridge. Here they deposited me and the baggage, till they should swim the horses over. In the mean time, others came up from the meeting, forming a company of some fifteen in all. The coming-out place lay rather up stream from us, and just below it, we were told, the bank, then under water, was too steep for the horses to rise when they should strike bottom. To avoid this, and procure a sloping bank to rise on, they selected a place below, where the bluff changed sides; so that after riding in till the horse was nearly covered, and arriving at the main channel, he suddenly and unexpectedly to himself, though not to his rider, stepped over a precipice, perhaps ten feet high, into a sweeping current, where horse and rider were violently immerged, but soon emerged some distance from where they first disappeared, and presently made safe landing. In this way the young brethren conveyed their own horses over, after which Richardson and Stemmons rode for the whole company, securing one horse and swimming back for another, making several trips each. This done, Richardson led me over the channel on the log; and leaving still between us and the dry ground a sheet of water some thirty yards wide, and three feet deep, he deliberately stepped in, took me upon his shoulder, and, notwithstanding much brush and drift-wood were on the way, placed me safely on solid ground. The whole was accomplished in a few minutes. Here we parted with all but our own company, with whom we first started from camp; and leaving the *Shallow Ford,* our way was clear before us to the next branch of the same stream,* only a few miles distant.

Our second crossing was like to prove more difficult than the first, having an equally rapid stream, without the advantage of any log. Having appointments ahead, it was important to get on somehow or other; and after a short consultation, it was thought best, on account of my condition, to head the stream, or at least go far enough up to ford. This being agreed on, we made the attempt, but were so much embarrassed by quicksand, especially where the ground had been overflowed, that we soon became weary of it, and determined to cross if possible. Finding a place where the banks were dry on both sides, the water being there confined within its usual channel, we dismounted, and were consulting about the mode of

* I regret that I have forgotten the name of this creek; brother Barger can tell.

crossing, when Stemmons concluded it was time to execute as well as plan. Fixing his large, laughing, blue eye on a tall, slim hickory, growing on our side of the creek, he deliberately began to ascend, which he did almost as easily and rapidly as a wild bear would climb a chestnut-tree on search of nuts. When he had left the ground about forty feet below him, and arrived where the sapling had scarce strength to support him, he turned on the side next to the stream, held on with his hands, letting his feet swing clear, and his weight brought the top down on the other side, and, with the assistance of another, who swam over to his relief, tied the limbs fast to the root of a tree. This bent sapling formed an arched bridge about forty feet long, six inches wide, and elevated in the center about twelve or fifteen feet over the deepest of the turbid stream, on which we crossed—*astride*—safely, pushing our baggage before us, and resumed our journey, leaving the Hickory Bridge for the accommodation of the public.

Such were our facilities for crossing in those days, when we had help; but when alone, there was often no alternative but to make the horse swim with his rider and baggage, and trust to Providence to get safely through; and such were the difficulties to which we were accustomed in carrying the Gospel to the poor, in the new countries then; and the same are doubtless realized now by many of our traveling preachers on the frontiers of the work. Now, for such work as this, I would rather have a half a dozen such young preachers as those above named, than twenty graduates of any theological seminary in the United States. A. H. Stemmons has gone to his reward, and J. S. B. and G. R. are still in their Master's work, though the latter has been for many years much disabled by hemorrhage from the lungs. Peace be with them!

OUR CIRCUITS.

THE reader has ample proof, in the preceding scraps, that I do not aim at regular chronological order, much less at writing a history of Methodism in the west. My object is only to furnish a few scraps of information respecting the preachers, and the circumstances under which their work was prosecuted in my day, illustrated by such anecdotes, and enlivened by such reflections as may seem edifying and proper.

The next point I shall touch, is the amount of labor which we used to perform as traveling preachers in the west. When I labored on Marietta circuit with the Rev. Marcus Lindsay, in 1816, it was a four weeks circuit, embracing what are now called Marietta circuit, Athens circuit, and parts of several others. It extended from Newport, sixteen miles above Marietta, to the west end of Athens county, a distance of some sixty-five miles in a straight direction, and was so arranged as to include the neighborhoods on the Ohio river as far down as Newbury; those on Duck creek; on the Big Muskingum, as far up as Big Rock, above Waterford; those of Little Hockhocking; Federal creek; Big Hockhocking, from the mouth to Minker's Bottom, ten miles above Athens; part of those on Shade river; and all intermediate points. To compass this plan, each of us traveled some two hundred and fifty or three hundred miles, preached forty times, and examined about one thousand persons in the classes every twenty-eight days; besides laboring extensively in prayer meetings, catechising children, etc.

The Muskingum circuit, when the Rev. Charles Elliott was my colleague, in 1818–19, included what are now called Zanesville station, Cambridge circuit, Putnam circuit, and parts of others; and the year following, when Samuel Brockunier and James Gilruth were my colleagues, we so enlarged it as to include Washington and Coshocton, and the intermediate settlements. Those familiar with the country can see the extent of our plan, by running a supposed line from Zanesville by Dilan's Iron Works, and curving round through the settlements on Jonathan's creek, to Wolf creek, below M'Connellsville; thence up the Muskingum, on the west side, to Putnam and Zanesville; thence south-east, by a zigzag route, past Chandler's Salt Works, and on to the head of Wills creek, and all the neighborhoods down to Cambridge; thence to Washington, Sugar creek, Wagoner's Plains, Coshocton, and Johnson's Plains; and finally, by numerous angles, right angles, and acute angles, back to Zanesville. This, when I went to it, was a four weeks circuit, but when I left, it required a tour of six weeks, and allowed but little rest for man or beast. Our first year's labor there resulted in a small decrease, chiefly on account of strictly enforcing the rules of Discipline, and laying aside many delinquent members; but the second year we received about two hundred new members, which, after deducting all losses, afforded some considerable increase.

I will name one other circuit which I traveled, to show the extent of the fields we used to cultivate. Christian circuit, in Kentucky conference, to which I was assigned in 1821–22, with Philip Kennerly, who died before I reached the circuit, embraced all of Christian and Todd counties, most of Muhlenburg, and parts of Butler and Logan counties, in Kentucky, and, in Tennessee, parts of Montgomery and Stewart counties. This was also a six weeks circuit, about three hundred miles round, with near forty appointments, out of which have since been formed Greenville circuit, Hopkinsville circuit, Montgomery circuit, Tennessee conference, and parts of several others. I have referred the reader to these circuits, of which I had personal knowledge, not as unusual, but ordinary fields of labor in those days, in the western country, which, however, when compared to the circuits of our fathers before us, were mere pea-patches. Still, they were sufficient to keep us busy. No account was taken of wet, cold, or stormy weather. When we had appointments to preach, we generally filled them, though often through much difficulty, and sometimes at the risk of life, on ice, or in crossing fearful streams. It was considered but moderate work to preach and meet class once a day, on an average, and ride eight, ten, or fifteen miles. And if we redeemed one or two days in the week, to stay with our families and rest, or, rather, work to make provision for them in our absence, it was by riding harder, and preaching oftener in the day, while out on the circuit. Our preaching-places were not only far apart in general, but the way from one to the other was often very difficult; being only a dim path, which frequently branched off, without affording the stranger any direction which to follow. Some of the preachers, in early times, carried a hatchet to mark the trees, in a certain way, at each place where they had to turn off from the main track, and others adopted the plan of splitting a bush, to enable them to recollect which path to take; but their enemies, finding out these things, made false signs to deceive and get them bewildered: so that, with all the care we could take, it was quite common to miss our way and get lost, till we became familiar with all the different routes and neighborhoods in the circuit. And when we were favored with plainer roads, they were not well improved; and we had to contend with mud, water, and quicksand, swamps and pole-bridges, and steep, difficult ascents and descents alternately. In the winter season, when the weather was rough, the mornings short, and the roads in the worst state, it required great effort to keep up with our appointments. Sometimes we had to travel twelve, fifteen, or twenty miles before the morning preaching, having no lodging-place on the way. To meet such engagements I have myself, when far from home, risen long before day, gone to the wood pile, covered with snow, and fished out the wood, a piece at a time, packed it on my shoulder, built a large fire, and then roused up the family to get me a hasty lunch, that I might be off in good time. Starting with the dawn of day, on a clear morning, it was pleasant to observe the sun as he appeared above the horizon, throwing his golden rays through the frosty boughs of the lofty forest trees, and spreading cheerfulness over all the works of God. But if the day was cloudy, and the temperature below the freezing point, it was tedious to climb the dreary hills, descend into the ice-bound vales, and plunge into the cold stream, perhaps breaking ice as we went. This we often did alone, and far from the habitation of man. When we reached the place of destination, it was very discouraging to meet only a few indifferent hearers, as was often the case; but very pleasant and encouraging to find a house full of patient, willing hearers, waiting to hail us welcome as messengers of truth in the name of Christ. In both cases it was important for the preacher to be punctual; in the former, that he might gather a congregation, and in the latter, that he might retain and increase the one already gathered. A few disappointments in one neighborhood would discourage the people, and destroy their confidence in the preacher; so that he lost his influence and his hearers together. Knowing this, it was expected of the preachers to attend, if possible, and preach, whether the hearers were many or few. I have frequently preached to three, four, or a half a dozen, as well I might, since Philip preached to the Eunuch on the road, and Jesus to the Samaritan woman at Jacob's well. And though it was usually dull work to speak to so few, it was not always so. I recollect, the second year I was on Christian circuit, of riding about nine miles, to a place called Dunham's School-house, where I had engaged to preach. The school-house was among the Knobs, north-east part of Christian county, situated on the west point of a ridge, in an exposed position, being an open log building, covered with clapboards. The north-west wind was piercing cold, so much so as to prevent the people from venturing out. However, four persons attended; old brother D—— and his two single daughters, all members, and a neighboring young woman, who was not a member of the society. These I found shivering round a small fire, at the time appointed to commence. But before I began, being very cold myself, I went to the woods, gathered as much dry wood as I could carry, and made on a large fire. The chimney was as broad as the end of the house, which was in our favor. I stood in one corner, the old brother was seated in the other, and the women in front of the fire, all in convenient distance. I read, sang, prayed, and preached, just as though the house had been full; afterward I proceeded to examine them as in class meeting. They all wept, one shouted for joy, and the non-professor being seriously affected, we finished with a prayer meeting for her special benefit. She became, from that hour, an earnest seeker of, and soon after obtained salvation. And though I suffered some with cold, and returned without my dinner, I did not regret going. The next time I preached there to a much larger congregation, and our new convert joined the Church.

Now, it would be easy, if necessary, to multiply anecdotes of this character, but I only wish to apprise the reader of the nature of our work as Methodist preachers in those days, and the circumstances under which it was performed. Our preaching was mostly in private dwellings and school-houses, having but few chapels; though in warm weather we preferred the open woods, especially on popular occasions, when very large congregations attended. And though this seemed to be a small business, it was laying a foundation deep and broad, on which to build subsequently, as the result abundantly shows.

OUR STUDIES.

ANOTHER part of our duty was, studying to show ourselves approved unto God, workmen that needed not to be ashamed, rightly dividing the word of truth. In this part of our employment we were rather embarrassed in cold weather. House-room was scarce; and, as is generally the case in new countries, families were large. In many places where we were kindly entertained, a small cabin, consisting of one room, served for parlor, dining-room, kitchen, bed-chamber, study, class-room, and chapel. Still, we did not neglect our books. After allowing a reasonable time for profitable conversation, we resumed our studies. While the family were employed at their business, we read and wrote; and if they became so loquacious as to interrupt us much, we read aloud, and explained, to the mutual improvement of them and us. And we had more facilities for gaining knowledge than might, at first, be supposed. The Bible, and most of the standard works which we have now, we had then, and made good use of them, being at that time but little affected with the extensive variety of light reading which now diverts the mind and heart from more important things. And owing to our peculiar mode of circulating books, these standard works got into the hands of all the preachers, and many of the members, together with a sufficient number of literary works to answer the purpose. To all these we applied ourselves diligently. In the winter, those whose eyes could bear it, read much at night. If they could obtain a lamp or candle, well; if not, they split boards and old fence-rails to splinters, and throwing in a piece at a time, read by the blazing light. And in warm weather we took for our study the shade of a tree; or, if the musketos became very troublesome, the preacher might be occasionally seen up in the fork, or on a large limb of a beech-tree among the boughs, where those insects suffered him to pursue his studies in peace. We also read much on horseback, occasionally closing the book, and reflecting on its contents; to which mode of study our long, lonesome rides were admirably adapted. But what rendered our studies most profitable, was the daily opportunity afforded us of turning immediately to practical, useful account, all the knowledge we gained from books, conversation, or meditation. The consequence of the whole was, many of the Methodist preachers who entered the work with very limited education, became not only grammarians, historians, philosophers, and orators, but what was much better, profound theologians and able ministers of the New Testament. When self-styled *competent ministers*, of certain Churches, brought up in literary and theological institutions, questioned our right to minister in holy things, on the ground that we were uneducated and ignorant men, we referred them to the hundreds and thousands converted to God under our ministry, living epistles, known and read of all men. Some, not satisfied with this answer, and self-confident in the support of their supposed orthodoxy, especially considering they were from the college, and we from the woods, provoked some of our preachers to public discussion of questions in controversy between them and us; but the result before the people seldom or never failed to help our cause at the expense of their own. After proscribing us as novitiates, fanatics, and heretics, till they became satisfied that their opposition was helping us and injuring themselves, they struck their crimson colors, commenced harping on the *union* string, and began to style us, one of the *evangelical denominations!* It was then, and not till then, that other denominations began to exert a deleterious influence on the institutions of Methodism, alluring our young members and young preachers from their Methodist simplicity, and putting into their heads notions of conformity to the world, and to those who had only a name to live, while they were dead. This has been an occasion of much grief to scores of old preachers and thousands of old members among us who have borne the burden and heat of the day. But as this train of thought would lead me from the original design of these scraps, I forbear.

OUR SUPPORT.

The next feature of the subject to which I wish to direct the attention of the reader, is the inducement which Methodist preachers had to engage and continue in the toils and hardships above referred to. This is the more proper, as every motive was attributed to them which malice could invent, or ignorance credit; each class of enemies having their own method of accounting for our conduct. Cold-hearted, half-hearted, and false-hearted professors of religion, in various denominations, finding their own craft in danger, charged us with being false prophets, whose object was to deceive the simple for the sake of the loaves and fishes, though we received but few of them. Many ignorant people, of the lower class, professed to think we were a lazy set of men, who wished to be fed and clothed without work, though no men in the country worked as hard as we did in our ministerial calling. Some, whose reading did not extend beyond the pages of a stale novel, or the advertisements of a country newspaper, suspected that we were spies or tories, sent by John Wesley to spy out the liberties of the people, under a cloak of religion. Politicians, who exhausted all the energy of their souls in the scrambles of party politics and the feuds of county elections, professed to think we were hired by demagogues—almost as corrupt as themselves—to influence the suffrages of the people; and this charge was preferred by men of all political parties, though we interfered with none of them. Pleasure-takers complained that we were officious meddlers with other people's business, because we preached against balls, horse-races, profanity, intemperance, and the like. Those who aspired to the high places of society, but were less popular and caressed than they thought they deserved to be, concluded our object must be fame; and, indeed, we were somewhat famous in their estimation, and the estimation of all whom they could influence, but it was for being every thing but Christians and gentlemen; while those whose god was mammon, wiser than all the rest, found out to their satisfaction, that we were fortune-hunters; that the chief object of our desire was money. This last was, upon the whole, the most common and popular allegation of our adversaries; for as self-interest governs the conduct of the multitude, it was easy to influence them to judge us by themselves. To this charge, therefore, I will briefly reply.

Any man who has intelligence enough to be a Methodist preacher, knows that ours is not a lucrative profession; and any man having sufficient energy of character to be a useful Methodist preacher, could succeed better at almost any thing else, if money were his object. This is true of most Methodist preachers now, and it was doubly so twenty years ago, when we were generally without parsonages, received nothing but quarterage, and but little of that. Some of us had families to support, but we asked no accommodations on that score—went in for the work as it came, and moved from circuit to circuit as occasion required, though often subject to difficulties and embarrassments, known only to God and ourselves. In the economy of Methodism, no arrangements could be previously entered into between the preachers and people in reference to their field of labor or support. The preachers knew nothing of their appointments till they heard them read out at conference. Learning to what circuits we were assigned, we went immediately to them, without inquiring whether the people to be served by us were wealthy or poor, liberal or otherwise, and provided houses for ourselves as we could. We did the work, pay or no pay, supplying our lack of support out of our own private funds; and when these failed, very many were compelled to locate, and work with their own hands, till they recruited their circumstances so as to resume their high and holy calling.

On the subject of making money, as a Methodist preacher, I beg leave to speak that I do know, and testify that I have seen. I entered the itinerant ministry with a family, in my twenty-second year, having first sold my little farm, and vested the funds for safe-keeping, so as to be at all times ready to go wherever appointed; and have been a man of one business for more than twenty-three years, not incumbered with any worldly business, which in any wise interfered with my ministerial calling. The whole amount appropriated by the stewards, during the first twelve years, as their books in the several circuits will show, was about $1,700; and if to this be added all my marriage fees and private presents, the aggregate that I received on every score, as a minister, for twelve years service, was about $2,000. This is not guess work. My private accounts were kept with great care; and, though some of them are lost, my recollection of them is substantially correct. The average dividend is $166.66⅔ per year. This was to pay house rent, buy fuel, and provisions, and clothing for the entire family, entertain company, educate the children, pay doctors' bills, public and private charities, and provide myself with books, and horses, and riding equipage for the circuit, etc. After appropriating all I received to these purposes as far as it went, the balance was drawn from my scant private resources, only for which we must have suffered till literally starved out of the connection. In confirmation of this, I will here detail a few particulars.

The year I was stationed in Hopkinsville, Ky., the stewards, with some difficulty, raised for me $30 quarterage, and $35 family expense, or $65 in the year; my expense the same year being about $450, and nothing received from conference. This was not owing to any neglect of the work, or the manner of doing it, that I am informed of. Nor was this the worst year of my life, in reference to support. The Green River district, to which I was appointed in the fall of 1825, was about one thousand miles round, including the journeys I made to visit my family occasionally between quarterly meetings. My way led through Henderson swamps and Jackson's purchase, and, consequently, across Cumberland and Tennessee rivers. My first quarterly meeting was one hundred and twenty miles from home, though I resided in the bounds of the district. Before I commenced this heavy work, I sold my pony and paid $100 for an able horse, on which I traveled that year, by computation as exact as could be made without measuring, three thousand, nine hundred miles. The same year, beside holding quarterly conferences, and administering the sacraments frequently, I delivered near three hundred public discourses, and, by the blessing of Providence, never lost an appointment, winter or summer, spring or autumn, day or night, sick or well. And now, gentle reader, what do you suppose I received for the whole year's labor? It was $66 and a few cents. And as I shared with the preachers of the several circuits my proportion of the whole amount collected, this was equal to the average support of the married preachers in the district. The next year two more circuits were added to the district, which, of course, increased both the labor and the amount of traveling. That year my horse began to fail, and I bought another for $80, and got through by riding them alternately, but not without losing a few appointments, by reason of family affliction. My receipts this year amounted to a few cents over $62. However, near the close of the year a few friends, incidentally learning my temporal circumstances, raised for me $120. This was unofficial, but I reported it at conference to the credit of the district, as a part of my family expense. Some time previous to my entering this work, in order to save the remnant of my little estate, I had laid out part of it in a small private residence in Elkton, and the balance in a small farm near the town. This farm of seventy-eight acres, the only productive stock I had, was rented out for about $65 per year, in produce, which, added to my salary, made an income of $130 yearly. But as my annual expenditure was not less than $400, it became necessary, at the end of the second year on the district, to sell my farm to pay the bills I had contracted to support the family, while I was serving the Church and public. By this means I was thankful once more to be clear of debt; and being next year stationed in Louisville, and subsequently transferred back to the Ohio conference, have never since been so much embarrassed for want of support.

Such were our facilities for making money as traveling Methodist preachers. Of course it became us, in those days, to be strictly economical. Costly furniture, silk dresses, and superfine black cloth coats were out of the question. We were glad of something comfortable to eat on poplar tables, and equally so to obtain new garments of *homespun.* Though it did not accord with our views of fitness, for ministers to appear in public dressed like country laborers, it was the best we could do under the circumstances; and as the people chose to hear us preach in jeans coats and tow-linen or linsey *pants,* rather than to enable us to provide better, our chief concern, in reference to that matter, was to have clothes whole and clean, which, by the way, was not always convenient.

Before I leave this money-making business, it is proper to observe, that in almost every circuit we found some noble souls, whose kindness and liberality ministered to our necessities, imparting consolation to us in the day of adversity, so as to keep our sinking heads a little above the waves of despondency. These few liberal souls contributed nearly all that was raised toward our support. I could name more than a score of such in the bounds of Green River district. Their names, I trust, are in the book of life, and the Lord will remember them when he makes up his jewels. But the great mass of our people were formerly very ignorant, or very neglectful of their duty in supporting the Gospel. In illustration of this, I will relate what occurred at a country quarterly meeting in Livingston circuit, October, 1826, while I presided and Clement L. Clifton was preacher in charge of the circuit. After passing through the regular business of quarterly conference on Saturday, the stewards proceeded to make their call on the leaders for the quarterly collections from their respective classes; and as it was a farming district of country, and some of our members were in quite easy circumstances, something pretty clever might have been expected, only that it was the first occasion of the sort after annual conference; but when the contributions from all the classes, containing several hundred members, were brought together, they amounted to seventy-five cents. There was due Clifton, for one quarter's service, $25, and myself $5; his traveling expense from conference, for which he had a claim on the circuit, was $2.50, and their proportion of mine was fifty cents, making, in the whole, sacramental expenses included, about $34, or if there were two preachers, of which I am not sure, it was $59, which the circuit should have raised. These bills so far exceeded the amount in the treasury, that it was thought prudent to defer any appropriation till after the public collection should be made on the Sabbath, of which due notice had been given. The weather on Sabbath was remarkably fine and pleasant, so that the house was full of females and the yard of men. I stood in the door and preached to the listening crowd, who paid very strict attention, and seemed to be interested. Sermon ended, I made a few appropriate remarks on the privilege and duty of supporting the Gospel, explained the object of the collection about to be lifted, and sent the stewards through the congregation, in doors and out. About that time change in Kentucky consisted mostly of individual notes on stores, ferry-boats, blacksmith shops, etc.; and when all the hats were emptied into one, and the money counted, it was ascertained to be exactly fifty cents in *shinplasters*. Total amount raised by the circuit that quarter, $1.25.

Now, if the reader will connect with this state of things the recollection that we were regarded, in early days, by many as idle strollers, or deceivers, having constantly to breast a storm of opposition and persecution, he can judge whether the love of gain, ease, or applause had any hand in causing men of good character and fair prospects in life to turn Methodist preachers. No, it was the love of God and man, and the desire of saving blood-bought souls, that rendered them willing to spend and be spent in the cause of Christ. Amidst a thousand nameless difficulties they persevered in their Master's work, till most of the obstacles were overcome; and, thank God! a brighter day has dawned upon us in this western land. Our preachers are now as much respected, and upon an average nearly as well supported as those of other Churches west of the mountains. And by comparing their present condition with the condition of those who preceded them in the cultivation of the Lord's vineyard, they may see sufficient cause to thank God and take courage, and go on their way rejoicing.

OUR ENJOYMENTS.

Those who look not beyond the things which perish, and take no thought for the life to come, might naturally suppose that the early Methodist preachers of this country, according to the preceding remarks respecting their difficulties, were very disconsolate men. And truly, in view of the things they suffered, there would be some plausibility in this supposition, if in this life only they had hope. But not so. They sought a better country, laying up a good foundation against the time to come; and their hope was anchored within the vail, whither Christ, the forerunner, was for them entered, as an advocate with the Father. When a man glories not, save in the cross of Christ, by which he is crucified to the world and the world to him—when he has a conscience void of offense toward God and man, and a good hope, through grace, of everlasting life in heaven, he will be happy under any outward circumstances. Now, this was the condition of most Methodist preachers, under the trying scenes alluded to above. There may have been exceptions; but the great body of them knew that their witness was in heaven, and their record on high, while they received within their hearts a kingdom which could not be shaken by the combined opposition of Satan and his children. The testimony of Paul, respecting the first teachers of Christianity, was quite applicable to them: "Even unto this present hour we both hunger, and thirst, and are naked, and are buffeted, and have no certain dwelling-place; and labor, working with our own hands: being reviled, we bless; being persecuted, we suffer it; being defamed, we entreat; we are made as the filth of the earth, and are the offscouring of all things unto this day." "But we have this treasure in earthen vessels, that the excellency of the power may be of God, and not of us. We are troubled on every side, yet not distressed; we are perplexed, but not in despair; persecuted, but not forsaken; cast down, but not destroyed; always bearing about in the body the dying of the Lord Jesus, that the life also of Jesus might be made manifest in our body."

Beside peace in believing, and joy in the Holy Ghost, they had some pleasant things connected with their work; for outward circumstances were not all against them. Far removed from the noise and bustle of commercial cities, the hurrying crowds of business men, and the frivolity of fashionable life, they enjoyed the sweet solitude of the woods, so favorable to pious meditation. This afforded a most delightful school, in which to gain the knowledge of God and their own hearts. How precious is the recollection still, of those evening hours spent in prayer and meditation, amidst the shady bowers of our western forests! For such exercise there is no place equal to the solemn, silent grove, whose spreading foliage conceals the kneeling suppliant from the view of all but God. It is true, we were not always in the country; for, as our commission was to "go into all the world, and preach the Gospel to every creature," the villages were not neglected. In them we had flourishing societies of living Christians, long before the "educated ministry" ventured to the "moral desolations" of this great valley; although some of them reported officially, that they had preached the first Gospel sermons ever delivered in certain places, where we had been regularly preaching for many years. But having preached our sermons, examined our classes, and visited the sick and serious in town, we resumed our wonted employment of searching for lost sheep in the wilderness. Exercise on horseback was our element and favorite recreation. When slightly indisposed, or debilitated by excess of public exercise in town or city, it served at once to invigorate the body and exhilarate the mind. Thus, this part of our work promoted good health and fine spirits. It is strange that any Methodist preacher should prefer a station to a circuit, in view of these things. And, moreover, our long, solitary rides were as favorable to study as to health and piety, affording the best possible opportunity to study a sermon, or to carry out any train of thought suggested by reading or conversation. Sometimes we enjoyed hours together almost uninterrupted, in this delightful employment, and consequently came before the congregation well prepared to discuss some profitable subject selected for their edification, and frequently had times of refreshing from the presence of the Lord. If the meeting was in a log schoolhouse, or under the spreading boughs of an oak, it was nothing the worse of that, so God was worshiped in spirit and in truth. Week-day congregations in the country were much larger then than now; for, though we were opposed by formalists, infidels, and libertines, very many of the people loved to hear preaching, and would gather in from a distance of several miles round, and hang on the lips of the preacher with solemn attention, as he stood behind a table or split-bottom chair, proclaiming peace on earth and good-will to man. Excuses about distance and want of time were less frequent, than complaints that the minister came too seldom, or made his sermon too short. We were frequently importuned to appoint a second meeting in the evening, to which we often consented, and had the cabin full of weeping hearers. After sermon and prayer meeting, when the people started home of a dark night, it was an interesting spectacle to step out into the yard and observe a score of torch lights diverging in every direction from the place of worship, to light the families to their different homes. But what interested the preacher most, was the simplicity and fervor of their devotions; because this was conclusive evidence that his work was not in vain in the Lord. While he lined the hymn, all the people stood up and sang the praise of God together; and though they had neither pitch pipe, note-book, nor choir, it was most solemn and impressive to hear them "singing with grace in their hearts to the Lord." And their prayers were as earnest as their songs were solemn and melodious. In those cabins and woods we often witnessed displays of awakening power, pardoning mercy, and sanctifying influence, over which angels might well rejoice. And after a few days in the country, laboring in revivals, forming new societies, enlarging his circuit, and witnessing numerous conversions, the preacher returned to town like a messenger of grace newly commissioned from on high, filled with faith and the Holy Ghost, and preached in the power and demonstration of the Spirit, till sinners trembled, wept, and turned to Christ, and saints shouted aloud for joy.

Now, if any one is tempted to doubt the excellency of this itinerant mode of operation, let him lift up his eyes and look eastward, westward, northward, and southward, and behold what God hath wrought by it. Where we were no people, we have become the people of the Lord, the wilderness has bloomed, and the fruits of righteousness cluster thickly round us. The handful of members have swelled to multitudes, and the place of the log hut, in which we once met to worship, is supplied with a spacious chapel, and is still full. Truly, "the Lord hath done great things for us, whereof we are glad;" and the blessed work is still going on!

INCIDENTS OF TRAVEL, 1836.

I SHOULD like to introduce the reader to the Black River Swamp, in the state of Arkansas, but not till I get to it, nor yet exactly as I was introduced to it myself.

In September, 1836, I left the Queen City, to attend the Tennessee, Arkansas, Mississippi, and Alabama conferences. It appeared like a long, fatiguing journey to perform on horseback, and alone; but there were points in view which could be reached by no other means of conveyance. There might be disease and danger in the course; but I was on lawful business, intimately connected with the welfare of redeemed sinners; and why should any man ever fear to go where duty calls, or remain till his work is done? Moreover, I was well mounted upon *Nick*, a fine pacing gray. He moved as if on elliptic springs, and bore onward with a strength of muscle, and power of endurance, which excited my admiration. Far removed, not only from wife, children, and friends, but from the crowds of strangers which usually throng the public lines of conveyance, it was a time for reflection on the responsibilities and difficulties of my new relation, and not wholly unimproved. Lonely reflection, however, was soon superseded by practical duties. While in council with the brethren of Tennessee conference, at Columbia, a call made for volunteers to supply the wants of the new conference just set off in the state of Arkansas, was promptly responded to by some noble-hearted, self-sacrificing young ministers. Three of them were ready to bear me company thither, immediately after the final adjournment. Their names were Randle, Duncan, and Simmons. Passing down through the western district of Tennessee, we came on the fresh trail of fourteen thousand Creek Indians, just then removing from Alabama to their new home in the far-off west. At one of their camping places, then vacated, was seen a standing hollow tree, out of the side of which had been taken a slab, by cutting above and below, and splitting it off, and which had been carefully replaced. A citizen, whose neighbors had made examination, informed us, that in the hollow of that tree was a deceased Indian, standing erect, with his gun, blanket, and hunting costume, as he appeared when living. We subsequently saw several of these depositories of their dead. As a matter of convenience, the Indians were separated into companies of fifteen hundred, and a sub-agent assigned to each. We came up with the rear gang in the vicinity of Memphis, were two days passing their extended line of companies, and slept three nights in sight of their camps. No nation of men ever exhibited more powerful muscles than were developed in the persons of the Creek warriors. Like other people, they bore the marks of inequality. Some had the appearance of abject poverty. Among this class the men rode on ponies, carrying their guns and camp-kettles, while the women trudged on foot, bearing heavy packs on their heads, and small children lashed upon their shoulders. A second class were better clad, had a better outfit, and presented more appearance of comfort. The third class, probably formed of the nobility of the nation, were gaudily attired in silk and jewelry, and exhibited the insignia of wealth and office.

After crossing the "Father of waters," at Memphis, we immediately entered the Mississippi Swamp, which, at that point, was forty-two miles across. The track was so worked up by the teams and pack-horses, that we found it more pleasant to avoid it when practicable. For miles together our horses waded, but generally found firm bottom, except about the sloughs, where many tired Indian ponies stuck fast, and were left to perish in the bog, and where our noble animals had to struggle hard to escape the same fate. On the evening of the second day, we emerged from the swamp, and crossed the St. Francis river. At a small, green bottom, two miles beyond the river, two companies of Creeks, numbering some three thousand in all, were camped for the night. We took lodging at a country tavern on the hill, about thirty rods from them. They had nearly as many ponies as people, and almost every pony wore a bell. The camp axes were roaring; dogs and children appeared to be alike abundant and alike noisy. The whole, taken together, produced a singular confusion of sounds, and presented quite a novel spectacle.

Next morning, about daybreak, we rode out through the encampment, in a north-east direction, on the Batesville road. Having cleared the great swamp, and reached an undulating surface, we congratulated ourselves that the worst of the journey was behind. For some twenty-five miles our course led us over desolate pine and oak ridges, which, nevertheless, formed an agreeable contrast with the sludge from which we had escaped. At noon the rain began to fall, slowly at first, but steadily. In the afternoon we came by a small company of men engaged in raising a corn-crib near to a cabin, which seemed to be full, and presented no appearance of comfort, when the following conversation ensued:

"How far is it to the next house?"

"Twenty-one miles; and three more to the tavern."

"What sort of road is it?"

"Not very good, nor bad; just middling."

"Is there any deep water to cross?"

"None that will swim, except Bayou de View, sixteen miles from here; and I don't reckon that will swim quite."

Then among ourselves we held a conference, on horseback, the rain still coming down. "It is two o'clock; say four hours till daylight will be entirely gone. Can we reach the point of difficulty before dark?" "Yes, I think we can." "If we fail to get through, we shall need our dinner by to-morrow." "Well, I have a little piece of corn bread," said one. "And I have part of a sweet potato," said another. "That is as good fare as we can get here," responded a third. It was suggested, if we had to camp out, there was no means of striking fire; but perhaps other campers might have left fire on the way. The case was finally summed up thus: our time in which to reach conference is short; there is no use staying here in the rain: come on. And onward we went, ignorant of what was before us. In a few minutes our road disappeared under water. What does this mean? Why, the Black River Swamp. "They said, last night, we should cross it, but it looks worse than we expected." The sludge increased, and the horses sank more and more. Presently, while passing a bad place, Nick, better acquainted with M'Adamized turnpikes than swamps, went down till he was nearly buried alive in quicksand and water. After a long and hard struggle, he came out and brought me with him, but my heavy saddle-bags were left behind in the mud. Having recovered them, we resumed the journey, but soon reached another slough, where, to prevent a greater evil, I dismounted, drove the horse, and followed on foot, through mud and water to the knees, by which we made a safe crossing. But the thought of its being twenty miles to the next house, wet and cold, my boots full of water, and the night approaching, was not very cheering. It was about the last of

October. The climate was supposed to be unhealthy. We had fairly entered a dismal swamp, thirty-two miles wide, and, in consequence of heavy rains, unusually full of water. Instead of traveling four miles an hour, as we had expected, our horses were unable to make three. The beaten track was the least dangerous, as it always is over quicksand; but for miles together it was wholly under water, varying in depth from six inches to three feet, and the bottom little more than a continuous quagmire, as deep as the horses could struggle through. While daylight lasted, we could follow the trace by the old blazes on the sides of the trees; but night closed in upon us long before we reached the main point of difficulty, and the rain still increasing. We lost the track, our feet dragged through brushwood, and the morass shook beneath us; but giving the affrighted horses loose rein, they returned to it. Again we took the wrong direction, and went plunging through water and alder-bushes, in danger, every moment, of being ingulfed in quicksand, but, after some time, found our road once more. A conference was then called, to discuss the question, "Shall we give it up, or try to proceed?" It was a solemn conference; and though darkness and storm prevailed without, order and peace were maintained within. The sum of our conversation was briefly this: to stay here all night, wet, cold, and hungry, without shelter, without fire, or a foot of dry ground on which to stand, is perilous: to proceed was only perilous; and the conclusion was, to try it again. After losing and regaining the beaten way a third time, at last coming to a bank of sand, and then a rapid descent of some feet to a sheet of deep water, we inferred that we were at the margin of the much-dreaded Bayou de View. The bill of direction was, to enter near a large tree, bear up to the point of an island, then, forming an angle downward, steer for a projecting log on the opposite shore.

But, alas! under the lofty trees and lowering clouds, the darkness was such that we could not see the animals on which we rode. What was to be done? To encounter the turbid stream at random, was bordering on presumption; to wait for daylight, when the stream was rising, was discouraging, and might defeat our whole enterprise. As it was a case in which life might be involved, a regular vote was taken, by calling the roll, and it was unanimous in favor of going ahead. It was also agreed that I should be commander. The line was promptly formed, as follows: brother Randle, having a steady horse, and being a light rider, was to lead off; brother Simmons, second; the writer third; and brother Duncan was to bring up the rear. It was further ordered, to keep two rods apart, so that if we struck a swim, every man might have sea-room, and a chance for life. "All ready?" "Yes." "Proceed. Cry soundings." "Knee-deep; up to the girth; mid-sides; steady: over the withers, but still feel bottom; more shallow now. Here is the point of the island." "Very well. Now form an angle to the left; down stream is easy." The latter channel was no deeper than the former, and all made safe landing. Thanks to kind Providence!

Our next direction was, to leave the old trace here, turn down the bayou some distance without any road, so as to intersect a new way, which had been recently cut out, starting from a point lower down. Between the ford and the new way we tore through brushwood, leaped over logs, and plunged into sloughs, at the risk of our limbs, but finally reached the road, when our horses gladly resumed the proper course. It was, to our great mortification, soon ascertained that the new way was more miry than the old. As we could see nothing, our quadrupeds had all the credit for keeping the road. Presently brother Randle's horse was heard plunging, at a fearful rate, for some time, when he announced a very dangerous place; "water up to midsides, and the bottom very boggy." Brother Simmons next put in, and was glad when he got out. He advised me to veer to the left; it might be better, and, he thought, could be no worse. It proved to be unfortunate advice, as it threw me on to a heap of logs, that had been rolled in to fill up a deep and dangerous bog, but which were then all afloat. Nick had a terrible scuffle over them. Once his foot hung fast; twice the water rolled over him, and the rider was well-nigh unhorsed; but, finally, he righted, and brought me out unhurt. Taking a position, as nearly as I could guess, opposite to where the others crossed, I called to brother Duncan to steer by my voice, and put in. He came near sticking fast, but received no damage. At a late period of the night, while groping amid darkness that could be felt, mingled with incessant showers, we were suddenly aroused by the joyful note, "A light! a light!" Approaching as near as some unseen obstruction allowed, we hailed. An old lady came to the door and demanded,

"Who is there?"

"Travelers."

"Ah! I thought my sons had got back from bear-hunting."

"No, madam, we are strangers; have been belated in the swamp, and wish to know if you will shelter us the balance of the night."

"Why, la, me! I wouldn't turn off a dog such a night as this."

Securing the horses to the trees, we joyfully entered the cabin of poles, about sixteen feet long, and fourteen wide. The chimney was unfinished. There was a place for a hearth, but it was not filled up, and the fire was down in a hole, some eighteen inches below the puncheons. Four of us, with our wet baggage, added to the family, and two other strangers that were there before us, scarcely left us room to turn round. At midnight we made a comfortable dinner on pork and corn-dodger; and having dried off a little, we held our evening prayers at two o'clock in the morning, and quietly laid us down to sleep, grateful for our kind reception. About daylight we asked the old lady for our bill, which was two dollars. When we inquired if she meant two dollars each, she said,

"La, me! I should be rich if I had that much. I mean two dollars for all four."

Having completed our preparation, we resumed the swamp; but the limbs of our animals were so lacerated by maple-roots and cypress-knees, that they took it very reluctantly. We reached the Cash river tavern, with hard toiling, in an hour and a half, the distance being three miles, where the landlady, in the absence of her husband, first served us with breakfast, and then ferried us over the river. When the boat had crossed the rapid channel, she grounded on the bank, which was entirely inundated; so that we had no alternative but to mount in the boat, and leap over the bow into the water. Eight miles more of wading and plunging, which consumed just four hours, brought us out of the Black River Swamp at Litchfield, thankful that we were alive.

After reaching solid ground, and obtaining lodgings, our first concern was to unpack our clothes, books, and papers, and dry them. This done, we preached, exhorted, and held prayer meeting in the village of Litchfield, where the inhabitants received us kindly, and requested regular preaching, which was of course provided for them. Our little party felt toward each other like a band of patriot soldiers, who had endured a hard and hazardous campaign together, and we distributed among ourselves small presents, as mementos of our mutual regard and providential deliverance. The last I knew of my companions in travel, they were all zealous and successful ministers of Christ. May they severally receive the crown of life!

In this narrative there is not a particle of fiction, nothing thrown in to fill up a chasm, but much omitted to shorten the article. Every man who adventured himself into that swamp in the condition it was then in, did it at his peril. Had I been offered one thousand dollars to retrace my steps, it would have been no temptation. Only for reliance on the providence of God, I should have despaired of getting safely out. In all the course of my life I have seldom, if ever, felt such a spirit of prayer and enjoyed such a power of faith in God as I did during the perils of that, to me, memorable night. How we were to be delivered I did not know, nor feel concerned to know, but felt the most unshaken confidence that God, in his own way, would bring us safely through. And after obtaining that confidence, I felt more of the spirit of rejoicing than is usual for me, even under more favorable circumstances. Such was the beginning of my first regular tour on what is sometimes called "the big circuit;" but I am happy to add, it was not a fair specimen of my journeyings, even in that new country.

TRAVELING, 1841.

THE writer, a native of the United States, has never visited any foreign lands, and does not desire to do so, as he prefers "the land of the brave and the home of the free;" but he has some experience in traveling in our own beloved country. Of course he writes not for the entertainment of those who have feasted their eyes on the mountain scenery of Italy, surveyed the catacombs and pyramids of Egypt, braved the sirocco of Arabian deserts, or wandered amidst the sacred relics of the Holy Land; but with the hope of benefiting some who have not traveled at all. Americans are a migratory people; the facilities for traveling are increasing; distant points are apparently brought near together; much conversation on the part of those who have been abroad, renders them familiar to all, and a general spirit of passing to and fro is cultivated. Many who have never been distant from the place of their nativity, seem to think they lack but one thing to render them happy; that is, to travel and see the world; and they long to be on the *go.* Some desire chiefly to behold the distant city with its domes and steeples; some to scale the lofty Alleghanies, those "majestic pyramids of nature;" while others are impatient to explore the new countries of the far-famed west, strangely supposing that the nearer they get toward where the sun goes down, the more paradisiacal will be their situation. Now, it is for the special benefit of those infected with this restless spirit of migration, that the author begs leave to submit a few thoughts.

That the American traveler enjoys some pleasures which he can not command at home, is readily admitted. In mid-winter it is decidedly grateful to the sense of feeling, to inhale the balmy zephyrs of the south, as they rustle through the boughs of the live oak and the broad, green leaves of the magnolia, wafting soft notes of melody from nature's musicians—the feathered tribes of every hue. It is no less delightful in summer to be fanned by the refreshing breezes of the Green Mountain or White Mountain of the north. Moreover, it satisfies one's curiosity to gaze on the extended prairie of the west; for, on entering it for the first time, the surprised traveler, like the inexperienced voyager, is ready to exclaim, "The sea, the sea, the open sea!" and when he reaches the middle of it, and passes some deep ravine, where the distant forest is concealed from view, he may carry out the figure by saying, "We are out of sight of land." It is equally pleasant to others to stand on the shores of our inland seas—the lakes—whitened with the sails of commerce and bordered with new and flourishing villages. To some it would appear at least novel, to be conveyed, perfectly at their ease, twenty miles an hour by a railroad locomotive; while others would regard it as quite desirable to traverse our eastern cities, thronged with moving multitudes of every nation—wander among the shipping of the crowded port, and see "old ocean heave." But all these objects soon lose their novelty, and with it much of their attractive charms, leaving the weary traveler possessed of few pleasures in comparison of his numerous discomforts.

Before commencing a long journey there are the expense, care, and toil of making preparation. Then comes the pain of parting with family and friends, it may be, to see them no more. Should the journey be prosperous and end in a safe return, still it will not be performed without corroding care and sleepless nights, on account of the home interest, especially if the absence be long, and the tourist unaccustomed to it. Females, particularly, are liable, under such circumstances, to become "home-sick;" and when this disease once gets firmly seated on the heart, it destroys all the pleasure of traveling, engrossing at once both thought and feeling.

The inconveniences and difficulties of extended journeys are not all imaginary. At one time the traveler is oppressed with heat, parched with feverish thirst, and nearly suffocated with clouds of dust; at another time he is stung with cold, impeded by ice, or in peril from the sweeping current of the swollen stream. Again: as soon as he leaves the M'Adamized road, he will find himself alternately contending with rocky hills and muddy vales, with a little sprinkling of Davy Crocket's railroad, made by laying poles crosswise in the track to prevent the carriage from being entirely swamped. It is said that riding on these causeways is good exercise for an invalid, especially one of congested liver, but it is certainly not a pleasant remedy. To these commonplace evils, which discount so largely from the pleasures of travel, must be added exposure to inclement weather. It is extremely unpleasant to grope all night in darkness, exposed to a chilly atmosphere, and the more so if pelted by a continuous storm of rain, sleet, or snow; for such wear and tear upon a passenger's constitution affects his spirit, and suggests thoughts of a severe illness, where he would be at the mercy of uninterested strangers. But suppose him to escape this, still he is subject to a score of nameless perplexities which must be borne, because they can not be avoided.

Among the trials of his patience are those which arise from delays and disappointed expectation of getting on his journey. A freshet may carry off the ferry or bridge, his only dependence for crossing some river, or he may be journeying where there is none to lose, and find himself at a dead halt till the flood subside. The coach may break down where it can not be repaired, or the boat may get aground or break a shaft, and leave him on a bleak sand-bar, or desolate shore, to shift for himself. What is still worse, deception will be palmed on him, by interested and unprincipled men. Systematic imposition on strangers, is a regular part of the trade of many individuals and companies, whose business is to convey passengers in steamboats and stages. The writer speaks here from woeful experience, and may be indulged in giving one or two examples, commencing with a trip on the Ohio river.

According to the printed bills, the boat will leave "this day at four o'clock," and, beside the bill, a positive verbal promise is given by the proper officer of punctuality. Deceived by fair speeches, smoking chimneys, and other appearances of preparation, you bring your baggage aboard, and, in conformity to the rules of the cabin, enter your name, with the full expectation of presently being under way. Toward dark they blow off steam and ring the bell, as if about to *clear;* but it proves to be only a maneuver to ascertain whether a sufficient number of passengers can be obtained to make a profitable trip. They fail to appear, the fire is lowered, and you are informed they can not get ready to leave till to-morrow morning; and if you really get off by to-morrow night, it will be well, unless they are forced out sooner by competition. Now, this, to one pressed for time to accomplish the object of his journey, or on his return trip, attracted by the consideration of

"Home, home, sweet, sweet home,"

is sufficient to put the virtue of patience to a severe test.

Again: on leaving this floating prison you hasten to the stage office, pay the fare, and are pleased to read on the bills, "Splendid Troy-built coaches, first-rate teams, steady drivers, good accommodation, and through in —— hours." Congratulating yourself on the happy change, you set off with fine spirit, in a fine new coach, drawn by elegant grays, and manned by a decent-looking coachman; but, alas! shortly after you are transferred to an old worn-out establishment, with ragged cushions, broken doors, polluted in appearance, drawn by old Ring-bone, Splint-leg, Club-foot, and Wheezer, which ought to have been discharged from the service years ago. The driver, degraded by dissipation and crime, is more to be pitied than his team. He stops at every tavern, except those which hang out the temperance sign; and when stimulated till he feels his own importance, but can no longer observe the difference between a level plain and a steep ascent, loses his temper, and curses and beats his jaded team for the mere love of the cruel sport.

Some relief is afforded the distressed passenger from his unpleasant situation for a few minutes, by arriving at the dinner stand, where he expects not only to be provided with a fresh team and sober driver, but also to be refreshed with some of the good accommodation referred to in the bill. However, the stage is behind the time, and what was lost on the last drive must be made up on the next; and before the hungry passenger gets fairly engaged at his dinner, the impatient driver blows his horn as the signal for starting; so that, in the end, the good accommodation turns out to be a very hasty meal, only half finished, on cold scraps and bread about half baked. They who keep stage passengers know that the customer is compelled to stop where the stage does, and to eat such as is set before him, or starve. Now, all this would be quite tolerable, if the expense was in keeping with the quality of the dinner and the time allowed for eating it—in a word, if the pay was in proportion to the accommodation, after the manner of a public house kept by an honest lady of whom I heard in the south-west, whose bill of fare and prices was in this laconic style: "Corn-bread and hominy doings, two bits; flour-bread and chicken doings, four bits." But not so, generally, at stage houses. Whatever the fare may be, the bill is always up to high-water mark. But let that pass—we are off again, and are making some headway.

After dinner is a dull hour of the day, especially to those who have lost rest and sleep, and the passengers are soon dozing; but their pleasure is very short-lived, for before they have half finished their nap they are roused by a modest request of the driver to get out and *foot it* up a long ascent, or over a layer of black loam too deep for the loaded stage to pass through, and rather soft for comfortable walking. It is not a little provoking, after paying for the privilege of riding, to be constantly afflicted with wet and muddy feet, by being obliged to walk over every difficult piece of road. Still it might be worse, far worse; for sometimes the stage gets wrong side up, and throws the passengers all in a heap; then all whose bones are not fractured, will be expected to take hold with the driver and assist in replacing it, which is not remarkably pleasant, to say the least, especially if the coach be very muddy. After all these difficulties you may get through, though long after the time appointed, and have at least this consolation left, you are still alive, which, under all the circumstances, is great cause of gratitude.

Exhausted with such scenes of toil, vexation, and exposure, the weary traveler longs for a change, such as will afford opportunity of rest and slumber. Well, here is the steam packet to convey him over the lake, or round the coast. This would be delightful, only for a few considerations, such as liability of being wrecked by storm, as in case of the HOME, or destruction by fire, of boat and life, as in case of the LEXINGTON, or by explosion, as in case of the MOSELLE. It is true, we may hope to escape such fearful calamities as these, when voyaging on the deep; but there is one scourge which seldom suffers any to pass unhurt; namely, the seasickness, the very thought of which is appalling for weeks after. It is the most deathly feeling which I ever experienced, and I can scarcely conceive how any one could live through it in crossing the main ocean.

Under the prostrating influence of this loathsome disorder, the voyager longs for the port of destination, that he may once more stand erect on solid ground, and feel composed. But when he arrives, trouble of another sort meets him; before he clears the deck, he is surrounded by a swarm of porters, ravenous as hungry wolves, clamoring and scrambling for his baggage, as if the life of each depended on obtaining a few cents for the service of carrying it to the hotel; and should it once get out of his sight for one minute, he might think himself fortunate if he ever saw or heard of it again.

Some of these difficulties, it is admitted, may be avoided by traveling in a private conveyance, as far as that mode is practicable, which, on some accounts, is much preferable; but it will require more sacrifice of time, impose on you much more care and fatigue upon the whole, and, taking the wear and tear of horses and carriage into the account, will not in any wise reduce the expense.

These are some of the ordinary discomforts of journeying. While suffering them you very soon get clear of hundreds of dollars, perhaps earned by the toil and care of years, and which might be laid out to much better advantage. The time is gone, the money is gone, your wardrobe is exhausted, your business neglected and deranged; and what is gained by this sacrifice? Why, a momentary gratification of curiosity, and the honor of saying you have been abroad, have traveled through more states than one, and have seen a few things which some of your neighbors have not seen. The pleasure of all this, if there be any left after deducting the discomfort, is too dearly bought. It costs more than it comes to.

To perform a journey when business, health, or duty requires it, is certainly well enough; but to me it is matter of wonder that any one should ever travel for pleasure, more especially any one who has any practical knowledge on the subject.

In reference to a Christian, the worst of the story remains to be told. Traveling is unfavorable to religious prosperity. It divides the attention and dissipates serious thought—breaks off the regular course of duty, depriving the Christian traveler of the means of grace and the society of his religious friends. Beside, it throws him into taverns, steamboats, and stages, crowded chiefly with the careless, fashionable, dissipated, and profane, with whom it is difficult to be associated in any way, except for the purpose of imparting religious instruction, without sustaining spiritual loss. On this subject I can speak, with the more confidence, a word of admonition to my Christian friends, having proved by experience the truth of what I say. There is nothing better for the Christian than to be generally at home, "Not slothful in business; fervent in spirit; serving the Lord." And now, if any of my readers, who are tired of home, and anxious to make an experiment of the blessedness of packing trunks and band-boxes over mountains, to visit places of fashionable resort, etc., can profit aught by these few hints from one who has journeyed much—not, indeed, for pleasure or profit, but on duty—they are heartily welcome, and the object of this article will be accomplished.

LAND TRIP FROM ST. LOUIS TO TEXAS.

LETTER I.

Brother Elliott,—Remembering your oft-repeated request to let you hear from me on this division of the work, I have at last concluded to write out briefly a few incidents of our land journey from St. Louis to Texas; but, from the circumstances in which I am placed, they must necessarily be few, short, and irregular as to the times of forwarding them. Writing these scraps may keep our brethren advised that the south-west corner of our Lord's vineyard is not only needy and worthy of more help, but also easy of access by all willing laborers, whether preachers or Sabbath school teachers, who may be influenced by considerations of usefulness. In the mean time, I may, perhaps, be indulged by yourself and others in a passing remark on any occurrence of interest which may fall under our observation, however small, for the history of human life is made up of little things.

Since I left home, on the 6th of last August, I have, by the Divine blessing, been enabled to meet my engagements at the Rock River, Illinois, and Missouri conferences. My route was through Indiana, Illinois, and partially through Wisconsin and Iowa territories and the north-east part of Missouri; but of that part of my tour I made no notes, and will, therefore, decline giving any particulars respecting it. When in Platteville, Wisconsin territory, last August, I entered into an agreement to meet certain brethren at St. Louis, after the session of the Missouri conference, to form a little party, and proceed on to Texas together, which plan we are now executing. Our company consists of Rev. John Clark, his wife, and little son, John Emory, about nine years old; Rev. Josiah W. Whipple, and myself. Brothers Clark and Whipple are regular itinerant Methodist preachers, noble spirits who volunteered to go as regular transfers from the Rock River to Texas conference, for the sole object of preaching the Gospel of the grace of God in that new and interesting republic. No other consideration, I am satisfied, could have induced them to tear away from their homes and country, amidst the tears and remonstrance of friends, numerous and strong, and encounter the toils and perils of a new and distant field of labor. We have one covered wagon, hung on elliptic springs, with baggage racks and all the necessary fixtures to render it a convenient and comfortable traveling wagon for a family, which is drawn by two substantial horses, and carries brother and sister Clark, and brother Whipple, and some five hundred pounds of baggage. Besides this we have a common-size buggy, drawn by one horse, which carries young Clark, myself and baggage, and some light articles for every-day use. Our buggy affords us a comfortable conveyance; and though without a cover, it is on that account the more safe and convenient in difficult road. Our outfit for this journey was partly arranged by brother Clark before he left his home at Mount Morris, Illinois; and completed when we met in St. Louis. It includes a markee, or linen tent, glass lamp, ax, hammer, tea-kettle, frying-pan, coffee-mill, patent coffee boiler, water bucket, provision basket, plates, knives and forks, spoons, etc. It is well for us that brother Clark labored some years as missionary among Indians at Green Bay, for no one but a practical missionary, accustomed to journey through desolate regions, could have thought of so many little notions adapted to our wants, and no one but the wife of a practical missionary could use them to such good purpose as does sister Clark. We laid in but a small store of provisions before we started, and for some time after scarce found use for that; being in a settled country and among hospitable people, we had no occasion to provide for ourselves, except the noon luncheon.

We left St. Louis, Tuesday, October 19th, passed the village of Carondelett, and some fifteen miles from the city crossed the Merrimack river on a beautiful gravel ford, where the stream was perhaps three feet deep and some eighty or one hundred yards wide. It was quite agreeable, after traveling over a muddy road, occasioned by rain the previous day and night, to have our wheels and horses thoroughly washed with so little trouble. We were kindly entertained that night ten miles from the river by brother Hunt and family, who resided in Marietta circuit, Ohio conference, when I labored there in 1817. Only one inconvenience was experienced here. Sister Clark, by sleeping in an open, unfinished room, took cold, and suffered some in consequence of it. The next morning, five miles onward, we descended a large hill and came down into Herculaneum, a village on the west bank of the Mississippi, above the mouth of a creek, and so surrounded by water and hills as to remind us of the prophetic description, "The city shall be low in a low place." Crossing the creek on an old ferry-boat, which reached from shore to shore, and served as a substitute for a bridge, we turned up the creek under a bold cliff covering our left, on the top of which was an old shot-house and furnace, so situated on the point of a projecting rock that shot might fall some one hundred feet, more or less, into a reservoir at the base. But the furnace was cold, the house inclined to one side and in a dilapidated condition. The appearance of this place and Carondelett above, afforded evidence of the truth of what we heard remarked by some citizens of the country, that the villages in south Missouri, which were settled chiefly by French Catholics, were in a declining state. St. Genevieve, for example, is said to be of less importance now than it was twenty years ago, notwithstanding the advantage of steamboat navigation. Leaving this creek, we ascended a very difficult hill where the road was steep, sideling, and badly washed, and still neglected; and nine miles from Herculaneum dined at Dr. Steel's, spent a pleasant hour, had prayers with the family, and baptized a child of German parents at their special request. In the evening we passed Valley's Mines, eleven miles from the Doctor's; and six miles beyond we reached Mrs. Poston's after dark, where we met with a kind reception and excellent accommodation. This lady, her daughter, and son, are members of our Church. The main difficulty of traveling in this part of Missouri is to find out your proper road, for at the numerous forks there is seldom any direction to guide the stranger on his way. When we inquired for the reason of this, the answer was, "We often put up finger-boards, but ill-disposed persons stone them down." Next morning we hastened to Farmington, thirteen miles, expecting to meet a congregation, and called on old brother David Murphey, who has resided on his farm adjoining town about thirty years, if I remember right; and he informed us that the meeting was postponed till night, with a view to obtain a larger congregation. In the afternoon he entertained us with many interesting anecdotes of Bishop M'Kendree and Jesse Walker, who used to make his house a resting-place after their excessive toils in that new country. His narratives of early Methodism were truly interesting. In brother Murphey's house, while waiting for the hour of public service, we met with brother Job Lawrence, deacon elect, and consecrated him to that office in due form. The evening proved stormy, and I preached a short sermon to a very small congregation in the Presbyterian church, with scarce light enough to discover whether our hearers were white or black; and brother Clark followed with exhortation and prayer. Farmington is a small village, and the county seat of St. Francois, situated in the best neighborhood of land we have seen south of Merrimack river; but our society, enfeebled by emigration, have no chapel here of their own. This sheet is well-nigh full, and lest I weary you and our readers, will desist for the present.

Yours, truly, T. A. Morris.

Missouri, October 22, 1841.

LETTER II.

Brother Elliott,—It will be recollected that in my first communication the narrative of our journey was broken off at Farmington. From thence we proceeded, on Friday, 22d of October, to Fredericktown, Madison county, distant eighteen miles, where a two-days' meeting had been appointed in view of our visit. On Saturday morning and night the congregations were quite small, owing, it was said, to the circuit court then in session, which did not adjourn till late that evening; but on Sabbath day our little chapel was well filled with attentive hearers, yet nothing of special interest occurred. During the meeting, we were comfortably provided for among our Christian friends. My lodging was at brother Tongue's, a short distance out of town. Among the new acquaintances we made there, were the Hon. Judge Cook, presiding judge of the district, and Mr. Davis, a respectable member of the bar, both citizens of Cape Girardeau county, and members of our Church, whose character and example, as we were informed by others, exert a beautiful moral and religious influence in the country, and afford additional evidence that gentlemen of the green-bag profession may be experimental and practical Christians. While other persons, who attended court, left on Sabbath morning, these two brethren remained and worshiped with us all day like Christians who know their duty and appreciate their privileges. Fredericktown is a clever inland village, surrounded by the second body of good land we have seen in south Missouri, and is only a few miles from the smelting furnaces of the lead and copper mines, which we passed on our way thither. From this place to St. Louis is about ninety miles.

Monday, 25th, we lunched at Twelve Mile creek, and lodged with Mr. Short, a clever Baptist, on reasonable terms, having traveled twenty miles. Here we got summer grapes of a good quality, which grow abundantly in the woods around the farm and along the creek. Excellent springs of water appear in this neighborhood; the land is of medium quality, and mostly vacant, only a few quarter sections being entered and settled; and deer and small game are plenty. Still they have a school in operation on the road-side, near Mr. Short's, and Baptist preaching in his house once a month.

Tuesday, 26th, we reached Greenville, the county seat of Wayne, a small village on St. Francis river, having traveled about twenty miles, and called on Mr. Smith, a native of New York, I believe, who received us with every expression of welcome, and entertained us in the best style gratuitously, recruited our little store of provision, and let us depart in peace next morning. Mr. Smith owns a large tract of river land well improved; and though not a professor of religion, has one of the best regulated and most interesting families we have met with in all our travels, evincing that true politeness and sterling moral worth may be cultivated in new as well as old countries. His house is one of the traveling preachers' best homes in this country.

Wednesday, 27th, we took our dinner on the south bank of Black river, perhaps fourteen miles from Greenville, out of our own provision basket—rested under the trees, and drank from the pure stream gliding down the vale between the hills, and had some conversation with a plain-looking man, who said he was one of a large company preparing to remove from the south-east part of Missouri to the north-east part of Texas. He was not a professor of religion, but said several of the company were Methodists, and brother Clark sent word to them, by him, to be sure to take certificates of their membership, and not to backslide on the way, but join the Church immediately on their arrival in the republic. Eight miles more brought us to sister Scott's, a widow lady, who was from home, but her sons and daughters received us very kindly. They had retreated from their first location on a creek to the high ground, to escape the ague, and lived in an unfinished house, but made us as comfortable as was in their power, and we felt satisfied and grateful.

No opportunity offered to try how well we could entertain ourselves all night till Thursday, 28th, when, foreseeing we should reach no suitable house of entertainment, in the evening we bought corn and fodder, and pushed on in search of water. About dark we reached a beautiful tributary stream of Black river, the name of which we did not know, and pitched our tent under a large cypress-tree growing immediately on its bank, the spreading boughs whereof afforded us a partial shelter from light showers of rain that fell while we were making preparation for the night. After taking off the horses and securing them with halters fastened to the trees, brother Clark plied his steel, flint, and spunk, in raising a fire, while brother Whipple cut tent-poles, and I gathered brush and drift-wood for kindling. This done, we hung on the tea-kettle; and while the others adjusted the tent, etc., sister Clark prepared for us a good supper, served up in real camp style, which we all enjoyed with more than common pleasure. Several companies of travelers passed our camp after dark, seeking their night's lodging. One of them was quite a procession of pack-horse movers, bound for south Arkansas, if they liked when they saw it; otherwise for Texas. There were several servants among them, and some appearance of style, from which we judged they were only the advance guard going on to make preparation to receive the wagons and families behind. We find the spirit of emigration to Texas prevails in the south-west to a considerable extent. Even in south Missouri, some of the people speak of being crowded, and think of moving to where they can have outlet. The ground was full damp for comfortable lodging, in consequence of rain that day; but we spread down first some oil-cloths or pieces of painted canvas, then our buffalo-skins and blankets, using our carriage-cushions for pillows, and we slept in peace and safety. Our tent is partitioned off into two apartments, one of which affords ample room for brother Clark's family, and the other for brother Whipple and myself. It was here I began to realize that my buffalo robe and Mackinaw blanket were among my best friends on this journey. Before we left, curiosity led us to run a line round the trunk of the stately tree under whose branches we rested, and found its circumference to be twenty-four feet, as accurately as we could measure without an exact rule. This place we called Camp Cypress. At the hour of offering up the evening and morning sacrifice, we had family worship, and like Jacob, when he had a stone for his pillow in the wilderness, felt that the Lord was in that place.

While here we saw, for the first time on this journey, large flocks of paroquets passing over and occasionally lighting on the trees around us. They are a small species of parrot, something less than pigeons, with plumage mostly green, but exhibiting all the colors of the rainbow; their greatest strength is in their yellow, hooked beak, with which they can sever small branches of fruit trees; they live chiefly on small grain and burs, and sleep in hollow trees, hanging by the point of the bill. Paroquets are noisy birds, but their notes are not melodious; yet, on account of their superior beauty, they are often domesticated, which is very easily done. Two of these birds were pets in my father's family on Kanawha river, nearly forty years ago, and were useful in destroying the burs. After ranging the fields and forest all day, they regularly returned to their resting-place in the evening, which was the side of a tall, cotton basket, where they slept, hanging by the beak to one of the splits. You shall hear again from

Yours, respectfully, T. A. MORRIS.

WAYNE COUNTY, MISSOURI, OCTOBER 28, 1841.

LETTER III.

Brother Elliott,—As we are not land-jobbers, nor going on a tour of observation, it will not be expected of me to say much of the country; yet I would like to afford some information for the benefit of our missionaries who may hereafter remove to Arkansas, or Texas, by this route. And before I take leave of Missouri, I would just say, our road from St. Louis to the southern boundary of the state passes chiefly over sterile hills, some of which are quite rocky, and the good land lies mostly on the creeks and small rivers; and on our route it is all a timbered country. What I saw, in 1839, of the land north of Missouri river, is generally preferable to what we have seen south of it. The road is often narrow, sideling, rocky, stumpy, and hilly, but free from swamp, and therefore passable. On the morning of Friday, 29th, about fifty miles from Greenville, we crossed the Missouri line, entered the state of Arkansas, and immediately after took the ferry-boat over Current river, at Dr. Pitman's, the place formerly known by the name of Hix's ferry; and in the evening camped some thirteen miles beyond the river, a short distance from the road, back of a field, on the bank of a large creek called Fourche de Mass—pronounced Foosh de Maugh. Mr. Johnson, who occupied the premises, not only gave us leave to camp and gather sticks for our fire, but kindly went and aided us in selecting a pleasant place on which to pitch our tent. We chose rather a romantic site on the point of a sloping ridge, just in the rear of projecting rocks, the strata of which so receded one over another as to afford natural steps to and from the water's edge. The evening was mild and calm; the full moon shone brightly, our log fire looked cheerful, and all the company were in fine glee, except brother Whipple, who was suffering under a severe attack of sick headache, of which, however, he was relieved by a comfortable night's sleep. It is true, our wheat loaf was exhausted, and all efforts to obtain flour had failed, but we had warm corn hoe-cake, fried ham, butter, eggs, sweet potatos, coffee, and Boston crackers; and considered ourselves among the best livers in the country. We did not, however, pretend to keep fashionable hours, and as soon as we could say prayers and make ready, laid us down and rested to purpose.

Our design was to reach Jackson the next day, and preach there on Sabbath; but a wise Providence ordered otherwise. About midnight the weather changed; a gale sprang up and brought clouds and rain, which pelted our thin habitation the balance of the night, and nearly all next day, so that we could scarcely leave our tent at all without getting wet. Much relief was experienced by putting up a Russia duck awning between the tent and fire, that afforded a shelter under which to sit and eat. Our chief difficulty was from smoke, which occasionally drove in with such violence as to affect our eyes severely, and sometimes force us out into the rain to get a good breath. Here, and in this condition, we expected to remain till Monday; and in view of that conclusion brother Whipple rode some miles in the afternoon, without a saddle, to ascertain whether we could obtain a congregation any where in that region to hear us preach on Sabbath. While he was gone, brother Clark chopped wood to avoid the sin of gathering sticks on the Lord's day. About this time, our camp was visited by a youth, nearly a man in years and size, on the singular errand, as he said, of buying sugar. We did not keep the article on sale, and could not accommodate him; but soon found him better employment. Some of the logs chopped off were very heavy: brother Clark placed a lever under the forepart, put the sturdy youth at one end of the lever, and myself at the other, and taking the tail-end of the log himself, we put forth our strength, straightened, and marched into camp. This operation was repeated till we had collected an ample store of fuel for the Sabbath. This done, we commenced shaving and other preparations for the day of rest, when all our plans were suddenly thrown into confusion. Brother Whipple returned, and brought with him old brother Spikes, a native of North Carolina, and for some ten years past a citizen of Arkansas, who insisted on our decamping and going home with him so kindly and earnestly, we had to yield to his entreaty. It was after four o'clock, P. M., when we changed our plan for the night: all possible haste was made in packing up and striking tent; the rain still coming down upon us with increased force. About a quarter past five, we bowed out from Camp Fourche de Mass, and reached our new quarters, three miles off, with some difficulty, after dark. The incessant showers of rain on the Sabbath rendered it impracticable to collect any congregation. We sang and prayed at the interment of a neighbor's child on brother Spikes's premises, but had no preaching. Monday we judged it prudent to lay by, in order to dry our tent, and replenish our store of provisions. Brother Whipple went to mill and bought flour, and while sister Clark kneaded and baked, brother Clark made us a portable table out of four new clapboards, shaved and jointed, which we carry on the baggage-rack without any trouble; the legs and frame, consisting of four small forks and two poles laid across, we can procure at any camping-place in five minutes, and the table is complete. As to the cloth, we need none; when the boards become greasy they are easily washed. Brother Whipple's friends, before he left home, presented him with a rifle and shot-gun, which he accepted for the sake of the small game in this new country. He is what the hunters call "a sure shot" with the rifle, and among hands a fine lot of squirrels and a fat rabbit were here added to our supplies. These, parboiled for the convenience of carrying, made us fine camp provisions.

Tuesday, November 2d, we crossed a small, rapid river, called Eleven Pines, because that number of pine-trees grow around the head spring of it, as we were informed. In the afternoon, we passed through Jackson, a small town, and formerly the seat of justice for Lawrence county, and, a mile and a half beyond, camped on the north bank of Spring river. While brother Whipple went with the buggy across the river in search of horse provender, we raised a great brush-fire against the fallen trunk of a large sycamore, and when rearing our tent before it. the owner of the land, Mr. S——, rode by, called at the camp, and remarked we had a fine fire. We asked if he had any objection to its being on his land, or kindled with his wood? He replied, "Not any;" and he would be glad if all the timber on his bottom land was removed; as well he might, for it was heavy clearing. On learning that we were preachers going to Texas, he invited us to his house; but not feeling inclined to repack and turn back, we declined accepting the invitation. Here we found our small fry, and other fresh provisions, excellent fare, spent the night pleasantly, and called the place *Camp Sycamore.*

Wednesday, 3d, having lost some time in the morning, getting our horses shod, and some after we started, by losing the tea-kettle and having to send back for it, we only gained seventeen miles. In the afternoon we passed through Smithville, the new county seat of Lawrence, and in the evening camped on the south bank of Strawberry creek. Here we improved our lodging by filling the tent with dry leaves before we laid down our bedding. While at Camp Strawberry, we killed young squirrels, which, with some birds obtained on the way, made us an excellent pot-pie; none of your fashionable articles, Doctor, baked in plates, but a real family pot-pie, such as our mothers made in days of yore, and good enough for missionaries on their way to Texas.

Thursday, we agreed to take the upper, usually called the new road; drove on till one o'clock, and came to one of the transparent streams of water which abound in this country; and raising a fire, dined on a quail, a young squirrel roasted, and the balance of the pot-pie. While there, a boy came by who could not tell us what was the name of the stream, or whether it had any, and we agreed to call it *Lunch creek*. Soon after we left this place, we ascended a dry ridge, at the summit of which we came suddenly in view of one of the beauty spots of nature; an assemblage of sand-rocks, resembling in form a group of ancient pyramids: some of them were quite large. The surface, except where it was covered with moss, was exceeding white, and, shaded by a forest of thrifty oaks, presented a commanding appearance. Some of them, by the action of the rain, had natural steps, and, being broader at the base than the summit, were easily ascended. We stood on one of the largest, being, as we judged, some sixteen feet high, and observed an excavation on the top, which would probably contain a bushel of water: whether it was formed by the operation of nature, or the hand of savage man, could not be determined. From this position we counted twenty of these singular formations of the larger size, beside many smaller ones, in the space of about one acre of ground. The site affords a commanding view overlooking a farm on the north-west. There was not a cloud in the heavens, but a lively breeze, rustling through the leaves and gently moving the unbroken forest, added solemnity to the scene. It was enough to inspire a poet. Fancy was called into requisition, and we indulged in speculation on the suitableness of the site for a park, and the pleasure of sitting on one of these monuments to observe the movements and study the nature of the deer and other animals. We know no name for the place; but in view of those extraordinary monuments of nature, I shall take the liberty to call it *Monumental Hill.* For some distance onward, we saw scattering specimens of the same kind of formation. Our expectation was, to stay that night with a brother Adams on our road, whose house had been recommended to us as one of the best places in the country for entertainment; but when we arrived, his house was unroofed and his chamber without a floor, undergoing repairs; and of course he could not conveniently shelter us; but the disappointment was not a serious matter: he sold us corn, and fodder, and chickens, and gave us sweet potatos for supper and breakfast. We passed on a half of a mile to Cury's run, and entertained ourselves in good style, on a quarter section of Government land, and felt as independent as *squatters* with a preemption right and peaceable possession. Brother Adams came down to our camp next morning, and sold to brother Whipple a handsome young horse for a circuit-nag in Texas. The night we staid there was cold; ice was formed in our water-bucket within a few yards of the log fire. However, with about twenty bushels of dry leaves, our blankets, and great camp fire, we got through quite comfortably.

Friday, 5th, we reached Batesville, the seat of the Arkansas conference, where we met a welcome reception, and found excellent accommodation among our Christian friends. I am quartered at Colonel Pelham's, one of the oldest settlers of the place, Clerk of Independence county, and a member of our Church, and has a pious, pleasant family. Batesville is a considerable town for this new country, and has improved greatly since I was here in 1836. It is situated on the north side of White river, which is navigable for small steamboats a part of the year to this place.

What we have seen of north Arkansas, on this tour, is one of the best watered countries in the United States, and has every appearance of being generally healthy. The upland is mostly poor oak barrens, and the hills quite stony; but the creek and river lands are rich, and covered with lofty forest trees. The climate is mild, and very pleasant. Batesville is situated between thirty-five and thirty-six degrees of north latitude. As to the people, they are quite as intelligent in Arkansas as in other new countries, and generally as well disposed. That there are some desperadoes in Arkansas, as there are in all the states, whose fame has gone abroad, must be admitted; but they are not true specimens of the general state of society. Wherever I have been in this state—and I have traveled through it considerably—the inhabitants have uniformly treated me not only civilly, but kindly, and in character as a Christian minister. And though a large proportion of them are not professedly religious, many are so professedly and in fact; and the others are generally willing to hear the Gospel preached. Methodism is evidently making some progress among them. Our society have erected quite a handsome brick chapel in this place. But of the general state of the work I may be able to speak more definitely after I shall have heard, in conference, the reports from every part. So far we have had much cause of gratitude on this journey. Providence has favored us in reference to good weather generally. No calamity has befallen us. The Lord has given us some favor in the eyes of the people, and our health has been wonderfully preserved. Sister Clark has been for many years in delicate health; but, by riding moderately each day in the carriage, and the morning and evening exercise of tent-keeping, she is evidently gaining health and strength. Brother Whipple, whose health was very poor before he started, is mending rapidly. Little John, who had long been subject to chills, is becoming strong and hearty. Brother Clark is growing fleshy; and as for myself, though I have no occasion to be any fatter, am nevertheless gaining.

This letter is already too long, yet I beg indulgence till I make one small addition. In most of our older conferences we have some good brethren in delicate health, who seem to think themselves unable to endure the toils and exposures of an itinerant life, and under the influence of mistaken notions of self-preservation, incline to linger about those places where roast beef, plum-pudding, and preserves abound in the greatest luxuriance; so that it would not be marvelous if they were to decline under the wasting influence of dyspepsy, hypochondria, and nervous debility. Now, for the benefit of all such young preachers, though not a professor of the healing art, I venture to make this prescription: Let them form themselves into companies of two, three, or four, and volunteer for the work in Arkansas or Texas conference, not to float down the river pent in the cabin of a steamboat, but to travel in light wagons, such as will carry themselves, tents, and baggage: let them camp out; kill, roast, and eat wild meat; study their Bibles; pray; and sleep with their feet to the fire. A few blankets are easily carried; and as for feathers, every oak and elm produces abundance of such as would be most healthy for them, and which they can have for the trouble of gathering, One such campaign, with the blessing of Providence, would make them sound men, buoyant in spirit, and ready for a frontier circuit, or mission, where they might have the honor of preaching the Gospel to the poor, and of aiding a noble band of brethren in their efforts to save souls. Who will get ready and make the experiment next fall? Healthy brethren are not excluded from the privilege of coming.

Yours, sincerely, T. A. MORRIS.

BATESVILLE, ARKANSAS, NOV. 9, 1841.

LETTER IV.

BROTHER ELLIOTT,—The Arkansas conference commenced its sixth session at Batesville, November 10th, in the court-house, the same building in which it first organized, November, 1836. Very few of the original members remain. In the short space of five years most of them have disappeared from the list by deaths, locations, division of conference, etc.; but others have fallen into the breaking ranks, and the conference has nearly doubled its numbers, having now about forty-seven names on the entire list, some thirty of them members, and the balance probationers. Their geographical boundary is extensive, embracing the state of Arkansas, the Missouri territory south of the Cherokee line, and a fraction of the northeast corner of Texas. To cover this vast extent of surface with such a small force, we have necessarily to form our circuits something after the primitive model, very large, from two hundred to four hundred miles round, and leave most of them with only one preacher; consequently, in many instances, the people have preaching only once in four weeks, in some circuits once in six weeks, and in others once in two or three weeks. This lack of service is supplied, to a limited extent only, by local preachers. Still they are a choice band of brethren, and are accomplishing a good and glorious work, both in the state and in the Indian country, especially among the Choctaws and Cherokees. For particulars on this point, I refer any who may feel interested to the printed Minutes. The Arkansas band of itinerants appear to be firmly united in their purpose of accomplishing the grand object of the Christian ministry, "to spread Scripture holiness over these lands," and they evidently gathered fresh vigor in the work while met in conference to report the result of the last year's labor. On Sabbath, being the only time I had opportunity to attend preaching, the services of the sanctuary were refreshing to many. The spacious chapel in Batesville on that day was crowded with people, who appeared to be intelligent, and deeply interested. That the word preached took effect, was abundantly testified, by fixed attention, general solemnity, showers of tears, and numerous responses breaking from the deepest recesses of the heart. The colored people were preached to in the court-house at the same hours, who seemed to enjoy themselves to the life.

Monday afternoon some of the brethren went out to hold a temperance meeting; and, it is said, about seventy persons signed the temperance pledge, in addition to about eighty that had signed it previously. I am told there is but one liquor establishment left in Batesville, and it is doubtful whether that will be sustained much longer. After the conference finally adjourned on Monday evening, the missionary anniversary was celebrated in the chapel. I regretted the necessity of being absent, but was happy to learn they had a meeting of much interest, which resulted in raising over $400, which was certainly very liberal for a village of some seven hundred inhabitants, these hard times.

Now, what we chiefly need in this country is a strong reinforcement of efficient traveling preachers, self-sacrificing men, whose sole object is to be useful, and who, in order to do this, are willing to give up country, home, and friends, travel difficult circuits, labor hard, peril their health, and receive only a moderate support: in a word, men who count not their lives dear to themselves, so they may finish their course with joy, and the ministry which they have received of the Lord Jesus, to testify the Gospel of the grace of God. We would not deceive any brother. They who come to labor as itinerants in Arkansas should know that the country is yet comparatively new, and, consequently, that chapels are scarce, and parsonages are scarcer; that the currency is depreciated, which renders it difficult to support the preachers and go on to erect the necessary buildings; and that some of the circuits are situated in a latitude low and sickly, though none of the preachers of the conference have died the past year. Still, to such as are willing to encounter these difficulties, there is not a more ample or promising field of usefulness in our extended connection, than in this region of country. And why should the minister of Christ feel afraid to serve on any part of the globe where duty calls him, or to remain till his work is done? Paul was willing not only to suffer at Jerusalem, but, if needful, to die there for the sake of the Lord Jesus.

There is one thing, Doctor, which I do not understand; perhaps you can explain it. Methodist preachers profess to be commissioned to go into all the world and preach the Gospel to every creature; and yet in some favorite sections of country, they throng together in such multitudes as to stand in each other's way, and crowd some out of the work, and leave other sections of the Lord's vineyard in a state of destitution. We have preachers enough to supply our entire home work, east, west, north, and south, if properly distributed; but some are not willing to go where they are most needed. Can this be fairly reconciled to a professed call to the work of the itinerant ministry? I allow there may be a palliation of such inconsistency in some cases, arising from the opposition of friends. Young preachers are generally disposed to do right in the matter; but older brethren, who should be the first to encourage them, get around and dissuade them from it, especially popular young men; and in this way we are often defeated in obtaining such transfers as we need from the older to the new conferences. This sort of opposition to the work is not founded in a deliberate intention on the part of senior brethren to do wrong, but in an unwillingness to part with their sons in the Gospel. Still it is mischievous in its tendency. Let them, whom it may concern, see to it, lest they hinder the work of the Lord.

We are about to resume our journey, and time fails to add more at present; but you may hear again, at some convenient time, from

Yours, sincerely, T. A. MORRIS.

BATESVILLE, ARKANSAS, NOVEMBER 16, 1841.

LETTER V.

BROTHER ELLIOTT,—When taking leave of Batesville in my last, I should have remembered the Male and Female Academy of that place, under the superintendence of Rev. Henry Hunt and his lady. Brother Hunt was formerly a member of the Kentucky conference, but is now in a local relation. His school is situated at the north end of town, in a high and healthy position; the rear ground extends into the edge of a very handsome grove of young cedars, which throws around the place an air of beauty and cheerfulness; the buildings are of respectable appearance, and the institution is favorably spoken of, and pretty well sustained. A committee was appointed by the conference to attend the examination.

On Tuesday, 16th, at a late hour in the morning, we left Batesville in a cold rain, not because we loved it, but for the reason that our engagements ahead required us to be diligent. When we arrived at the ferry, it was difficult crossing, on account of the freshet in White river: however, after being detained two hours, we were safely landed on the opposite side. Usually the water of White river is of the most transparent sort, but then it was turbid and rapid. Before we got aboard, the company accumulated till there were three full boat-loads of Methodist preachers and their horses, including our own. After we resumed the road, the brethren on horseback passed us, and we were left with our usual company. The afternoon was pleasant; and in the evening we sought and found a retired spot off the road for our camp, with a view to dodge the pigs, as they had been very troublesome on previous occasions; and the experiment was successful—they did not find us till next morning. Our camp was on the north bank of Sally Doe, a name suggested by a singular occurrence. Among the pioneers of the country was a heroine named Sally, who, observing a female deer in the water, stood on the bank, and with a gun killed it, from which achievement the settlers agreed to name the creek Sally Doe. It is about three rods wide, the water clear and pleasant, and, near our camp, passes over a ledge of rocks, producing a monotonous roar favorable to refreshing sleep on a calm night.

Wednesday afternoon we crossed Little Red river at Crolman's ferry, thirty-two miles from Batesville. It is a deep, rapid stream, about ten or twelve rods over: the boat is worked across by a hand rope, extending from shore to shore, in a very short time; and appears to be profitable to the owner, as I paid for one horse and buggy sixty-two and a half cents in silver; a circumstance not worth naming, only as a specimen of ferriage-rates in this country. After we left the river, we inquired at each house we passed that evening for corn, but they had none for sale; nor did we blame them, for they appeared to have very little for themselves; till we reached Indian creek, about dark, where Mr. Magness, one of the first settlers, accommodated us with three half-bushels of ears, or about three pecks of corn, for a dollar, which we find to be the usual price of late. This, however, is more than the ordinary price of the country, and is occasioned by the summer drought this year. When the next band of Texas missionaries come this way and cross Indian creek, if they will form an angle to the right, and pass along the south bank about one hundred and twenty yards, they will see the remains of our camp-fire, where we spent a very pleasant night, and they shall be welcome to our chumps to kindle their fire. Perhaps we should have stopped on the north side, but it was preoccupied by a company of movers from the state of Mississippi to White river. Their fire made some show as we passed them; but we soon raised an opposition line, which rather threw them into the shade.

Thursday we lunched at Bayou Dezark, and camped in the evening near Mr. Walker's, where we had nothing to annoy us whatever, except our swine visitors. These ravenous animals appear to be well versed in the art of filching from movers' camps, and have no doubt been practicing their feats of roguery from the time they were weaned. One of the ringleaders of the gang came that night while we were asleep, and dragged our bag of corn from the mouth of our tent, and getting a little the start of us before we awoke, gave us quite a chase to recover it. Friday evening we were kindly received and well treated at Mr. Covvey's. Saturday we crossed Arkansas river in a steam ferry-boat, and arrived at the capital of the state, where the brethren received us with true Christian courtesy. The river here is some six hundred yards wide, and is at present in fine condition for navigation by steamboats. The distance from Batesville to Little Rock by the old military road which we came, is one hundred miles. The country between, except the creek lands, is very poor in general, consisting of oak barrens, oak ridges, and pine hills alternately. Many of the hills are long, steep, and difficult to ascend and descend, on account of the masses of broken free-stone, which cover the surface. The inhabitants are few and far between, which, together with the want of time, may account for our having no appointments on the way for preaching. We are here in the midst of Indian summer. The weather last week was frequently too warm to be comfortable. On Friday the temperature was nearly up to summer heat. We had occasionally to shed our coats, and even then, leading our horses up the rocky ascents produced perspiration equal to "Dr. Thompson's Cayenne" and "No. 6." The small flies worried our horses as if it had been August; and on Saturday and Sunday night in the city, the musketoes played a merry tune around our heads. Such a state of weather the latter part of November is rather remarkable even in Arkansas. Still I have no doubt but this is one of the finest climates in the United States, forming a medium between the extremes north and south, so as to secure its inhabitants generally against the winter fever of the former, and the yellow fever of the latter. If climate only were to be considered in selecting a permanent residence, it should be located between thirty-four and thirty-five degrees of north latitude, a range which includes Little Rock, and stretches across the Chickasaw purchase in the state of Mississippi, north Alabama, the up country of Georgia and South Carolina, and the south-east corner of North Carolina. But why should people be so difficult to suit in countries? When in the north I am delighted; when in the south, if I had my family with me, I should almost be willing to remain; and when I return to my native west, it still appears to be the best of all. As traveling preachers, the world is our parish, and wherever duty calls, we should be willing to go. On the Sabbath, according to previous appointment, we met the congregation in this city. The morning was stormy. Thunder-showers were passing over and around us, such as you have in Ohio at midsummer; but as it was not raining at eleven o'clock our little chapel was well filled. After sermon the sacrament was administered. All the brethren filled the table around the altar only twice. There was preaching again in the afternoon and evening. We also ordained brother Rezin Davis a deacon, in the house of brother S. Sanger, where I lodge. Little Rock has improved considerably, since I saw it five years ago, in appearance; but our society has not increased in proportion. Still they have peace among themselves, exhibit some fruits of true piety, and there is ground to hope thev may so increase in numbers and grace as to become a strong people. To-day we expect to resume our journey, having a series of appointments in advance. At some convenient time you may hear again from

Yours, respectfully, T. A. MORRIS.

LITTLE ROCK, ARKANSAS, Nov. 22, 1841.

LETTER VI.

BROTHER ELLIOTT,—We left Little Rock Monday, November 22d, and took the military road leading off in a south-west direction. Very soon we entered an extensive forest of pitch pine; the trees tall and straight, and many of them quite large; and from their contiguity to the city and to the Arkansas river, they must be valuable. This pinery extends south-east to Pine Bluff, and south-west, with some intermission, to the Red river. Six miles from the city we passed the cabin in which I slept in 1836, the night before I entered the forty mile wilderness on my way to Mississippi conference, which was then occupied by an excellent Methodist family, named Hoover; but on inquiry I learned that the master of the family was dead, and his widow and orphans had removed to a distant part of the country, and the place was in possession of strangers. In one corner of the little field adjoining the cabin, was a neat white paling, which inclosed the remains of brother Wells, who, some years since, came as an itinerant from Tennessee to labor in Arkansas, and died in the work. He was the same brother Wells whose name is identified with the history of the arrest of the missionaries in the Cherokee nation in 1831. While his fellow-laborer was driven on foot before the mounted guards, brother Wells followed on, leading his horse for him to ride back, in case he should be discharged on examination; and for this act of kindness to the prisoner, the heroic Colonel of the guards struck him over the head with a club. He is now where the wicked cease to trouble, where the weary are at rest. These brief but solemn items of the past, afforded for some time a profitable theme of meditation. We spent that evening pleasantly at the house of Mr. T. Rolands, who, some four years since, emigrated from Alabama. He and his family are members of our Church.

Next morning several of his family accompanied us to Benton, the seat of justice for Saline county, where we preached to a small congregation in the court-house. Benton is a small village, twenty-five miles from Little Rock. After dining with Mr. Hockersmith, we proceeded on to the house of brother H. Cornelius, formerly a member of Arkansas conference; but, from a sense of duty to a large and increasing family, located, and commenced farming and raising stock. On our way to his house, and near Benton, we forded a heavy stream of water, called Saline river.

Wednesday we ferried the Washitta river, where it is, perhaps, one hundred and fifty yards wide, but not navigable for steamboats, though an excellent river for steamers from Ecorefabre down, and ate our luncheon on the south bank. This ferry is twenty-one miles from Benton. In the afternoon we bought provender of Mr. Stubling, entered the Twelve Mile Stretch, so called, because for that distance the road passes over pine hills so poor that no one lives near it; and having penetrated the wilderness four or five miles, and found a running brook named Bayou de Sale, pitched our tent. About half-past eight o'clock a violent storm of wind and rain broke upon us, attended with sharp lightning and heavy thunder, so that for some time we were amidst all the terrific grandeur of a hurricane at night in an unbroken forest. For some time before it reached us we heard the havoc which it was making among the pines; but fortunately we occupied a favorable position for the occasion in relation to standing trees, there being no large ones between us and the creek facing the storm: when it struck, it smote the four corners of our house, the tent pins gave way, and the tent cloth twisted up into a whirling heap around us, and, doubtless, would have gone off, had we not secured the corners by throwing our whole weight upon them; and before we could replace the pins and bring the tent to its proper form, the rain dashed through and gave us a wetting. However, we got sufficiently dry before midnight to lay down and sleep comfortably. When we observed next day how the trees were thrown along and across our road, and saw the providence of God in our preservation, amidst crashing timber and warring elements, we felt our hearts swell with emotions of gratitude. At the south end of this stretch, we came down, on Thursday morning, to Bayou de Roche, which, as its name is intended to express, is remarkably stony in the channel and on either shore, and only a few miles further on, found it sufficiently deep fording a very rapid little river, called Fourche Caddo; and as it was turning cold, we raised a fire, by which to warm and eat, on the other side, in what had been a cane-brake, the remnant of which was fine grazing. In the evening we turned off the road to the right, about one hundred yards down a small brook, seeking a good place to camp, when our buggy, in which was the bag of corn, suddenly broke down; the fore axletree, both wood and iron, gave way at the king bolt, and let me down softly within one rod of where we judged best, upon thorough examination, to build our fire. Next day we lost from our journey getting the buggy repaired, and, consequently, we remained two cold nights at Camp Mishap. When not otherwise employed, we walked round the camp and shot birds for a pot-pie.

Saturday morning we resumed our journey, and soon found that all the mud and water which adhered to the wheels became congealed. It froze all day—was cloudy, windy, and unpleasant. In the evening we forded a large creek called Antoine, and soon after reached Wolf creek, where we had appointed to preach on the Sabbath. We called, as previously advised, on Colonel John Wilson, who keeps a public house, but had the kindness to entertain us gratuitously. His wife, children, and servants, are members of our Church. This was in the corner of Pike county. The Colonel has on his place two valuable springs, one chalybeate and the other weak sulphur, and pleasant to the taste.

On Sabbath, at eleven o'clock, we commenced public service in Wolf creek meeting-house with eighteen persons; others came during sermon, some after sermon, while brother Clark was exhorting; and after the congregation dispersed we met others going. This irregularity, as to the time of meeting, grew partly out of a misunderstanding as to the hour appointed for preaching. Moreover, it is a free house, where some appoint to commence at noon, and then delay as much longer as suits their convenience. As this is said to be the best chapel in the south part of the state, it may be of some interest to read a brief description of it. The walls are made of hewed logs, about twenty by twenty-four feet in extent, with a wooden chimney in one end, and a place cut out for a chimney at the other end, which is partly closed up with slabs. In the front is a large door, with a center post, and double shutters, on the principle of a barn door. Immediately opposite, on the other side, is a pulpit, which projects some six feet from the wall, the forepart of which is so high that when the preacher kneels to pray he is nearly concealed from the view of the people. Behind this pulpit is a window without glass, the shutter of which is neither long nor wide enough to close it, and, consequently, lets a double stream of air upon him. The roof is made of clapboards, between which and the floor there is no ceiling, though there are some naked poles laid across on the plates; and the cracks between the logs are neither chinked nor daubed; and though they were once partially closed by nailing on thin boards, these have been mostly torn off, to afford light and a free circulation of air. The day was cold, and the people appeared to suffer. In the evening we found a large fire kindled in the front yard near the door, to which the people could retreat when too cold to hear the preaching; when one class were warmed they would return into the house, and another cold set would give place to them. No blame was attached to them for this procedure; for, judging of the feelings of others by my own, it was an indispensable arrangement. We had truly a chilly time that day throughout, temporally and spiritually. Next morning we concluded to measure the temperature of the atmosphere, hung out the thermometer, and the mercury stood only eleven degrees above zero, which was certainly extraordinary weather for this country the last week in November.

Monday morning we crossed Little Missouri river, about five rods wide, for which we paid $2. The ferry-boat is keeled at the ends, and has nothing attached to conduct the wheels from the boat to the shore, so that where we led out, the carriages had to make a pitch of some fifteen inches; and the consequence was, the main bar of the hind spring of the buggy snapped in two; but we splintered and wrapped it with small cord, and in an hour resumed our journey. This was on the old road, which, for about two miles south of the river, is nearly impassable on account of mud, broken bridges, etc. That night we staid at Mr. Pates's, and the next morning came into Washington, Hempstead county, where our Christian friends received us cheerfully and treated us kindly. Washington is situated on a high sandy plain, which was, from appearance, originally a pine forest; the town is compact and of respectable appearance, and, except the capital, is one of the largest in the state. There is here a respectable male and female academy, under the superintendence, I learn, of the Rev. Mr. Hoge, of the Presbyterian Church, and a convenient, substantial court-house, in which we preached several times to a congregation respectable in size, appearance, and orderly attention. There is no chapel in the place, nor is there any regularly-organized Methodist society, though we have a few members in the town and its vicinity.

Wednesday evening brother Clark and I, accompanied by brother Gregory, presiding elder of this district, who met us at Wolf creek, and has attended us since, went to Columbus, eight or ten miles distant, and preached evening and morning to a small congregation. Columbus is a small village of some taste, and has a male and female academy, both white frames of neat appearance, under the tuition of Rev. Mr. Meloy and his lady, of the Cumberland Presbyterian Church. In this village there is no chapel; and though we have some Methodists there, they are not organized, and have no class meetings. This state of things is much to be regretted. Our brethren never did, and never will, prosper long in any place where class and prayer meetings are lightly esteemed or neglected. After sermon here, on Thursday, deacons' orders were conferred on three local preachers, and the case of one, namely, John Henry, was remarkable. He was converted under the ministry of the Rev. David Young, when he traveled the old Merrimack circuit, Missouri, in 1810; has been a faithful local preacher twenty-nine years, and presented a certificate of election to deacons' orders, signed "John Scripps, secretary of Missouri conference, September 16, 1819," which he had carried twenty-two years without an opportunity of presenting it; during which time his license was regularly renewed every year, and from the long good standing which he has maintained, is every-where in this country called Father Henry.

On our way to Columbus we passed the far-famed Mount Prairie, which gives name to this circuit. It is a small prairie, the only one we have seen this side of Illinois, is chiefly under cultivation, and has a notable mound, which is the building-site of the farm. The soil is black, rich, and lies on a bed of rotten limestone, and when wet will adhere to the wheels of a carriage like kneaded dough. The most remarkable circumstance about it is, the surface abounds with sea-shells—clams, oysters, etc.—so thick, we were told, in places, that a plow can scarcely be forced through. These shells, in many instances, are in a perfect state of preservation, while, in others, they are in a process of decomposition. How they came on a high, dry prairie, more than three hundred miles from the Gulf of Mexico, is a question which I leave for the learned to answer.*

* This is the best neighborhood of land we have seen in Arkansas.

Thursday evening we returned to Washington, where brother Clark preached again to an increased congregation, notwithstanding the evening was rainy.

Yours, truly, T. A. Morris.

Washington, Ark., Dec. 2, 1841.

LETTER VII.

Brother Elliott,—We left Washington Friday, December 3d, and came to Spring Hill, a village on an elevation among the pines in Hempstead county, so called from the fact that numerous springs of excellent water break out of the hill, in various directions, around the village. Many of the citizens of this place are planters, whose cotton farms are on the low lands of Red river, a few miles distant, and afford excellent society for each other. The site, being high and well watered, is healthy and pleasant for family residences; and their children have the benefits of male and female academies, under the superintendence of Rev. Mr. Banks and lady, of the Presbyterian Church. While in Spring Hill we enjoyed a fair specimen of old Virginia hospitality, which of course was very grateful to us weary travelers, and in turn we exerted ourselves to be useful among them. There is no Methodist society organized there, and very few persons who were members of our Church, nor have they any chapel of any sort; but we had the pleasure of preaching two days in the female academy, which accommodated quite a respectable congregation; and from the number present, the attention given, and the interest apparently taken in the preaching, we can but hope that some beneficial effects may follow.

Monday, 6th, we left our kind friends of Spring Hill, and took the Minden road, which leads through a country forming a striking contrast with Hempstead county, in some particulars. It should be observed that we left the military road near Greenville, some forty miles beyond Washington, and formed a curve westward, in order to visit several important points; and instead of returning directly east from Spring Hill to our former road, we aimed to strike it obliquely by a nigher route. In the evening we passed Lewisville, the seat of a new county named Fayette. This is a new establishment in the woods, consisting of a log court-house, with a brush arbor in front, an indifferent log school-house, and the commencement of a wooden jail, the walls of which were partly raised. One mile beyond Lewisville, between Dr. Wilson's and Mr. Lemay's, we lodged by a small ravine, where the light-wood was abundant, and called the place Pinot Camp. Here we ate breakfast by candle-light, and at an early hour on Tuesday entered a wilderness of about thirty miles, without a house. Soon after we heard the keen crack of a rifle, and presently saw a buck fleeing as if wounded, and immediately afterward met a young Indian with his hunting costume, attended by a well-trained dog on his track, who, without manifesting any surprise at our appearance, went on in pursuit of his game. While observing him, his father and mother, as we supposed, and some younger children, came up with a train of small ponies packed with skins and meat, in real hunter's style. This was a family of Choctaws returning from their fall hunt, made in the wild regions of the Bodcaw, which is still the abode of wild beasts. Some days previous we had been told by brother Gregory, presiding elder of the Red river district, that wild cattle were still to be found in the cane down Red river, and that he had recently rode nearly into the midst of a large drove of them before they observed him, but when started by his appearance, they made the brush and cane crack like a gang of buffalo; and to-day we had a confirmation of the correctness of this intelligence. Only a few miles on our day's journey, we met a wagon drawn by two mewly oxen, attended with hunters, who informed us they were going after a wild bull, which they had just killed near that place, to bring him into their camp, which we would presently pass; that he was very fat, and they judged would weigh about seven or eight hundred pounds. It is presumed that these cattle originally strayed from the French and Spaniards, and have been increasing in their wild state for ages past. Soon after passing them, we came to the Bodcaw, a large bayou, full of cypress, and difficult to pass. At our crossing, it parted so as to form an island, on which we saw the hunters' camp among the cane, which, in the absence of its owners, was occupied by ravens and buzzards, feeding on the offal. The banks of the Bodcaw are nearly perpendicular, and the water so deep that to secure our baggage we had to prop it up on blocks, and then lash it on with ropes to keep it dry. Twelve inches more and our horses would have been covered, if not floated; but, by the blessing of kind Providence, we got all over safely. Had we been men of leisure and sport, the temptation to stop here and exhaust our little store of ammunition would have been strong; but we had another and more important object in view than hunting deer, bear, and wild cattle. Indeed, we had to pass the wilderness that day, or let our horses suffer for grain. Why no body settles along on this road it is difficult to account for, only on the supposition that the land is owned by non-resident speculators. Between Bodcaw and Dorcheat there is an extensive body of the most beautiful pine-land I ever saw. It lies handsomely, is dry, of dark complexion, mellow, and apparently rich; and though rather sandy, it would doubtless produce cotton, corn, oats, peaches, and sweet potatos, in great abundance; and from the character of the timber it is easily cleared. The water on the road is scarce this dry season, though we saw some springs. Many flocks of deer scampered before us during this day's journey, but we paid little attention to them. After pushing on all day, we reached Dorcheat at dark, a bayou some forty yards wide, and too difficult crossing to pass in the night, and we were content to stop in rather an inconvenient place on the north side, about two rods from a deserted Indian camp, made of cypress bark; but we preferred our own tent on fresh ground. Our camp was in sight of the house of old Mr. Moss, perhaps the first settler of the neighborhood; but he was buying corn at one dollar a bushel, and hauling it forty miles. However, with some persuasion, he let us have one bushel for two dollars in par funds, but would spare no fodder at any price. The water of Dorcheat is so colored with cypress leaves, etc., that it is nearly as black as tar, though it is cold, and tolerably pleasant to the taste. The cypress grows not only on the banks, but in the channel of the sluggish stream, starting generally in conical form, and then shooting up a trunk tall and straight, with foliage similar to pine, though not so heavy, and subject to fade and fall off about the first of winter. Around each large cypress are scores of knees or excrescences, like little cones, from the roots, which are hollow shells of a spongy nature, that grow from one to five feet high above the ground, or water, as the case may be; and, when sawed off, answer for bee-gums or well-buckets. The cypress wood, though soft, is durable, and answers well for boards, palings, etc. While at Camp Dorcheat, the hooting of owls and howling of wolves made us music enough for one night.

Next morning, by blocking up our baggage as before, we forded safely, and, within one mile beyond it, passed two smaller bayous with some difficulty; the ford of one being so blocked up with drift, that we had to seek a new crossing, and cut a road to and from it. The first mile of our road from Dorcheat presented a novel appearance to a northern man: the undergrowth was cane and bay-shrub, shaded by a dense forest of holly, with an occasional pine from three to four feet in diameter. This forest of evergreens, in connection with the mildness of the weather, reminded us of summer. The bark of the holly-tree resembles the northern beech, while its boughs are ornamented with deep-green foliage, and clusters of blood-red berries about the size of cherries. Leaving this flat, we came over poor pine knobs to Mr. Rice's, seven miles, where we bought a nice piece of a fat cub, killed the day before; and half a mile beyond saw a large sweet-gum marked "A. and L.," which we recognized as a line-tree between the states of Arkansas and Louisiana, where we let our horses feed on the cane, while we took our luncheon. This was in latitude thirty-three degrees north.

Yours, respectfully, T. A. Morris.

State Line, Dec. 8, 1841.

LETTER VIII.

Brother Elliott,—While taking leave of Arkansas, it may be proper for me to add one or two general remarks to those already made. The south part of the state is a more interesting country, on some accounts, than the north part. The land is rather better, and the climate milder, of course; insomuch that the stock is generally wintered on the wild range, without the expense or trouble of feeding, especially where the cane has not yet been destroyed. This circumstance, together with its China-trees and numerous evergreens, gives it the characteristics of a southern country. It is also a planting region, and produces cotton in abundance, and exhibits more appearance of wealth and intelligence. All that I have said of the civility and hospitality of the inhabitants heretofore, has only been confirmed in my mind by passing through the south-west part of the state. Methodism, I am sorry to say, appears to be less efficient in its operations, and therefore less influential, in Arkansas generally, than it should be, but there is no necessity for this state of things being perpetuated. The people are generally well disposed to receive our views of Christianity, and the teachers of it whom we send to labor among them; and even in the towns, where we have accomplished but little, with a few exceptions, much might be done if proper attention was paid to them. I do not know of a better opening for usefulness, by an enterprising Methodist preacher, than in the villages of Hempstead county.

On Wednesday, December 8th, we entered Claiborne parish, Louisiana, and in the evening passed what is called, on the maps, Allen's Settlement, nothing of which is seen from the road but Mr. Allen's field and cabin, and lodged that night in the pine woods a mile and a half beyond; having traveled that day only twelve or thirteen miles, on account of the road being so blocked up with timber that we had frequently to cut our way through or around it. The place where we staid that night afforded so many conveniences and comforts, that brother Clark suggested to call it Camp Felicity, to which all the company agreed, of course. The ground was handsome, water good, fuel abundant and convenient. We had bread and butter, milk and sugar for our tea, sweet potatos, stewed peaches, boiled ham, fried cub, etc. Who could desire better living?

Thursday, 9th, was a rainy day: quick, heavy showers fell upon us, especially in the afternoon: the road was rough; houses few and far between; and to crown all, we got lost: took a wrong road, and got some miles out of the way; but in the evening got right, and came to a creek called Flat Lick, having gained fifteen miles that day. This place we called Camp Holly, because it was ornamented by trees of that name on every side. In the evening we were visited by a Methodist brother, named Frederick Grounds, who had resided in that neighborhood eighteen years; though his house was behind us, and off our road. He appeared to be a friendly, good-natured man; and it was fortunate that he was so, for he weighed two hundred and twenty or two hundred and thirty pounds, and possessed much muscular strength. Subsequently he brought us a chicken, some butter and eggs, and helped to cut and carry our wood, all gratuitously. The ground here was rather wet, in consequence of the rain; but we borrowed four bundles of blades from our horses till morning, put them under our buffalo-robes, and slept in safety. Next morning we passed a neighborhood of good upland, and better improved than any we had seen this side of Spring Hill: the soil was black and mellow, and the natural growth pine, oak, and hickory. Thirteen miles brought us to Minden, which is ninety miles from Spring Hill. This is a new, but neat and improving village, chiefly inhabited by planters and merchants. It was laid off in 1836; but has been mostly built since 1838. Three miles further on is Overton, the seat of Claiborne parish, said to be sickly, and nearly deserted in favor of Minden, to which place it is thought the county seat will be removed next session of the legislature. Here we saw the first long moss on our road, which I have never observed in a higher latitude than thirty-two and a half degrees north. Just beyond Overton, we crossed the track of a tremendous hurricane, which, for some half mile, had destroyed nearly all the timber. It was not of very late occurrence, so that our road was clear. When we reached the next farm it was after three o'clock; and, on inquiry, we found it was twelve miles to the next house on our road: we bought provender, proceeded on to the middle of this desolation, and slept quietly and sweetly under the pine-bushes in *Camp Solitude.*

Saturday, 11th, brother Whipple took his rifle, mounted his colt, and proceeded in advance of the wagons; saw abundance of deer; shot twice, and wounded one mortally; but, for want of time and skill to follow the trail, did not obtain it. His squirrel-balls are too light for bucks. About noon we passed a camp of Indian hunters. Their ponies were belled, and grazing: an old Indian was lying in camp on his stomach, resting his chin on his hands, like a lazy dog sleeping with his head upon his paws, and scarcely opened his eyes to see us pass: skins were drying over a smoke-pit: two squaws were working outside of the camp; and three small children were sitting round a little fire some distance off, who observed us passing, but manifested no alarm or surprise. The hunters were probably on the chase. In the evening, after going nine miles without seeing a house, we reached brother Manning's, who keeps a house of entertainment, where we remained till Monday morning, and were accommodated. On the Sabbath we rode four miles to a log meeting-house, where there is a small Methodist society, and preached to about twenty persons, including our own company. These were nearly all the persons in the neighborhood, and we had a pleasant little meeting. We fell into the old military road at Thompson's, twenty miles back, which is very much cut up by the wagons of emigrants, chiefly to Texas. They have here a weekly horse mail from Natchitoches to Washington, and a post-office at this place. For a week past, the weather has been exceedingly mild and pleasant, except one rainy day: part of the time it was oppressive to ride with our coats on; and as for cloaks, they were an incumbrance. Last evening, we had a heavy shower, and the weather is like to be cooler. H. Johnson, Esq., Ex-Governor of Louisiana, staid here last night. He is the Whig candidate for governor the next term, and is performing the tour of the parishes on an electioneering campaign, and from *stumping*, or some other cause, is rather indisposed. We are now thirty-seven miles from Natchitoches, and about one hundred and ten from San Augustine. Time fails to add more at present.

Yours, truly, T. A. MORRIS.

MANNING'S, CLAIBORNE PARISH, LA., DEC. 13, 1841.

LETTER IX.

BROTHER ELLIOTT,—My last letter was dated at Manning's, Louisiana, December 13th. We left that place the same day, and immediately after passed out of Claiborne into Natchitoches parish, and in the afternoon reached brother Randolph's house of entertainment, south of the Big Bayou, having traveled seventeen miles over a country so poor that it is entirely desolate. While at Randolph's, we met with three men on their return from Texas, whose observations had been chiefly confined to Jasper county, and reported that the land there was rich in spots, and the balance poor. These appeared to be civil men, and conformed very respectfully to the rules of the family at evening and morning prayers; but one of them carried a deadly weapon, such as we had not seen before—a pistol and Bowie-knife in one solid piece; the back of the knife was welded to the under side of the barrel, and the blade projected some seven inches beyond the muzzle, and the but of the pistol answered for the knife-handle. It had a percussion lock, and the whole was carried in a case made to suit its form, and worn on the side under the vest. When the owner of it undressed for sleeping, John Emory Clark, who had been put to bed in the same room, saw the instrument taken out and examined, and concluding that he was in dangerous company, slipped out of bed, opened the door, and, in his night clothes, ran across the porch and entry to the door of his father's bed-room, and called for quarters; and, when taken in, was evidently much agitated, being only nine years old, and having never seen the like before. Next morning he very shrewdly remarked, that he did not like the looks of that thing; it would kill a man twice, first shoot and then stab him. It is to be regretted that public sentiment does in any part of the United States tolerate the savage practice of carrying frightful instruments made on purpose to destroy human life, such as pistols, dirks, and Bowie-knives. The history of the origin of the latter should be disgusting to every decent man. A desperado in west Louisiana, some years ago, named Bowie, took the blade of an old mill-saw to a common blacksmith, and got part of it made into a huge butcher-knife, to which he fixed a rough, wooden handle, and with which he soon after spilt the heart's blood of his enemy on a sand-bar, east side of the Mississippi, near the city of Natchez. Other desperate men, seeing the success of this experiment, had similar weapons made, and called them Bowie-knives; and mechanics, seeing that the business was likely to become profitable, commenced manufacturing fine articles of the same name, so large, of such material, and fine polish, as to cost from twenty to fifty dollars. Nearly every other instrument can be applied to some useful purpose; but these are made for the special and exclusive purpose of committing murder. It is true that many individuals carry them, who intend to make no other use of them than to defend themselves when attacked; but the whole system is erroneous in principle and ruinous in practice. He that carries a Bowie-knife must expect to be met by Bowie-knife men on his own ground, and run the risk of being killed or involved in prosecutions for homicide; which he might otherwise avoid. Beside, the appearance of the thing is shocking to all the better feelings of our nature, and renders a man liable to suspicion. Who can travel as a stranger through the country, armed with the instruments of death, and not be suspected by the better part of community as a blackleg or desperado! The best way to get safely through a strange country is to travel unarmed, and treat every body civilly. Most of my life has been spent in journeying among strangers, without any weapons, except the shield of faith and the sword of the Spirit, and no man has ever assaulted me.

Tuesday, 14th. Shortly after we left Randolph's, the woods suddenly became a shade darker as we entered the long-leafed pine, which grows on the poor hills: we then came down to Compte, a French village on Red river, where they really cut a singular figure with their mud-houses, blanket coats, capos, spotted ponies, Spanish saddles, and great wooden stirrups. At the lower end of the village we met some Choctaw women and children, with a load of cotton-baskets for sale; and a little further on we saw the camp where they were manufactured, in which an Indian man was resting horizontally, while the squaws were shaving splits and weaving baskets. The chief difference we observed between these and the Spanish Creole ladies, was, the Choctaw ladies were rather fairer, and their pappooses wore more fringes and finery than their Spanish neighbors. As we passed along down the bank of the river, it was reviving to our spirits, after coming so far over pine hills, to observe the extended fields of luxuriant cotton, the drills running parallel with the road, the stalks as high as the fence, and so thick as nearly to conceal the ground from the sight of the eye. From the quantity of ground planted, and the number of negro huts and ginning establishments, we judged that an immense amount of cotton must be produced on the Red river bottoms. The plantations are handsomely improved: some of them separated by long lanes, shaded by continuous rows of China and catalpa-trees; while others had preserved fine patches of cane, by inclosing them so as to exclude the stock. Here, too, we saw the pecan-trees, large and apparently fruitful. Six miles from Compte brought us down opposite Grande de Core, which, a Frenchman informed us, means the grand hill, a name suggested by a bold, prominent bluff at the upper end of the village, covered with pines. This is the usual crossing place; but we passed on to the lower ferry, in order to avail ourselves of a new boat and better road, and crossed at the head of the cut-off, two miles below Grande de Core, and three or four above Natchitoches. This cut-off comes in sixty miles below, and is now becoming the main channel, so that boats, to avoid the raft on the old channel, come up the new, and then turn down to Natchitoches; and, from present appearances, Grande de Core must finally become the prominent business point on the river. The ferry in which we crossed is kept by a Frenchman, slow-motioned, surly, and exceedingly profane. If he prove faithful to the principles taught him, it is to be hoped that the next time he goes to confession he will remember the profane oaths which he swore in our presence, and do the penance which his confessor may award him. Red river here, as in other places, with its turbid waters, rapid current, and whirling eddies, suggests the idea of a river of cider in a state of fermentation: its breaking shores of red clay imparts to it a reddish hue, which, no doubt, gave rise to its name. We were glad to be safely landed on the south side of it, and passing out half of a mile, we kindled our fire by a pine log on the point of a hill near to a sort of spring lake, three miles from Natchitoches, and called the place Long Moss Camp, the weather being exceedingly mild and pleasant.

Wednesday, 15th. Brother Whipple went by the city

to deliver and inquire for letters, etc., and the balance of us came directly across to the Texas road, and forming a right angle, turned our faces toward the west, and after going twenty miles over pine hills, without seeing any thing specially attractive, slept at Baytree Camp, by a sluggish stream of poor water.

Yours, as ever, T. A. MORRIS.

NATCHITOCHES PARISH, LA., DEC. 15, 1841.

LETTER X.

BROTHER ELLIOTT,—The road from Natchitoches to the Sabine is broad, much traveled, and though passing over a broken country, would be tolerably pleasant, if it were not torn to pieces by the cotton wagons; but we were almost constantly meeting teams of horses, mules, or oxen, mostly from Texas, drawing ponderous loads of this staple to Natchitoches, the great cotton depot for eastern Texas, as well as its own vicinity, in consequence of which much of the road was in bad condition.

Thursday, 16th, in the forenoon, we passed Fort Jessup, on high, dry ground, twenty-five miles from Natchitoches. The houses are built of wood, and the walks shaded with China-trees, but present nothing striking in appearance, or materially different from other military posts on the frontier. Much money, of course, has been expended here by the Government, but how profitably to the country I am not prepared to say. We saw five or six soldiers only; some of these were standing about the street, and the others at a considerable distance from the fort, walking about leisurely: we saw no other persons, except two men at the hotel, and some very rude children romping about the post-office. It is supposed by some that if the best of these houses were rented out for a tavern-stand, and the fort converted into a yard to accommodate the wagons of emigrants and cotton-planters, it might save some expense to the General Government, and do more real service to the country. Of this, however, I profess to know nothing. A few miles beyond the fort we met a small drove, say twenty fat bullocks, large and handsome, driven from the Trinity, and going to the Natchitoches market. Such exports of cotton and stock from Texas must bring into it large sums of good money. That night we lodged at the Dry Camp, on a fine ridge, where it was difficult to obtain a sufficiency of good water for ourselves and horses, though in all other respects our location was comfortable, and the more so as we were well sheltered from the north-west wind, which was cold enough to form some ice in the water bucket.

Friday, 17th, we came down to Sabine river, at Gaines's Ferry; stopped on the east shore; took our last luncheon in the United States; crossed over and were within the limits of the "virgin republic." Sabine is about ten rods wide, its banks steep and high, and has fourteen feet water in the channel. The bottom lands adjoining are wet and poor, producing water-oak, gum, and cypress. Pendleton is the name of a poor village on the west bank, containing some six or eight houses, most of which are empty. Leaving this we passed over level ground, plowing through white sand, which tried the strength of our teams for four miles, when we rose on to high ground and entered the border of that interesting part of Texas called the Redlands, which is thickly settled and well improved. Our first night in the republic was passed in Redland Camp, near a pure fountain of excellent spring water, clear, soft, and pleasant to the taste, a short distance east of Milam. Here we found ourselves in a pleasant and plentiful country. Whatever we desired for ourselves, or horses, was readily obtained, and on reasonable terms, compared with what we had been paying for the same articles in Arkansas and Louisiana. We added to our imported provisions a mess of sweet potatos, which were to us the first-fruits of the land, and an excellent omen of its good things. The night was cool, but clear, and so perfectly calm, that the smoke went up from our hickory-log fire as straight as if it had passed through a stone chimney. Our camp was handsomely illuminated by driving down a stake at each front corner, splitting the top and introducing torches of lightwood. We had one of our best camp suppers, felt every way cheerful, happy, and joyful; spent the evening in our own quiet habitation, singing the songs of Zion, among others the Jubilee of the Israelites, and with some emphasis when we came to these words:

> "Though Baca's vale be dry, and the land yield no supply,
> To a land of corn and wine, we'll go on, we'll go on," etc.

Also the verse which refers to their crossing Jordan, and entering the promised land, the last of which is,

> "Jehovah rules the tide, and the waters he'll divide,
> And the ransomed host shall shout, we are come, we are come."

Saturday morning, 18th, before sunrise, the mercury fell to twenty-four degrees above zero, and the leaves were handsomely frosted over, but all melted away as soon as the sun shone upon it. After breakfast we passed through Milam, the seat of justice for Sabine county, which is built on the red clay, and contains from twelve to twenty houses, nearly the color of the dust in their streets. In sight of town was a gallows still standing, where there had recently been an execution, the particulars of which we did not learn, and I only advert to it to remind bad people in the United States, that if they do not wish to be hung, they had better keep away from Texas. Just at the west end of Milam is a handsome stream of water called Boreyas creek, where the white sycamore and large, green magnolia-trees formed a contrast at once singular and beautiful. The Redlands are undulating, rich, and judging from the stocks of corn and cotton, they must be about as productive as the "bottoms" of the Mississippi and Red rivers. They are also remarkably well-watered, abounding with small streams from never-failing springs. East of the Sabine we had muddy roads and dry brooks, but west of it we had dry roads and plenty of running water. These lands are likewise well timbered with hickory, oak, and, in some places, pine on the ridges. In the richest land, however, the most common growth is young hickory, white to the very center, and nearly as hard as lignumvitæ. The top limbs of the hickories have a whitish appearance; and, standing on an elevation where we could see over the forest trees for miles, the vales white with hickory, and the ridges green with pine, the whole presented the appearance of a striped carpet, beautiful beyond description. We occasionally saw quarries of building-stone on the points of ridges sloping down to the runs, but none in the road, which, in all places on the red sod, whether level or hilly, was perfectly firm, and nearly as smooth as a waxed floor. That it becomes soft and muddy when wet, there is no doubt, though it very soon dries into hardness by the action of wind and sun; but when we came through it was perfectly dry. There are in this part of the republic an enterprising community, and strong indications of growing wealth among them.

Saturday evening we reached San Augustine, the seat of justice for the county of the same name. This is one of the largest towns in Texas, containing some eight hundred or one thousand inhabitants. It is situated on the east side of the Ayish bayou. The houses are mostly frame, and painted white. There is in the town an academy of respectable appearance; also a new Methodist chapel about forty by thirty feet, just brought into use, but not finished. We were glad to finish this tedious journey. My traveling companions had come from the extreme north part of Illinois, more than one thousand miles, with the same teams, and I had accompanied them from St. Louis to this place, about seven hundred and fifty miles. Our time from St. Louis through was two months; but deducting the Sabbath and other days on which we stopped to preach or rest, we were actually on the road thirty-seven days, and slept in our own camp twenty nights. Still the journey has been, upon the whole, quite a pleasant one. We were much favored as to weather and low waters. Our company was pleasant, and when in camp we were not annoyed by cigars, whisky, or rude language. We were often weary, and sometimes wet and cold, but, by the blessing of a kind Providence, preserved from any severe sickness.

Yours, truly, T. A. Morris.

San Augustine, Dec. 20, 1841.

LETTER XI.

Brother Elliott,—The Texas conference met on the 23d instant, in the city of San Augustine. Most of the members were present: two were absent, and one or two of those in attendance were in poor health. There has been no death among them the past year; but some of the first band of missionaries are nearly worn out. The conference was reinforced by four transferred, one readmitted, and three young men admitted on trial; one located, and two probationers were discontinued. The whole number of names on the Minutes is twenty-three—sixteen are members of conference, and the balance are on trial.

On the day that conference commenced its session, we were receiving the full force of a *norther*, which was preceded by a heavy fall of rain the day before. It continued quite cold for this country the balance of the week; and on Sabbath morning, hail, or round snow, commenced falling obliquely from the east, which continued till afternoon, when it assumed the form of a cold rain, producing a very chilly state of atmosphere, which of course lessened our congregation: still the house was tolerably well filled morning and afternoon. Seven deacons and two elders were ordained; all local brethren, except three of the deacons.

When the Texan mission was instituted in 1837, it was scarcely to be expected that in four years we should see here an annual conference, with twenty-three traveling and thirty-six local preachers, and a membership of two thousand, seven hundred and ninety-five; but so it is in fact. The prospects of this young conference are truly encouraging. Their way is open to nearly every neighborhood and village in the republic; and in most places Methodism appears to be favorably received by the people. We have the ascendency over all other denominations; and if we do not keep it, the fault will be our own. An itinerant ministry, which is best for all countries, is specially adapted to this, in the present scattered condition of the inhabitants; while the climate, to some extent, supersedes the necessity of chapels. Camp meetings have been held to advantage, the past year, in December, when the people were healthy, and free from the annoyance of musketoes, and other troublesome insects.

The missionary meeting was held on Monday night; and though the weather was damp and chilly, it was well attended: the amount collected was seventy-four dollars and forty-four cents. Some jewelry was thrown in, after which one gave four town lots, another fifteen lots; one one hundred acres of land, two others three hundred and twenty acres each, and one a quarter of a league. All these donations, it is presumed, will be available. The lands given at the missionary meeting, last year, have been legally conveyed, and will some day bring the cash into the treasury.

Tuesday evening, the conference terminated a harmonious and pleasant session of five days, and every man repaired to his own field of labor, ready to spend and be spent in its cultivation.

To-morrow I am to leave for Austin, distant three hundred and fifty miles. My health is good, and spirits cheerful.

Yours, as ever, T. A. MORRIS.

SAN AUGUSTINE, DEC. 29, 1841.

LETTER XII.

BROTHER ELLIOTT,—The Redland, which I attempted to describe in a former communication, includes several counties up and down the Sabine river, and extends west to the Attoaye, which is the line between San Augustine and Nacogdoches counties. After passing this stream, the land assumes more of a chocolate hue, and soon ends in sand, of which very much of the last-mentioned county consists. It was on Thursday, December 30th, that we resumed our journey; and having been detained one day over our appointed time, by reason of a cold, north-east rain, we made a long drive to reach a brother's house on the way. It was dark before we got there, and learned that the good man of the house was from home, and the good lady was sick, and of course could not receive us, but gave us horse-provender, and we soon found shelter under our own tent. Brother Carl, on his way to Victoria circuit, lodged with us that night. When the sun rose upon us, next morning, we found ourselves in the city of Melrose, just laid out, and two or three cabins erected for a commencement. Whether we were on Main-street, or on somebody's lot, is not known to us; but in either case we advanced the improvement of the city, by cutting down, logging off, and burning up a snarly hickory-tree, to keep us warm and cook our supper and breakfast.

Friday, 31st, we passed through Nacogdoches, originally a Mexican town, and at present a mixture of American and Spanish houses. One of the latter, built of stone, is said to be nearly one hundred years old. The town is small, containing some three or four hundred inhabitants, and is situated on a plain of white sand, between two small creeks, which may be a half of a mile asunder; the poor ridges setting in on both sides. When we came through a crowd of people had collected, partly to pay their last respects to a deceased fellow-citizen, and partly to witness the examination of a man charged with having committed murder a few days prior at a horse-race, the result of which examination we did not learn. That night we lodged at the house of a Mr. Greer, a clever Cumberland Presbyterian, and were charged nothing.

Saturday, January 1st, we passed through Douglass, a small village, near which a company of men were collected to try the speed of their quarter-nags, and spend their surplus shillings at the place of strong drink. Such meetings are disgraceful to any community; but what better could we expect of Texans, seeing they come mostly from the United States, where horse-racing is encouraged by law? In the afternoon, we put up at Mr. M'Night's, to rest over the Sabbath, and to preach, if opportunity offered.

On Sunday we went to a school-house at the Union camp-ground, two miles from Douglass, to hear the Rev. Mr. Watkins, a Cumberland Presbyterian minister, preach; but, at his special request, I had the honor to become his substitute, and brother Clark preached at the village in the evening. There are in this neighborhood some Methodists, Baptists, and Presbyterians, and plenty of sinners.

On Monday sister Clark was so much indisposed, that we were obliged to remain another day with Mr. M'Night;

however, as he is a good old Presbyterian, and we had preached twice, and served at his family altar every night, he let us off with fifteen dollars in par funds.

Tuesday, 4th, we crossed Angelina and Neches rivers, both small streams, such as would be called creeks in the western states. Between these rivers there is a body of handsome land, and tolerably rich, being nearly all the good land we saw in Nacogdoches county. The old San Antonio road, which we traveled here, is the south line of what is called the Cherokee land, which was said to be given by the Mexicans to the Cherokees for their service in fighting the Camanchees and Texans; but the Texans never acknowledged the claim of the Cherokees, and finding them troublesome, drove them off, and are settling it themselves. When we crossed Neches river, we entered Houston county, and some eight miles beyond lodged at a good house of entertainment, kept by Mrs. M'Lean, whose husband was one of the first American settlers in the republic. The fare was both cheap and comfortable.

Wednesday, 5th, we passed Crockett, the county seat of Houston. The town is new and small, but apparently improving. That evening we called on brother Box, a short distance beyond Crockett, who cheerfully received and entertained us as well as he could.

Thursday, 6th, we halted at a new Methodist campground, and filled our vessels with water to serve us through an unsettled region of eighteen miles, where no water is to be obtained. In the afternoon we crossed Big Prairie—high, dry, and handsome, but not rich—and saw large flocks of deer, but so wild, that we could not approach within four hundred yards of them. Leaving the prairie, we came down through poor pine woods, and in the evening, while crossing a deep ravine, broke the tongue of the wagon, which detained us some; however, about dark, we reached the house of Mr. Stephen White, who resides near Trinity river, east side, a few miles below the town of Cincinnati, on a league of excellent land, which he obtained for settling it, and on which he has a mill, ferry, etc.

Friday morning we crossed the Trinity, which is perhaps twelve rods wide, and occasionally affords water enough to admit steamboats as far up as the three forks, but as it was quite low, and we had a pilot, we forded on a smooth rock, just above a sudden fall of some two or three feet. Here we took leave of eastern Texas, which, with the exception of the Redlands and Cherokee lands, is generally a poor country, so far as it came under our observation. The bottom-land of the Trinity is about four miles wide; on the east side low, but rich, and covered with cane and lofty timber; on the west side the bluff is high, which immediately lets into prairie and open woodland, both fertile and beautiful. Next to this, we passed poor ridges of pine and oak for three miles, and then entered a beautiful, undulating country, of prairie and woodland alternately, which continues, with but slight intermissions, across the entire county of Montgomery. The soil is black, deep, mixed with lime, and exceedingly productive. That evening, unable to reach our intended quarters, we camped in the edge of a cane-brake, near the house of an honest Dutchman, a little east of Huntsville, where we fared sumptuously, having, among other good things, a wild duck and two young squirrels served up into a pot-pie, which cost brother Whipple a hunt of about fifteen minutes.

Saturday morning we passed through Huntsville, a little city and few men within it, and most of them collected at the house called tavern, to enjoy the pitiful entertainment of hearing a trifling fellow pat his foot and draw his fiddle-bow, to kill time and chase dullness from the city.

In the afternoon we came down to the house of brother William Robinson—where we were to preach next day—who had gone in search of wild honey, and returned at night without success; but brought in some excellent venison. This old brother has lived here eleven years, on a league of excellent land obtained by head-right; has a wife and ten children in Texas, all members of our Church, and twenty-two grandchildren, who are natives of Texas, and four out of five sons-in-law are also Methodists; the whole forming a most interesting family. We were here overtaken by brothers Richardson, Summers, and Sullivan, going to their fields of labor. Our congregation of Sabbath morning was respectable in size and appearance, and we gave them two sermons at one sitting, some of them having come ten miles. In the evening we walked over to the new camp-ground, one mile off, to unite a worthy couple in the honorable relation of husband and wife; both members of our Church. The bride's father, being a new-comer, had taken his winter-quarters in one of the double log camps. After I performed the marriage ceremony, the company adjourned to the stand, where some others had assembled, to hear brother Summers preach. During sermon it commenced raining; but the congregation and preacher were all under a good shed, and experienced no inconvenience from the rain till they dispersed. Let it be recollected this night meeting at a camp-ground, without any fire, except pine torches for light, was on the ninth of January. Returning to our lodging, however, through rain, mud, and darkness, on foot, was not very pleasant to one so heavy and clumsy as myself.

Monday, 10th, was much colder; and the rain continued all day, and detained us within doors, except brothers Richardson and Whipple, who left in the afternoon.

Tuesday, 11th, we crossed San Jacinto, where it is

quite a narrow creek, and reached the hospitable dwelling of brother Porter, father to the preacher of the same name in the Mississippi conference, on the main Washington road. The game was so plentiful in this neighborhood, we concluded it was no marvel that most men who emigrate to Texas become hunters, and especially when it is considered that provisions are high; but this practice greatly retards the business of the country, by leading to idleness and the neglect of more important pursuits. And yet, in view of the present condition of the vermin and savage men, the practice of keeping guns and dogs at every house should not be hastily condemned.

Wednesday, 12th, we traveled twenty miles, to brother King's, in a neighborhood which, for rich land and beautiful sites, excels any thing we had seen in the republic. The prairies of Illinois are frequently wide and without timber, except on the water courses; but here the timber is irregularly distributed, without any reference to the small streams, except that the red cedar grows mostly along the branches and ravines, and the deep, black soil continues from the tops of the ridges to the very edge of the water, so that there is scarcely any waste land. In some places a rich prairie will have green borders of pine, growing on sandy ridges, so that a man can build on white sand amidst evergreens; and, immediately adjoining his yard, cultivate fields of the best marl-lime, entirely free from timber. And where the pine begins to fail, the red cedar comes in, affording abundance of the best timber for shingles, posting and railing, and even lumber for barns and houses. Near brother King's we passed the body of an unfinished meeting-house, and close by saw a circular cluster of cedars curtained with Spanish moss, and in the midst of them a neat stand with benches conveniently arranged for public worship, with an open prairie on one side and a dense cedar forest on the other. This was one of the most lovely spots I ever saw for outdoor worship, and is designed not for camp meeting, but ordinary circuit preaching. May Methodism long shed its heavenly influence around this consecrated and enchanting green chapel!

Thursday, 13th, the country appeared less inviting as we neared the Brazos river, though the bottom, on the east side, about three miles across, is rich enough to be very muddy. The river is, perhaps, eighty yards wide, and the banks very high and steep, but at present not much depth of water. As we ascended the hill from the ferry on the west side, we entered the town of Washington, late the seat of justice for Washington county, which contains, probably, about fifty or sixty houses, and is apparently on the decline, though in the midst of a fine country. Having proceeded west to the middle of the town, we turned at right angles to the north, about three hundred yards, to the old graveyard, which is situated on a dry ridge in open woods. Our business was to seek out the grave of Dr. Ruter, the apostle of Methodism in Texas, who died at his post May 16, 1838. The mournful spot sought for was easily found without a guide, the grave being inclosed by a stone wall, and covered with a white marble slab, three feet wide and six long, with a suitable inscription. At the foot of the slab stands a small hickory-tree, hung with Spanish moss, waving in the breeze over the charnel-house. As we stood under this tree reading the solemn epitaph, the sun was disappearing in the west, while a thousand thoughts of the past rushed upon our minds, and forcibly reminded us that our own days would soon be numbered. With Dr. Ruter I had often united in preaching the Gospel to crowded assemblies in Ohio and Kentucky. He now rests from all his toil, enjoying the promised reward; and if faithful to the grace given, may I not hope soon to join with him in the song of final and everlasting triumph? When we read on the cold marble, "thirty-seven years an itinerant minister of the Methodist Episcopal Church, and superintendent of the first mission of that Church in the republic of Texas," and then remembered that the same mission had already become a respectable annual conference, and was still increasing, the thought arose, whereunto will this mission grow, and what cause of rejoicing must this be to its first superintendent forever? Our visiting the graveyard at sundown in a village where we knew no one, and where no one knew us, seemed to excite some curiosity. A colored boy, sent no doubt for the purpose, came and inquired whence we journeyed? Our answer was, "Into all the world." That night we were kindly received and entertained at the house of brother Lynch, sheriff of the county, two miles west of town.

Yours, truly, T. A. MORRIS.

WASHINGTON, TEXAS, JAN. 13, 1842.

LETTER XIII.

BROTHER ELLIOTT,—As we came west from the vicinity of Washington, the scenery was delightful; every sensation of pleasure which extended plains, spotted with clumps of evergreens, grazing herds, and cultivated fields, all basking in the bright beams of a calm sunny morning, could inspire, was ours. A little east of Independence we gained the most commanding elevation which our eyes beheld in the republic. Standing on this most lovely eminence, the eye calmly rested on many objects of beauty near at hand, such as small islands of timber, farm-houses, and the village below, while the general appearance was that of boundless expanse, filling the mind with pleasure and admiration. Passing through Independence, we arrived, on Friday evening, at Dr. Hoxey's, near the academy, where we were expected to preach the two following days. This is one of the finest neighborhoods we have yet seen in Texas. The meeting was well attended; but having no place of worship, only the academy, which is occupied in common by all the religious denominations of the country, our prospect of usefulness is rather limited, till our people shall build a chapel in town, of which there is some prospect. Still, there is much cause of gratitude in what has been accomplished. A revival of religion, which, I believe, commenced under the preaching of brother F. some time ago, resulted in the conversion of several families, some of whom joined our Church. May they walk in Christ as they have received him!

Monday, 17th, we proceeded on, amidst scenes of beauty and grandeur peculiar to this region of the republic, to Capt. Crisman's, and preached in the evening, where we had more hearers than house room, who listened attentively to our plain talk. The Captain was an early settler in Colonel Austin's colony, and has resided in Texas nearly twenty years, and gave us many interesting incidents connected with the history of that colony. When Capt. C. arrived, there were only about forty families on the two rivers, Brazos and Colorado, most of whom went out with himself, and the few Mexicans about Nacogdoches and San Antonio were a long distance off. The colonists suffered much; some lived six months, and others a year or more, without ever eating a bit of bread, depending on deer, turkey, and the like, for a subsistence. As for himself, he was four years without a shoe, sock, shirt, or any clothing, except what he made of skins; and for the first ten years never heard a sermon. He is now in easy circumstances, well fixed for good living, and, with his family and many of his neighbors, happy in the enjoyment of religion after the Methodist sort; and, of course, rejoices exceedingly in the civil and religious improvement of the republic.

The next day we were received and entertained very cordially by brother H. Kerr and family, after our day's journey. The old gentleman is a native of Ireland, quite intelligent and communicative, and somewhat conspicuous as the author of "A Poem on Texas," which purports to be a history of the republic in verse. In the evening his neighbors came in, and filled the room, to whom we delivered a short sermon and exhortation.

Wednesday, 19th, we reached Rutersville, in Fayette county, and were made welcome by our Christian friends. Rutersville is a village situated on an elevated prairie, but contiguous to groves of timber, five miles from the Colorado river, and is distinguished chiefly by the location of Rutersville College in its immediate vicinity. The enterprise, I believe, originated with Dr. Ruter, during his short but glorious career of missionary operation in that country. A preparatory school was commenced in 1840, and had last year some eighty students. The Faculty are organized, and ready to organize regular college classes: the teachers are the Rev. Chauncey Richardson, President; Rev. Charles W. Thomas, professor of ancient languages; Mr. Bell, *tutor;* and Mrs. Richardson has charge of the female department. The college edifice, which is a frame building, but quite respectable for a new country, is nearly finished, and stands on a hill in the edge of a forest south of the village, while the academy occupied by the female teacher and pupils is situated on the west side, where the ground is less elevated, but more retired and picturesque. This institution is under the patronage and supervision of the Texas annual conference, but open to the public generally on the same principle of our colleges in the United States, and has flattering prospects of extensive patronage and usefulness. Congress has granted them a regular college charter, with the usual prerogatives of conferring degrees, and a donation of seventeen thousand acres of land, which has been increased by individual donations, obtained chiefly by the agency of President Richardson, till the whole amount of land owned by the College is about seventy-five thousand acres. If the Board can raise funds to complete the necessary improvement, and pay incidental expenses, without sacrificing the real estate, the institution will ultimately be well endowed. The charter exempts the College lands from taxation, and allows the corporation to hold property to the amount of $100,000, exclusive of the buildings, library, and apparatus. The Rev. Littleton Fowler, and the Rev. John Haynie, are regularly-authorized agents to collect funds for Rutersville College this year. On Sunday, January 23, we preached in the college chapel, crowded with attentive hearers.

The country between the Brazos and Colorado rivers, by the route we came, is one of exceeding beauty and fertility, much like the country between the Brazos and Trinity, except that the former affords more prairie and less pine than the latter. But the entire country, from the Trinity to the Colorado, is, with the exception of some limited sections, an excellent one. If a man wished to engage in planting cotton, or raising stock, or both, he could scarcely find a substantial objection to it, except the inconvenience of getting his produce to market, which would apply forcibly to much of it. In this part of the republic Indian corn grows tolerably well, and nearly all sorts of culinary vegetables, except Irish potatos, are easily produced in great abundance; so are peaches, plums, grapes, melons, etc.; but for wheat flour, the only certain dependence is importation from the states.

Monday, 24th, I resumed my journey, and traveled up the Colorado, on the north-east side, twenty-five miles, to Mr. Middleton Hill's, where I was very kindly entertained. That night it rained, and next day turned quite cold, of which I had ample proof while riding against the storm. After preaching to a small congregation at Gage's school-house, where brother Whipple met me, we rode in company, crossed the river, dined at brother Wiley Hill's, and spent the night at Mrs. M'Gee's very pleasantly. I was delighted with the people of this neighborhood. They reside in a circle around a small but beautiful prairie of excellent land. That night the Indians, who had been for some nights collecting a drove of horses in a pen on Cedar creek, came to a house, in sight of where we lodged across the prairie, and stole five: also, several, the same night, from the opposite side of the river. Indeed, it was said by the citizens, that they had not left enough horses and mules on the river to enable them to raise their crop. Most families, who did not watch or lock up their horses, lost them. It was matter of accommodation to us on our journey that they did not take ours.

Next day we preached at Bastrop, under the roar of artillery, the signal for collecting minute men to go in pursuit of the Indians. Our congregation was quite respectable for a week-day, and very attentive, considering the circumstances; but at each report of the cannon many of them would involuntarily spring from their seats; and after all we had a very comfortable meeting to many. The same afternoon we recrossed the river and proceeded on fourteen miles, through an unsettled and poor region of country, to brother Haynie's, where we tarried for the night; and on Thursday, 27th, finished our journey to the neighborhood of Austin City. This day several objects attracted our attention: the muskeet grass, which continues green all winter, resorted to by herds of cattle, and covered with flocks of geese and cranes to an extent incredible to any one who has never seen them, the Onion creek lands, with the Colorado on the right, the Pilot Mountain and Austin City ahead, and apparently a boundless waste on the left, presented a prospect of inimitable beauty. In the afternoon we reached the country residence of Judge Webb, two miles below the city, which is situated in a grove of live-oaks, on a handsome eminence, overlooking his cultivated fields and forests on the lowland, and is remarkably pleasant and inviting. Here I spent several days pleasantly with the Judge and his family, and my own son, whom I had not seen during the three years he had resided in Texas. Only one thing embarrassed me, and that was a heavy cold settled on my lungs, which entirely disqualified me for any public service for some days, in consequence of which I did not attempt to preach in Austin, nor was I in the city at all, only long enough to hear one sermon on Sabbath morning, by brother Clark, the presiding elder of the district. The capital, situated in the Colorado Valley, and in full view of the only mountains we saw in the republic, presents an air of beauty, and appears somewhat romantic. I made no examination, however, and decline any particular description of it. The arguments in favor of the location of the capital must be drawn chiefly from considerations of beauty, romance, and solitude, for between it and the populated part of the country there is no connecting ligament but a narrow string of settlements along the Colorado. To reach Austin City from Galveston requires a journey of two hundred and seventy-five miles, and to reach it from the Sabine on the east requires a journey of about four hundred. It may be geographically central, but it certainly is not so to the inhabited parts of the republic.

Yours, truly, T. A. Morris.

Austin, Texas, Feb. 1, 1842.

LETTER XIV.

Brother Elliott,—On Monday, 31st of January, we commenced retracing our steps, and returned to Rutersville by nearly the same route, crossing the river at sundry places. The Colorado is a rapid stream of clear water, about twenty rods wide, passing over a gravel bottom, between prominent bluff banks, through one of the finest sections of the republic, affording, perhaps, more picturesque and elegant building sites, and more fine groves of red cedar, ash, and elm, than any other part which came under my observation, and with at least as good a prospect of health as any interior point. The range on this river is exceedingly fine: beside the prairie grass common to the country, there is the finest sort of rye bottoms for the stock in winter, as green and fresh in January as a field of tame rye in April. The scenery of the Colorado is wild, but lovely and inviting. Much of the land is rich and cheap, and would probably be settled as fast as any other part of the republic, were it not so exposed to Indian depredations. This is at present a formidable difficulty: there is no barrier between the settlements and the Indian country, nor any provision of Government for their defense. If the Camanchees were like the northern Indians that resisted the settlement of Kentucky and Western Virginia, they would very soon destroy all the inhabitants of the Colorado; but they are wild, cowardly, and, having but few guns, are slow to attack the white man with his fire-arms, except when they have a decided advantage, then they will let their pointed arrows fly, and often with fatal consequence. These wild Indians live like Arabs; they have no certain dwelling-place, pass much of their time on horseback armed with spears, and having a vast extent of country to range in, it is difficult to dislodge or subdue them. Perhaps in thirty hours after the commission of theft or murder, they may be one hundred miles from the scene of atrocity, and so scattered that they can be trailed no further.

Friday, February 4th, brother Alexander met and proceeded on with me toward Houston. That night we staid with Colonel Thomas, and next day reached the neighborhood of Center Hill, where our congregation on the Sabbath was quite too large for the school-house, nearly one-half having to remain out of doors.

Monday, 7th, we passed the ruins of the late residence of Colonel Austin, which was destroyed during the revolution, and spent the night with Dr. H. Matthews, formerly of Lancaster, Ohio, in San Phillipe, which, by order of General Houston, was burnt by the Texan army as they retreated before the enemy, but has been since rebuilt. It is the seat of justice for Austin county, and stands on the west bank of the Brazos river. Dr. Matthews's family were in mourning for the recent death of Mrs. Hill, their only daughter; still our interview with these esteemed old friends was cheerful and pleasant. The country across from the Colorado to the Brazos is nearly such as I have endeavored to portray before between these rivers. On crossing the river next morning, we took leave of the undulating section of Texas, and passed fifty miles over a level plain, generally wet and without timber, or any thing of interest to rest the eye on or break the monotonous scene, except the immense flocks of deer which range over this desolation like droves of sheep. Wild horses also are here, it is said, though I saw none of them.

Wednesday, 8th, we reached Houston in safety, and were kindly and comfortably entertained at Miss Morgan's boarding-house while waiting for a boat. Here we parted with brother Alexander, who very kindly accompanied us to take back brother Clark's buggy, in which I had traveled from St. Louis to that place, a journey of more than thirteen hundred miles. Houston contains some three thousand inhabitants, and presents quite a business-like appearance.

Thursday my son and I took passage on the steamboat

Patrick Henry for Galveston. The Buffalo Bayou is, in many places, just wide enough for the steamboat to pass, brushed by the boughs of trees on both sides. Its banks, shaded with cypress, pine, magnolia, and wild peach-trees, are more enchanting than I was prepared to expect. The town of Harrisburg, twelve miles below Houston, presents some specimens of good taste in the arrangement of buildings and their appurtenances. Night fell on us just before we passed the far-famed battle-ground of San Jacinto. Next morning we awoke on the bay, and were soon in the city of Galveston, the grand port of entry to the republic. The island appears to be a dry sand plain without timber, but covered with grass and flowers like other prairies, and has the smoothest and most beautiful beach I ever saw. It is said to be thirty miles long, and one and a half wide, is surrounded by salt water, and is thought to be one of the most healthy places in the republic, or any where else. The city resembles a New England village, as to the arrangement of lots and houses; but the docks and shipping give it the appearance of a commercial city on the sea-board. Its inhabitants made a very satisfactory showing of intelligence and refined hospitality during our sojourn among them, while waiting for a passage across the gulf, and, from the attention which they paid to preaching, do not seem to be indifferent on the subject of religion.

Before I lose sight of Texas, I wish to add a few general remarks. I went there prepared to see a mixed country, containing rich, poor, and medium land, and was not disappointed, only the proportion of good country is larger than I supposed. The country, of course, is new, but as a new country I consider it inviting; and though the improvements are yet limited, I must say that, in my opinion, they are underrated abroad. The climate, taking the calendar year together, must be more pleasant than that of Cincinnati; the days being nearly an hour longer in the winter, and an hour shorter in summer, bring the temperament of the atmosphere within less extremes of heat and cold, producing more uniformity. The water, whether from springs or wells, is rather warm, but, to me, pleasant, except in a few places, where it is too strongly impregnated with lime. After performing a tour of seven hundred miles through the republic, and making diligent inquiry in every place, I came to the conclusion that, as a whole, it was healthy for a new country, of which the number and robust appearance of the children are conclusive evidence. That some sections of it are sickly, must be admitted; but much affliction, which some people charge to the climate, should be put to the account of their own imprudence, living in open houses, exposing themselves to inclement weather, etc. The facilities for making a living in Texas are such, that if the people would use half the diligence which is necessary to prevent starvation in the older parts of the United States, they might render their circumstances easy and independent in a few years. If any one doubts this, let him reflect on the following items: good land from fifty cents to one dollar an acre, no clearing to do, just fence and plow; and instead of toiling six months to raise what is indispensable to keep his stock alive the other half of the year, his cattle are fat all the year without a feed of grain, or fodder, or a lick of salt. Any man in Texas, who can build a cabin and raise breadstuff, can live after the first year, and if he will be industrious and economical, he can thrive. Indeed, the ease with which a mere living can be made has retarded the improvement of the country, led to idleness, dissipation, dependence on loans, speculation, and hunting; but the people are becoming convinced that this plan will not do, and have gone to plowing and digging, making new farms, and extending old ones rapidly. It is thought from fifty to seventy thousand bales of cotton have been exported the past winter, and that the number will be doubled next. They have, also, cut down the expenses of the government largely, done away with the government scrip as a circulating medium, and require gold and silver, or its equivalent, for all impost duties and nearly all other government dues, are determined to rub out the old score and begin anew. If they hold on to the ground they are now taking, in three years they will be beyond the need of a loan, unless in case of war with some foreign power. The character of the Texans, I beg leave to say, is not generally understood abroad. He who goes to Texas presuming on his own intelligence and their want of it, will find himself mistaken. I am acquainted with no community of the same number, which embodies more shrewd, intelligent men than that of the single star republic. We know as little of their moral as of their intellectual character. Because some men, bankrupt in morals, have been promoted to office in Texas, some have concluded that they were all scoundrels together; but the same mode of reasoning would blast the moral character of the United States. The laws in Texas are comparatively few and simple, and are better enforced than our own. For example, every man familiar with steamboats and taverns in the United States knows that most of them are infested with *blacklegs*, a perfect nuisance to society, carrying on their iniquitous trade with impunity; but in Texas, any man playing with cards in any place of public resort, whether for money or amusement, is liable to be fined and imprisoned, and the proper authorities are not slow in punishing him as the law requires. But are there not robberies and murders committed in Texas? Yes; and so there are in our own country. The common notion that all the bad people go to Texas can not be true, or there would not be so many of them left among us. But I can not pursue the subject farther, lest I weary the reader.

When we arrived in Galveston, we were agreeably surprised to meet our friend and brother Sehon, agent of the American Bible Society. He returned with us to New Orleans in the splendid steamship Neptune. We suffered the usual amount of inconvenience from head winds and seasickness; but the urbane commander, Captain Rollins, and his amiable family, did all that could be done to render us comfortable, during a difficult passage of fifty-six hours from port to port. I here close my long series of letters written in haste, by piecemeal, as I could redeem time on a difficult journey.

As ever, yours, truly, T. A. Morris.

New Orleans, Feb. 21, 1842.

A TRIP TO THE INDIAN MISSION CONFERENCE.

NUMBER I.

Brother Elliott,—The Missouri conference having closed its protracted session on the 4th of October, I took passage the same day on the steamboat Yucatan, bound for Weston, fàr up the Missouri river. The desolating effects of the spring and summer freshet were constantly visible, and produced painful impressions on every reflecting mind. With the exception of a few elevated points, the table-lands adjoining the river had been deluged from hill to hill, by a sweeping current, the main body of which appears to have come out of the Kansas, as the Missouri above that was not so much swollen. Most of the fencing and many of the farm-houses were entirely destroyed; and, instead of the expected crop being realized, the rich soil was washed away, or left covered with a layer of sand from twelve inches to two feet deep. The amount of property lost is incalculable. A few persons were endeavoring to repair their premises, but most of the proprietors appeared to have abandoned them in despair. One consequence which followed was, much sickness in the country adjacent; and the Wyandott Indians, who reside at present on the township of land immediately in the fork of the Missouri and Kansas rivers, where the overflow was deep, were perhaps among the greatest sufferers.

The Missouri river, at the time we ascended, formed a very striking contrast with what it had recently been. On several bars, the men who flung the lead-lines reported, "three feet scant" on both sides of the boat; still the water was turbid, and, in appearance, resembled boiling soap; and the vast numbers of snags and sawyers with which the river abounds, increased the difficulty of navigating it. However, after the usual amount of sounding, grounding, floundering, sparring, backing off, and going ahead, our vigilant and persevering commander and crew brought us safely to the landing, one mile below the mouth of the Kansas, and four hundred miles above the mouth of the Missouri, on the 10th, between sundown and dark. Here I came ashore alone, in a strange land: the ten or twelve preachers who embarked with me at St. Louis, having left at different points for their new circuits. It was not very cheering to reflect that I was far from my family and friends, on the border of the Indian country, where I knew no individual, without porter or guide, with the sable shades of night falling upon me, and my lodging yet to hunt; but knowing that my business was not only lawful, but benevolent, and believing that I was in the path of duty, I was not afraid to trust my heavenly Father for all I needed. Shouldering my baggage, which consisted of a heavy carpet-bag, cloak, umbrella, and a small bundle, I ascended the steep hill, between the base of which and the river there was scarcely room for a warehouse and a few other small buildings; and after resting several times by the way, much heated, and nearly out of breath, I reached a new cabin on the summit, occupied by Colonel Chick, who, having been "washed out" by the late freshet, removed far above high-water mark. The Colonel was very sick with chills and fever, and several members of his family were but just recovering from the same disease; yet, I was very cordially received by him and his interesting family, and treated like a Christian brother. Next morning Colonel Chick kindly sent me on horseback seven miles, to the Indian Manual Labor School, in the Shawnee nation, where I had appointed to meet a party of missionaries, to proceed on together through the Indian country to the conference. The land from the Missouri river to the Mission is well timbered, and is as fertile and beautiful as can well be conceived of; but the Mission Farm itself is partly in the prairie. The school is patronized by several neighboring tribes; but the largest number of scholars are children of Shawnees and Delawares, who, being thrown together, ignorant of each other's language, more readily adopt English as the ordinary medium of communication. Since the establishment of this great central school, the small schools previously connected with each tribe have been discontinued, though their respective missionaries continue in the regular missionary work of preaching and visiting, which contributes much toward keeping the central school well filled with children. The students vary in age from ten or twelve to twenty years, and in number from one hundred to one hundred and fifty. I was in time to witness part of the examination exercises at the close of the regular term, and to address a few words of approval and encouragement to them. Their performance in spelling, reading, arithmetic, geography, composition, autography, and vocal music, was such as would do credit to any of our city schools in the United States. Children, who one year previous knew nothing of letters or of the English language, read the New Testament well. Besides obtaining a knowledge of literature and science, the boys are learned practically the business of agriculture; and some of them the more useful mechanical arts; while the girls are taught to knit, spin, weave, cut and make garments, and the important business of housekeeping, which, I have no hesitation in saying, is a better course of education for all practical purposes of life, than is observed in most of our collegiate institutes. But the best of all is the religious influence brought to bear on the children by the daily reading of the Scriptures, morning and evening worship, the Sabbath school, and regular Sabbath preaching. Some of the boys hold prayer meetings in the woods by themselves; while the girls have prayer meetings in their own chambers, and often get unspeakably happy.

The improvements on the premises are quite respectable. Besides some comfortable frame buildings, there are two large, substantial brick buildings, one on either side of the spring. The boys and their teachers live in one of these houses, and the girls and their teachers and governesses in the other. The outbuildings, barn, etc., are comfortable and convenient. The Mission Farm, too, is extensive and productive. The whole number of acres inclosed with strong fencing, is five hundred, of which three hundred are well cultivated, and the balance in grass and pasture. It is well stocked with horses, cattle, sheep, hogs, and poultry; and among the stock are three native buffalos, which were captured when young, and subsequently purchased for the Mission. Two of them are perhaps two years old, and the other a calf six or seven months old. The mode of capturing these animals is very simple. A gentle cow, with a young calf, is driven into the buffalo range, the calf killed, and its place supplied with a young buffalo calf, which she adopts, and it follows her home. By the way, those three woolly captives on the Mission Farm, are missionary stock; and I am authorized to say, if any friend of missions would like to give the Missionary Society a handsome sum, say three hundred dollars, and take them, he can be accommodated. There is also connected with the Indian Manual Labor School, a steam flouring mill, capable of grinding three hundred bushels of wheat a day, and does good work, which cost the Society four thousand dollars, with four years to pay it in, the net profit of which, the past year, amounted to more than one thousand, eight hundred dollars; at which rate it will soon pay for itself, and become very productive stock. At the earnest request of some of the Indians in their official council, the superintendent is about adding machinery to saw lumber—they engaging to furnish the lumber at the mill for half of the sawed lumber—which, it is supposed, will increase the profits of the mill. This establishment, while the improvements were in progress, received from the Government four or five thousand dollars, and from the Missionary Society ten thousand dollars a year; but now, with five thousand dollars from the Society, and nothing from the Government, it gets along comfortably; and it is probable the sum may be gradually reduced till it can support itself, though the expense of feeding, lodging, clothing, and educating one hundred and fifty students, must necessarily be considerable.

After the interesting spiritual exercises of the Sabbath, we left on Monday, the 14th, for conference. While some brethren on horseback steered through the border settlements of Missouri, four of us, in two buggies, took the military road through the territory, which was once a comfortable road for a new country; but the bridges were mostly destroyed by the freshets, and the sloughs were extremely boggy, which rendered the traveling difficult. Our company consisted at first of Rev. L. B. Stateler, missionary to the Shawnees, Rev. Thomas Hurlbut, late of the Canada conference, and missionary among the Chippewas, Rev. E. T. Peery, superintendent of the Indian Manual Labor School, and myself. We got a late start the first day, and after proceeding about twenty-five miles, took lodging at the Hickory Camp, near a small branch. Our tent was made of domestic cotton, circular, after the form of the habitations of Northern Indians, supported by one center pole, and the base extended by cords and pegs, with an opening fronting the fire. It shed rain well, and afforded some shelter from the wind. We had two buffalo-skins for beds, a blanket each for covering, carriage cushions for pillows, and passed the night in safety. The next day, having journeyed about thirty-eight miles, we camped on the south bank of Mary de Zine, in a quiet and pleasant place, sheltered by the tall trees, with but little to break the stillness of night, except the tingle of the horse-bell, and an occasional report from a neighboring camp of Potawattomie Indians, who were sojourning there, probably for the benefit of the fall range. Next morning, while brother Hurlbut was making our coffee, and the other brethren were hunting the horses, which had lost their hopples and wandered out of hearing, I went to the Indian camp to inquire if they had seen any horses. It was a double camp, containing about a dozen individuals. While the children were gamboling about the creek, and the old man and his numerous dogs were lying down at their ease, the women were busily employed, some preparing breakfast, and the others making flag mattresses. I was favored with a true Indian reception, and having accomplished the object of my visit, soon retired. If the brethren, accustomed to Indian society, should feel disposed to laugh at this unimportant item, I have only to say, it is not written for their benefit. And lest I be over-much tedious, I will relieve your readers for the present.

Yours, truly, T. A. Morris.

Missouri Territory, Oct. 16, 1844.

NUMBER II.

Brother Elliott,—Having recovered our horses at Camp Mary de Zine, we resumed our journey, and, at Osage creek, overtook Rev. Thomas B. Ruble, missionary among the Potawattomie Indians, and Washington, son of chief Boashman. Young Boashman was educated at the Indian Manual Labor School, is a professor of Christianity, acts as interpreter, and it is thought may become a useful man, if faithful, in the missionary work. Thus reinforced, our three carriages formed a little procession, and we found it necessary at night to raise two camp fires. Early in the afternoon we were caught in a north-eastern storm of rain, attended with such wind as rendered it difficult to hold an umbrella; which, in an open buggy, was rather unpleasant. However, I was much relieved by the use of a Spanish blanket, with a hole in the middle to let my head through, so as to screen my shoulders and knees. Late in the evening we reached the Mamita, near Fort Scott, where we could procure fuel and water, and took our quarters for the night, chilled and wearied with the cold journey. The storm beat all night upon our frail habitation, and occasionally whirled the smoke and ashes into it. This was not the worst trouble: two of the horses gave us the slip, and detained us next morning about three hours searching for them; a difficulty against which we subsequently guarded. Thursday morning we called at the fort, and procured horse-provender for the next night, being the last opportunity for the next fifty miles. There were at the fort three companies, one of dragoons and two of infantry, though they appeared to have but little to do, as we saw some of them miles beyond, sporting with greyhounds. This day the wind, crossing the prairies, was quite chilly. When we reached the last skirt of timber on the Drywood Fork, though early in the afternoon, it was too late to encounter the Big Prairie, twenty-three miles across; and we concluded to wait till morning, shave our beards, readjust our equipage, and take a fresh start. We had replenished our store of provision with some beef, sweet potatos, and a chicken, and having full time to broil, roast, and eat, we fared well that night. In the evening we were warned, by the northern lights, of a coming storm. About three o'clock next morning, the sleet and hail commenced falling, which soon turned to a regular snow-storm; and when we left our camp, at daylight, the snow was about two inches deep, and still coming down on us. This was the only day of real suffering we experienced on the journey through the territory. We started with wet boots, exposed to a severe north-west wind, and soon became chilled, while the snow prevented our warming by running on foot, as we had done the day before. On reaching the Cow Fork, we found a fire ready for us, which some movers had just left, where we took our luncheon; and having cleared the range of the snow-storm, and reached dry ground, we resumed our journey under more favorable circumstances. Still it was very cold. When we arrived at Spring river, where we ended our day's journey of thirty-eight miles, the bottom was so crowded with the camps, teams, and stock of emigrants to Texas, that we had some difficulty in finding a suitable place to pitch our tents. As for myself, I was so affected by the cold, that I could not hold a limb of me still; but the work of preparation for night, a good log fire, and a supper of broiled jerk and hot tea, made of spice-wood brush, relieved all the difficulty, and we slept soundly

Saturday, 19th, we passed through the Quapaw lands, a small principality about eight by twenty-four miles in extent, in which we have a mission and mission-school in a tolerably prosperous condition. We also passed the Little Shawnee village, occupied by a small band of Shawnees detached from the main body of the nation. On the way we overtook several companies of Indian women mounted on ponies, well packed with bags of corn, going to mill, which, though not fashionable employment among white ladies, is far preferable to the old style of pounding corn with a pestle. In the evening we arrived at Mrs. Adams's in the Seneca nation, by whom we were kindly received. We rested over Sabbath in her house. Sister Adams is of the band of Stockbridges, and her husband, Rev. Daniel Adams, was a Mohawk. He was our missionary among the Senecas, an excellent man, and died at his post during the past year. His widow is a well-educated, intelligent, and pious woman, and, for her opportunity, keeps a comfortable house of entertainment. Our religious services in her house, on Sabbath, were, to me, at least, peculiarly interesting. The congregation contained about sixty persons only, yet among them were seen Senecas, Stockbridges, Shawnees, Cherokees, Africans, Canadians, and citizens from several of the United States; and during the exercises of preaching, prayer, and praise, all appeared to be "baptized into one Spirit;" while tears of joy, and half-suppressed exclamations of triumph, told the deep feeling of many hearts. It was here the Rev N. M. Talbott, missionary among the Kickapoos north of the Kansas, joined our traveling party, and continued with us to conference.

Monday, 21st, we resumed our journey, and soon passed the Seneca Mills; but, for want of water, all was still. In the afternoon we went through Baetie's Prairie, one of the best settlements in the Cherokee nation; and in the evening camped at Spavanaugh, a beautiful stream of clear water. About dark, while eating our supper, an Indian, on whose heart the light of the Gospel had probably never dawned, came to us in a bad humor, and though he could not clearly express his meaning in words that we understood, his countenance looked terrible; and by violent gestures, and an occasional word of broken English, we at last learned that he was offended at us for cutting and burning his wood. We, however, soon hit upon a successful mode of compromise: with two crackers and two dimes, we effected a satisfactory treaty of peace, which relieved the whole difficulty.

Tuesday, 22d, after traveling thirty-five miles, late in the evening, we reached Tahlequah, the capital of the Cherokee nation, commonly called the Council Ground. It is a little city, but full up to our expectation. The most important building is a new brick court-house. There is, in the midst of the village, a stand, with temporary seats arranged for public assemblies, and covered with an arbor, serving as a kind of forum for political orators, and perhaps for a place of religious worship. The National Council was in session. It consists, I understand, of a lower house, or popular branch, of twenty-four members, and a senate, or upper house, of sixteen members, occupying very ordinary buildings, but talking of erecting a more spacious capitol. It was said they were rather retarded in the business of the Council by the absence of the Hon. John Ross, head chief of the nation, who was, however, expected daily. The Supreme Court was also in session. From all I could learn, there is a strong feeling in the nation in favor of law, and a determination to enforce it. The Cherokees are progressing in education, civilization, and Christianity, all of which are forwarded by means of the press among them; and they might do very well in their new country, if they could permanently settle some internal difficulties that have long embarrassed them. In their political and social relations it is said that party feelings and party measures are strong; very much like those among their white neighbors of the United States. At Tahlequah we learned that the conference was to meet in Riley's Chapel, two miles distant, and that "headquarters," from which we were to be distributed to our respective lodgings, were near the chapel, at the house of Rev. Thomas Bertholf. Fortunately for us, my "cabinet" and self were all billeted to the house of George M. Murrell, Esq., at Park Hill, one of the finest neighborhoods in the nation. We were only two and a half miles from the chapel, with the privilege of riding to and from, and had as comfortable a home as could be desired in any country.

Here I close this number, with one or two general remarks. The distance from the mouth of the Kansas to Tahlequah is about two hundred and sixty miles by the military road, and about seven-eighths of the way are dreary barrens, or prairie, mostly of inferior quality, being arms or skirts of the almost boundless plains of sand, stretching toward the Rocky Mountains, which afford neither timber, water, nor soil sufficient to sustain any considerable population, and will, therefore, never be inhabited to any great extent. Even on the east border of this vast territory there is comparatively little to engage the eye, the ear, or the mind of the enterprising pioneer. One fox, one gray squirrel, and a few ducks and geese, were all the game we saw on a journey of two hundred and fifty miles. The character of the country west of the civilized Indians is greatly in their favor, as no considerable settlements are likely to be soon formed beyond them.

Yours, respectfully, T. A. Morris.

Park Hill, Cherokee Nation, Oct. 22, 1844.

NUMBER III.

BROTHER ELLIOTT, — The Indian Mission conference commenced its first session at Riley's Chapel, near Tahlequah, in the Cherokee nation, on Wednesday, October 23, 1844. The name of the house is intended, I learn, to perpetuate the precious memory of the first Cherokee converted to Christianity. It is a respectable frame building for a frontier country. There are in this conference seventeen elders, all of whom were present but one, six deacons, and four licentiates: total, twenty-seven; and all tried men in the Indian work. About one-fourth of them are native preachers. There are also several natives not yet admitted into the conference, who act as helpers and interpreters on the circuits. The conference, as a whole, will compare well with other conferences as to ministerial qualification, in proportion to their numbers. This little band of missionaries live and labor together in the bonds of Christian affection. All their work is missionary; and, consequently, there is no scrambling for popular appointments, or city stations. After arranging the work for the ensuing year, we stationed the whole conference in less than two hours, and had no occasion afterward to change a single appointment, nor did any one complain that his lot was hard. The religious exercises at the opening of each day's session were conducted in English, and at the close of the session, in Choctaw or Cherokee. We reached the point of final adjournment on Saturday afternoon; all the business having been fully considered and done up, except to ordain the preachers, which was done on the Sabbath. Two of those ordained were full-blooded Choctaws; and one of them, being a good English scholar, interpreted the questions to the other in presence of the congregation.

As this was the commencement of a new state of things in the Indian missionary work, the conference thought it best to take decisive measures at once, being determined not to encourage or countenance any mere hangers-on, or inefficient men, who might desire, under the name of traveling preachers, to be employed as teachers of neighborhood or Government schools, not under the control of the conference. And though they gave a supernumerary relation to one brother in feeble health, it was without claim on the missionary funds. Any brethren who may wish to become identified with the Indian Mission conference must calculate to go in for the work, the whole work, and nothing but the work, or to be furnished with "walking papers" in short order. So it should be in every conference. And the fear expressed by some that the missionaries, when once the power was put into their own hands, would make a prodigal use of the missionary funds, is perfectly groundless. On the contrary, the mission committee of five leading men, whose report of estimates was cordially approved by the conference, and concurred in by myself, manifested a scrupulous regard to economy. The whole amount appropriated for all the conference this year is, fourteen thousand, four hundred and ninety dollars, and thirty-two cents. And this, let it be observed, is not only to support the twenty-seven missionaries and their families—for most of them have families, and all of them should have—but also their helpers, interpreters, teachers; to pay for necessary improvements, and feed, clothe, lodge, and educate the children in the mission schools. Three of these schools, alone, required seven thousand dollars; nearly half of the whole amount. It is worthy of remark, that the appropriation for the Indian work, this year, is less than it usually was when connected with the other conferences. And yet much fear is entertained, that in the present excited state of the Church, the means may not come into the hands of the Assistant Treasurer to take up the drafts without difficulty. Still we hope better things, though we thus speak. The conference organized itself into a Conference Missionary Society, auxiliary to the Parent Society of the Methodist Episcopal Church, and reported two hundred and seventeen dollars, and some cents, obtained during the year, and at the first meeting. They will more than double this sum next year, I presume.

Now, if any one doubts the propriety of expending so much money on the Indians, to effect their conversion from heathenism and sin to civilization and Christianity, let him visit the work, make observation for himself, and his doubts will be removed. If he can not do this, we refer him to the official minutes of the Indian Mission conference, where he will see that, beside a few white and some hundreds of colored members—for some of the Indians are extensive slaveholders, and are likely to become liberal supporters of the missionary cause—we have nearly three thousand Indian Church members. Moreover, we have very many of the children in a course of training in day schools and Sabbath schools. But while much has been done, much remains to be done. Thousands are yet heathen sinners, and perishing for the bread of life. We owe them much, as an injured people. The land is before us. Great and effectual doors are open unto us; and there are many adversaries. Some of these doors may be shut, or entered by others, while we delay operations. The far-famed Nannawarrior fund has slipped out of our hands. By official action of the Choctaw Council, it has been diverted to other channels, not under our control. And from the best information we can obtain, this movement was intended by the leading men before they requested us to postpone our operation in the premises last spring. After all, it is questionable whether we shall have lost much in the end, as there is some prospect of other and more inviting fields of labor. In such an enterprise as that of converting the heathen, there will always be difficulties and discouragements, beyond what may be reasonably expected in our ordinary circuit work among our own countrymen; and these difficulties have been increased by the system of connecting the Indian missions with ordinary work in the conferences, which has led to frequent changes both of men and measures. We trust, however, the difficulties will be relieved, in part, by the organization of the Indian Mission conference, which will certainly afford those having the management of the missions more time and better means of information, in arranging and carrying out their plans of usefulness. Another thing greatly to the advantage of the work was ordered by the late General conference; namely, the appointment of a superintendent to reside in the Indian country, overlook all the missionary interests, and act as an agent for the Church to negotiate with Indian councils and the Government of the United States, in regard to Indian education funds, etc., as occasion requires. As the bishops were charged with the responsibility of making such appointments, both for the slave missions in the south and Indian missions in the south-west, they met in New York the day after General conference adjourned, and appointed Rev. William Capers to the former, and Rev. Jerome C. Berryman to the latter. (This is my answer to a communication, signed by some twenty-five or thirty worthy ministers of the Ohio conference, on the subject, received last September.) Brother Berryman had long been identified with the Indian missions, and was already a citizen of the Missouri territory, within the bounds of the Mission conference, which gave him some advantage in his new office. He entered upon his work immediately, and before the conference met had been to nearly every mission in its bounds. Those who know him best, think he is the right sort of a man for the work; and I trust he will make full and satisfactory proof of his ministry.

Upon the whole, dear brother, I am much pleased with my visit to the Indian Mission conference; and it would be ungrateful in me not to acknowledge the kindness which I have constantly received. I was not only conveyed by the brethren to conference, as I have elsewhere explained, gratuitously, but was subsequently sent by the hospitable family, who had the trouble of entertaining me, in a fine, close carriage, with handsome match horses, driver and escort, nearly forty miles, to this neighborhood, where I can obtain a stage to Van Buren, and thence to Little Rock. Such kindness I shall never forget nor cease to acknowledge with gratitude.

Yours, respectfully, T. A. MORRIS.

CUMMINGSVILLE, ARKANSAS, NOV. 1, 1844.

TRIP NORTH-WEST, 1848.

IN this article no report of official duties will be inflicted upon the reader, nor any thing but a few notes of travel, with such observations and reflections as may be deemed appropriate.

Our last day of sojourn in the Queen City, June 27, 1848, was memorable on account of heat. While the mercury rose to ninety-five in the shade, and the south-west wind drove clouds of dust, not only through the streets, but into our sitting-room and bed-chamber, we longed to be off, that we might gain a more elevated position, and inhale a purer air. How opportune were the gentle showers of rain that night, which brought relief at once from heat and dust, and were succeeded by a calm, refreshing morning! At eight o'clock, A. M., our train cleared the narrows of Fulton with its world of lumber and clattering machinery. Even there the eye found relief by resting upon the placid Ohio on the right, and the hights beyond it, dotted with objects of rural beauty. A few minutes more and we were gliding amidst the shadows of lofty forest trees, along the fertile vale of the Little Miami, enlivened by birds of various notes and flowers of every hue. How delightful the change! The stillness of the country contrasts pleasantly with the bustle of a crowded city. Riding in an elegant car, even at the moderate speed of fifteen miles an hour, is quite as agreeable as spinning street yarn on foot over burning hot brick and stone, employing one hand in supporting a silken shade overhead, and the other in relieving the eyes from dust and perspiration.

We could not have selected a more pleasant time for our flight across the state of Ohio: the growing fields of Indian corn were spread out before us in richest verdure; the fields of golden wheat, some waving in the gentle breeze, some falling before the sweeping cradle, and others arranged in clustering shocks, all indicating the greatest abundance, presented a cheerful appearance to the passing traveler. Farm-houses, factories, and fresh-looking villages, were passed in quick succession, till we halted for dinner at Springfield, eighty-five miles from the city. From this to Urbana, fourteen miles, the railroad was not quite completed, but in rapid progress. Stages were ready to convey the passengers and their baggage. The usual practice appeared to prevail, of filling the coaches outside and in with large passengers, and then putting in the children and sachels for chinking, to keep all steady. To avoid this inconvenience, we chartered a hack, which afforded ample room. As stage after stage came up, and received its well-packed load, our trunks still remaining on the side-walk, some guessed that we were at our journey's end. Last of all came our hack, nimble ponies and jolly driver, and moved us off nicely. As we passed the rear stage, reeling and screaking under its ponderous load, our fellow-passengers seemed, by their looks and manner, to say, "What lucky favorites to secure all that comfortable room to themselves, and move on with so much ease, leaving us to inhale the dust!" The real cause, however, was neither good luck nor favoritism, but the extra shillings. They put us through to Urbana in an hour and three-quarters, where we slept comfortably in the house of our much-respected friend, Judge Reynolds, while the crowd passed on in the night train.

Next day we took the morning line, affording us, among other pleasures, a full view of the wild meadows, or savannas, of Champaign county, interspersed with lucid streams and fragrant flowers, and swarming with horned cattle, colts, and lambs, contentedly cropping the luxuriant herbage. Another object of interest that day was the Wyandott Reservation. The dust of their fathers and noble chiefs slept there, but the remnants of their broken tribe were beyond the Kansas. What was recently their hunting-ground, and more recently a mission station, is now visibly changing into cultivated fields and flourishing villages. How rapidly the aboriginals of America are wasting before the march of civilization! Already scattered and peeled, in a few centuries more they will be numbered among the nations that have been and are not. Surely, as Christians and patriots, we owe them a debt of kindness.

As we neared Lake Erie the face of the country assumed more beauty, both of nature and culture. On reaching the depot at Sandusky City, in the afternoon, we witnessed the usual amount of noise, confusion, and clamor, of porters and agents for baggage and passengers, swearing at and pushing each other with violence, and each affirming, with a zeal worthy of a better cause, that he represented the best hotel in the city. As usual, we favored those who clamored least, went to the Sandusky Exchange, and found it an excellent house. After taking a room, it afforded us some entertainment to sit at our front window, which overlooks the bay and outlet to the main lake, and view the sail vessels with white canvas spread to the breeze, and the steam packets arriving and departing, laden with surplus produce, and crowded with passengers. These Americans, what an enterprising and migratory people! If true to their civil institutions, they must become the greatest nation, and if faithful to their religious privileges, the happiest people on earth.

The line from Cincinnati to Sandusky has been unfavorably represented, probably under the influence of canal and stage-line interests; but it is unjust. There are faster lines than it is, but I have found none more pleasant in the United States; nor is the speed even now to be complained of, as they who wish to do so, dine in Cincinnati, breakfast next morning in Sandusky, and proceed on immediately to Buffalo or Detroit, as the case may be. After the whole line shall have been completed and put in good order, the passenger cars may run through in eleven hours, distance two hundred and eighteen miles.

On Friday a small steamboat brought us to Detroit in seven hours. The scenery on the Lake, among the islands, and along the Detroit river, was imposing. At Malden, on the Canada shore, we landed to put some Indians out. They were from Missouri, and brought with them two young prairie wolves, coupled together in leading-strings, which attracted as much attention as their owners. On reaching Detroit we stopped at the National Hotel, but the Hon. Ross Wilkins soon called for us with a carriage, and removed us, bag and baggage, to his own quiet home. He is the Associate Judge of the United States Court for the state of Michigan, and a local minister of the Methodist

Episcopal Church, and no drone in either office; for, after sitting all the week constantly on the bench with Judge M'Lean, he preached twice in the country on Sabbath, and met class, felt refreshed in spirit, and was ready to resume court business on Monday morning. The Christian simplicity and hospitality of himself and lady caused us to feel perfectly at home, and as happy as visiting relatives. Their home is one of those delightful green spots where weary pilgrims love to linger and rest. The Sabbath brought us abundant privileges, and passed off pleasantly. Detroit is a growing and business-like city, of some twenty thousand inhabitants, situated on the American side of Detroit river, but in full view of the Queen's dominion in Upper Canada. The city is supplied with pure lake water from the river, and is considered quite a healthy place. From this point travelers west can choose between railroad and stage across the peninsula of Michigan, and a voyage round the lakes, as business or fancy may suggest.

The Fourth of July was celebrated in Detroit with the usual amount of hilarity and folly. Large boys fired cannon, and small boys fired squibs; both took aim at nothing and missed the world. The cold east rain-storm that day spoiled much of the sport in the city, and the blow upon the lake defeated the parties on excursions of pleasure, not in paying for their costly dinner, but in eating it, the seasickness having allayed the gnawing pains of hunger before it was ready. As for ourselves, we remained in doors by a comfortable fire, reading and preparing for our voyage on the lakes.

After waiting the arrival of our boat all night, in a state of preparation to move on the shortest notice, our coachman called for us about four o'clock in the morning, and hurried us on board of the Niagara, just in from Buffalo, and bound for Chicago; but they soon got over their hurry, and did not slip cable till half-past six. That day we took it leisurely through Detroit river, the Flats, Lake St. Clair, and St. Clair river, stopping two hours at one place for wood, and as long at another for coal, preparatory to the long runs ahead. Late in the afternoon, however, we cleared Gratiot, and bore northward on the broad bosom of Lake Huron. We had hoped to see the sun as he hid himself amid the waters, but a heavy bank of clouds, nearly stationary in the western horizon, obscured him, and changed the appearance of the lake from a bright sky blue to that of a somber purple. As night fell upon us, grave thoughts intruded themselves—three hundred souls aboard, with only a few inches of timber between them and a sheet of water two hundred and twenty miles long and one hundred and seventy-five broad, with the ordinary risk of collision, explosion, and fire. The visions of other years came up, and among them the Euroclydon, with which Paul and his fellow-voyagers had to contend on his way to Rome, as a prisoner in chains for the faith of Christ. In that storm no sun, moon, or stars appeared for fourteen days, during which time they labored, prayed, and fasted, till Paul assured them there should be no loss of life, but only of the vessel and cargo, for which he gave a satisfactory reason: "For there stood by me this night the angel of God, whose I am, and whom I serve, saying, Fear not, Paul; thou must be brought before Cæsar: and lo, God hath given thee all them that sail with thee." What a relief in their extremity! And how comfortable our condition in comparison of their perilous one, all at liberty, all well, on board of a noble steamer, well manned and provisioned, walking like a thing of life on the smooth surface, and affording all the luxuries of life! Of course we had much to comfort and but little to render us discontented.

The voyage of the lakes, from Buffalo to Chicago, is

one thousand and seventy-five miles. Niagara was a new boat of the line, on her sixth trip, and perhaps nearly equal in strength and speed to any other, and free from any unpleasant noise or motion, so that, while running from twelve to fifteen miles an hour, we scarcely heard her engines, or felt her move. Her forward keel was ornamented with a full length figure of an Indian chief, with his flowing robe, raven locks, jewelry, and cap of feathers. He stood erect, with lofty bearing, his right foot in advance, a bow in his left hand, and a quiver projecting behind the left shoulder, his right hand firmly grasping the handle of a scalping-knife, with the point downward; and with his piercing eye fixed on some distant point, he seemed, by a most determined air, to say, "Follow me." The man at the wheel wielded a strong and steady arm. There was no indication of storm, and all promised well. But we looked beyond all these visible means of safety, and committed ourselves for safe-keeping to Him who said to the sea, "Thus far shalt thou come, and here shalt thy proud waves be staid."

Our boat was a little world of itself. On the lower deck were crowds of foreigners, with their piles of chests and movables, figuring in quaint costume, and making their first observations upon America, to whom every thing appeared to be novel, but not unpleasant. Their children acted like young birds just venturing out of their nest, and gave their mothers ample employment to keep them out of danger. In the cabin were men of leisure and pleasure, with their families, seeking new sources of enjoyment—men of business, intent on its accomplishment—invalids traveling for health—peddlers of books and maps—tourists exploring new states—ministers and agents on ecclesiastical business, and smoking, loquacious politicians—some promenading the deck in solitude, some clustered together in social chitchat, others attracted by the sound of music and song. Some were in their state-rooms, praying and reading their Bibles, while such as wished to relieve each other of their cash by games of hazard, went aloft to the hurricane deck, and took with them the "History of the Four Kings." But after the tea-table was removed, the headquarters of amusement appeared to be in the ladies' cabin, where many assembled for the purpose of killing time, which hung heavily upon them. The moving agent of the whole operation was a son of Ham, patting his foot, and drawing a horse-hair across a piece of cat-gut, which made a kind of screaking noise. He must have been a captain; for so soon as he commenced tossing his head about and moving his right arm to and fro, though he gave no other signal or word of command, a number of individuals rose to their feet, commenced running past each other, and facing about, with a regular step to the sound of cuffy's violin. The characters under the influence of his enchantment were diversified—boys and misses, dandies and flirts, men and women; but one who witnessed the affair, declared that the commander of our boat beat them all; that he was the best dancer among them; and no one seemed disposed to dispute the fact. There was one thing, however, which appeared mysterious to us, who were unacquainted with such matters; namely, how the captain of the Niagara could spend his time in the silly dance, consistently with his responsible duties. Suppose, while he was capering about and measuring his steps by the motion of cuffy's elbow, surrounded with the stamping noise of a crazy multitude, the boat had suddenly taken fire, ten miles from land, who, amidst the darkness and peril of that hour, would have been responsible for the souls aboard, and prepared to meet the emergency with discretion? It is needless to say any thing respecting the rudeness of such conduct toward the civil part of the passengers, who had gone aboard with reasonable expectation of safe conveyance and excellent accommodation. The act defines itself.

On the morning of Thursday, 6th, near Thunder Bay, was witnessed one of nature's most beautiful exhibitions. It was a thin cloud forming a regular arch, which spanned one-fourth of the visible heavens, the ends resting upon the north and south, and the greatest elevation over the east. The face of it presented every possible hue, scarlet, deep purple, golden yellow, silver white, pea green, and all intermediate shades. It was apparently stationary, and for one hour increasing in beauty and splendor, till the luminary of day slowly emerged from the "vasty deep," immediately under the center of this triumphal arch, and threw his beams of light over the sparkling waves toward the lofty peaks of the Rocky Mountains. One such manifestation of infinite Wisdom affords more real pleasure than all the galleries of paintings this world contains.

About noon we rode into Mackinaw on a moderate swell, and went ashore, anxious to see what we could during the half hour allowed us. The island is small, and on the north side forms a bold bluff, shaded with deep-green foliage. On the east side, where the village is, the ascent is easy. The great object of attraction to strangers is the military fort, the appearance of which, at a distance, is quite handsome, and, from its elevated position, rather imposing. Afraid to encounter the hill in such haste, we contented ourselves with examining the stores of Indian curiosities, but found the variety so exhausted, that but little of interest remained. The number of Indians about the village appeared to have been greatly reduced since 1844; but few tents were standing in sight of the wharf; their birch-bark canoes were mostly hauled up on the beach above the swells, and very few of the Indians made their appearance. Some of the passengers ventured up to the fort to obtain a hasty view of it, but the tolling of our bell soon brought them back faster than they went, and we were off again.

Leaving Mackinaw, we headed south, up Lake Michigan. The breeze which had sprung up in the forenoon steadily increased till evening, when it became a gale, and finally a regular eastern storm of wind and rain. About eight o'clock we attempted to land at Manitou, one hundred miles from Mackinaw; but the storm drove us off without effecting it. We had just time to crawfish out into deep water, and get the proper course, before it fully broke upon us. For the next twelve hours the boat was rolling and pitching, till many of the passengers got "half seas over," and the lake appeared in general commotion, which corresponded exactly with our internal feelings. When the breakfast bell rang, most of us had no occasion to appear at table, till we landed at Sheboygan, about nine o'clock, and the motion which had destroyed our appetites ceased, then we revived in feeling, and the second table was well filled, and all lost time made up. Soon after this the wind shifted its course, met the rolling billows, and in a few minutes laid the entire surface as smooth as a level prairie.

At Sheboygan we saw the scanty remains of the steamboat Phœnix, which was destroyed by fire last fall. The calamity occurred eight miles out, when the boat was crowded with passengers, as we were told, some of whom reached the land on planks, ladders, and floating fragments; some were picked up by another steamboat, but many of them were lost. The burning keel was towed to the beach, where it is nearly buried in sand, and presents an appalling spectacle. The wreck of the Boston, which was driven ashore by a terrible storm at night near the same time, lies partly on her side near Milwaukie. The passengers on her, after much suffering in the cold water, reached land with their lives. These manifest tokens of destruction strongly admonish the passer-by of the perils of the lake.

We reached Milwaukie on Friday afternoon, where more than two hundred deck and cabin passengers were landed, to disperse through that new country. We stopped at the National Hotel, but were subsequently removed to the house of a kind friend, where we remained till Monday evening. Milwaukie is about twelve years old, and contains about fifteen thousand inhabitants. It is situated at the mouth of the small river of the same name, which affords a safe harbor. The improvements are very respectable for so new a place, and rapidly advancing. Its chief peculiarity is the color of the houses. The bricks are all of a light cream color, owing, probably, to some unusual substance in the natural formation of which they are made, and when in the building, look as handsome as ordinary bricks painted white, and are said to be very hard and durable. The wooden houses are nearly all white, which imparts to this young city a general air of cheerfulness. Many citizens and visitors suppose that Milwaukie will soon become a large commercial city.

At Southport we were put ashore at two o'clock in the morning amidst darkness that could be felt, because of a dense fog, and were conveyed to the Temperance House; but when daylight came to our relief, we found ourselves in a beautiful village of some two thousand five hundred inhabitants. The more it rains there the better the walking becomes; for, when dry, the sand is deep, and makes the travel heavy, but when closely packed, by beating showers, the walking is pleasant. This village is fifty-five miles below Chicago, and is a very inviting place at which to reside.

A COLD TRIP.

Rev. Dr. Simpson—Dear Brother,—When leaving Cincinnati, several friends requested us to inform them by letter when we should have safely reached this place; and, to save time and labor of writing, I have concluded, with your consent, to report to all of them at once, through your paper.

We took passage for Pittsburg on the 14th instant, on board of the Telegraph No. 1, and got under way at three o'clock, P. M. Our accommodations were excellent throughout, and we made good headway till next morning, when we met small flakes of floating ice, which were soon followed by larger and heavier pieces, as the cold increased, till roods became acres, and acres became fields, covering the entire width of the river. As the solid ice formed along the shores, and the channel for the drifting masses contracted, the friction was terrible, and the prospect of ascending constantly diminishing. At some of the short bends we found the channel gorged, and the ice nearly stationary for miles; but our noble steamer still plowed her way onward and upward, against the strong current and all the massive obstruction which it bore. After the iron sheeting was worn off from the bow, the captain substituted planks, and when they were cut to pieces their places were supplied by others; and when the paddles were broken, new ones were put in. Beside this difficulty we had too much freight, or too little depth of water on the bars, and were several times badly grounded. The hope of reaching Pittsburg was soon cut off; but, after a determined and persevering effort of nearly four days, we got to Wheeling without injury, where I had the pleasure of preaching, on Sabbath evening, to a large and attentive congregation.

At this season of the year, or when navigation is obstructed, there is but one way to reach Baltimore; that is, by stage to Cumberland, thence by railroad. The only point for us to settle was the time of leaving. After a severe snow-storm, the weather became very cold on Sabbath night, which occasioned some misgiving as we looked toward the elevated peaks of the Alleghany; but loss of time presented other difficulties worthy of consideration. The anticipation of one whom the people delight to honor, and his traveling party, just behind us, was already putting the multitudes in motion. Office-seekers and pleasure-takers were preparing to swell the train of him who "never surrenders," and to be at "headquarters" in time to witness the inauguration of General Taylor; all of whom had to travel the same road by stage, in anticipation of which the stage fare was already on the rise. To go with that multitude of aspirants after political pleasure and official distinction did not serve our convenience, nor suit our notion of comfort. We did not wish to follow the train after every thing was eaten and worn out, neither had we time to wait for all the eastern-bound pilgrims to pass on before us; and, as we were in advance, we resolved, if possible, to maintain that position, by leaving on Monday morning. New bills were distributed, promising, of course, superior accommodations, on a "splendid line of Troy-built coaches," etc.; so that crossing the mountains might have been regarded, by one not familiar with the practical operation, as a mere pleasure-ride on a summer's morning; but experience had taught us to throw in one-half for shrinkage. Some of our fellow-passengers on the Telegraph, forming a choice party, were promoted to the mail-line, with the flattering prospect of getting on in quick time; then four coaches of the accommodation line were loaded, of which ours was one. From appearance it had once been a second-class coach of its size, but had seen its best days, and bore evident marks of a veteran mountain pioneer; having inscribed upon its shield, in small capitals, the significant title, "Rio Grande." It was just large enough to accommodate six passengers of ordinary stature, and more should not have been required of it; but its unreasonable task-master piled on about one thousand pounds of baggage to commence with; and then about fifteen hundred pounds of humanity were stowed away inside, consisting of ten passengers, or, more technically, "nine and a half," one being under size, but not as much under as some of us were over; so that it was not respectful in our way-bill to call us nine and a half, for, on an average, we compared respectably with any ten passengers in the train. Beside, we were favored with the usual supply of baskets, sachels, extra robes, etc. Our concern did not do a way-side business; we were all through passengers; and when once crowded in, and the door forced to upon us, we experienced the practical definition of a *squeeze*. I will venture to say that the same lot of individuals were never before compressed within the same narrow space, and it is to be hoped they never will be again. The word was given, "All set," and we dashed off at a merry step, but not in a merry mood. To endure the pressure we then felt during a trip of one hundred and thirty-one miles, was a serious affliction, but one for which there was no remedy. The state of the temperature did not admit of any one riding outside. On reaching Washington, Pennsylvania, some of the mail-coach party becoming indisposed from exposure, remained; the balance held out to Uniontown, but were so affected with the intensity of cold as to abandon the coach, and lie over. While at Washington we procured heated bricks for our ladies to place under their feet, and a new blanket to spread over them, which enabled them to endure the cold to Union-town, where we renewed our preparations for the night, and set off for a lofty tumble over the mountains, having to ride sixty-three miles to Cumberland, the next place where we were allowed to warm, or receive any refreshment, which took us from half-past six in the evening till half-past seven next morning. A night's ride of thirteen hours, in the elevated and frozen regions of the Laurel Hill and the Alleghany Mountains, in our cramped condition, was really tedious, and attended with positive suffering from both cramp and frost. The road was firm, and tolerably smooth; too much so for our safety on the mountains. The icy descents were the more dangerous from being covered by the recent fall of snow, concealing the points of difficulty from the driver's view till the wheels commenced sliding. The lamps went out early in the night, and were not relighted; the road was but partially beaten down after the last snow, so that it was difficult to determine by sight when the stage was in the right track, as every place had nearly the same appearance. This was one source of danger. Another was the rapidity with which we descended, to regain the time lost in ascending the high mountains. Our drivers complained of having "a salty load," meaning heavy. One driver, while creeping up a long hill in a slow walk, became cold and impatient, and, having gained the summit, and reached the turning-point, jumped down, adjusted his check-blocks, gave his horses an awful cursing to wake them up, and a few lashes to raise their mettle for a lively run down the mountain. The checks had some control over the fore-wheels, but the hind ones would slide which ever way the weight of baggage leaned in the rear boot, changing sides as the ground changed. The diminutive old vehicle, reeling and screaking under its ponderous load, went sliding down with fearful speed, and, sometimes, almost sidewise, which, of course, was extremely perilous. We often had occasion to remember the Bible truth, "A horse is a vain thing for safety;" though, in some cases, the teams are more civil than their drivers. Neither was to be trusted; therefore we committed ourselves to the safe-keeping of the Most High, and pleaded that his presence might go with us and keep us from evil. To his superintending care, alone, we attributed our safety, amid perils visible and invisible to us.

On reaching Cumberland we felt thankful for whole bones. As we crept out of the stage the bell summoned us to breakfast. There was no time to rest or warm, as it was near the regular time of leaving for Baltimore, and we hurried in to the table, where we found only scraps left from the regular breakfast. Those who preceded had saved us the trouble of eating much. Our work of gleaning the fragments was soon accomplished, and we made for the depot, mending our pace at each note of the whistle, and just had time to pitch in our trunks and get aboard before the train moved. The change from the hard seats of our old, rickety coach to cushioned seats, in a warm and spacious car, was very grateful to us cold and weary travelers. The same evening we met a welcome reception by our Christian friends in Baltimore, where our perils are past, and our toils are ended, for the present; and, though nearly "used up" by the journey, we trust no serious injury to our health has been inflicted. Mrs. Morris endured the entire trip better than could have been expected under all the circumstances, but suffers with soreness and pain.

Yours, truly, T. A. Morris.

Baltimore, Feb. 22, 1849.

RURAL SCENERY—WHITE MOUNTAINS.

How striking is the contrast between city and country! The former is preferable for winter residence, on account of its facilities for business pursuits, social intercourse, and church privileges; but, in summer, the country is altogether more desirable. The few stinted shrubs and shade-trees, seen about the city mansions of the wealthy, are no more to the forests and gardens of nature, than the maps of countries and the pictures of landscapes are to the originals. Then the idea of being confined, during a long summer, to a city, with all its noise, and dust, and heat, compares indifferently with the freedom and pleasure of the cool country shade. It is only because the few months of relief allowed us from official business come in the cold season, that we are willing to spend them amid the bustle of crowded cities, while such a vast range of rural territory is accessible, where one may roam in peaceful contemplation among the beauties and grandeur of this wide world.

We have occasionally attempted brief sketches of western life and scenery, not for those familiar with them, but for distant friends and readers. Now we propose to reverse the order, and let our friends in the west have a glimpse of some things which have come under our observation in the east. In doing this, we hope to afford some entertainment for esteemed friends that never saw those things, and thereby discharge, in part, a debt of gratitude justly due them. All we assume, however, is to note down a few observations made in the summer of 1849, during a transient sojourn in "the land of steady habits." We kept no journal, and were not on a tour of observation particularly, but partly on a Gospel mission, and partly on a tour of health and recreation, after a long and severe campaign of official duty. Yet some objects lying in our course made so strong an impression on our mind, that we could not forget them, if we would, and would not, if we could. A few of those scenes which made the deepest impression on our memory, without attempting any connected narrative, is all we think of embracing in this article. Even on this limited scale, it is embarrassing to decide where to begin, and where to end. The Atlantic coast, with its bays and harbors, its capes and fisheries, its commercial points and fashionable bathing establishments, must all be omitted. Nor can we allow room for a description of the Penobscot and the Kennebec—those bold channels, with their islands, indentations, and promontories, their bluff shores, abrupt peaks, sloping borders, and fertile plains, ornamented with villages of white habitations and steeple-churches—however pleasant it would be to do so. The beautiful hights, and inclined planes between them, must share the same neglect. Neither can we linger, gentle reader, along the shady banks of the Merrimack, to examine its factories, growing young cities, rural retreats, and green valleys, though this would be delightful. We must hasten along the iron road, crossing hills and vales, alternately edging along cultivated plains, and cutting through extended ledges of solid granite, till we reach Lebanon, New Hampshire. Here let us pause awhile, amid the combined beauties of nature and art.

Lebanon is a small place, uniting the manufacturing and agricultural interests. In the center is a large hollow square, on a clean sand-plain, partially covered with a green grass-plat, bounded on two sides with business-houses, and on the others with tasty private dwellings, from which broad streets lead off in various directions. The plain on which the village stands appears to be inclosed all round with gently-rising hills, which are used as pasture-lands, dotted with numerous rocks, and shaded with forest-trees, and enlivened with grazing herds of cattle. There are, however, winding passes between those hills. The Mascomy, a narrow river, fed by a small lake of the same name a few miles east, cuts the west end of the village, where, in passing about a hundred and fifty yards, it falls some forty or fifty feet, over successive ledges of rock, and thence, by a rapid movement of some miles, loses itself in the Connecticut river. On one street, leading west, you cross the falls, about midway, on a substantial bridge, affording a fine view of the descending torrent. The railroad crosses near by, at the upper end of the falls, on a covered way, and leads up, through a deep cut, to the depot, in the north-east corner of the village. On this line, connecting Boston and Montpelier, six long trains pass daily, at regular hours; four of them crowded with passengers, and two conveying produce, lumber, and live stock—sheep and cattle—to the Boston market. The whole, taken together, renders Lebanon one of the most romantic little places we have seen. It affords excellent society, and, like most New England villages, is well supplied with churches and seminaries. Withal, it is remarkably healthy, in general; in proof of which, we made the acquaintance of some citizens over eighty years old, and one over ninety. From this point we hailed some two weeks in August, and found it a delightful summer retreat.

Now, suppose we roll down to the White river junction, then turn north up the Connecticut Valley, along the state line, between New Hampshire and Vermont, viewing a series of green meadows and lovely villages on either side of the river, altogether appearing as a vast, continuous garden, inclosed with a wall of mountains. Among the noted places, perhaps Haverhill, New Hampshire, and

Newberry, Vermont, are the most handsome. Here we spent a pleasant Sabbath, attending religious service in both places. In the latter is an excellent and flourishing seminary. We, however, can not linger, even on this beautiful landscape, lest we be tedious. A few miles above Newberry we leave the cars, and pass, by stage, up the Amonoosuc, through Lisbon and Littleton, toward the mountain region. But without regard to exact order, let us digress across the hill country, through that elevated, uneven, but cultivated section of gardens and meadows, cottages and stone fences, including the towns of Landaff, Bethlehem, and Sugar Hill, and first take a view of Franconia, a southern section of the general range of White Mountains.

The most natural way to approach this group of wonders is from the east. Coming up the narrow thoroughfare, between Mount Lafayette and Mount Jackson, along the Pemegewasset, a tributary of the Merrimack, the first stopping-place of note is Mr. Taft's Temperance Hotel, a quiet, well-kept house. From his front piazza north, the mountain view is at once grand and lovely. Here we obtained a guide, who conducted us over hills and hollows, by a winding path, through devious wilds and roughs, across the river, some three-fourths of a mile, to the Flume. This is a sheet of pure mountain water, two rods wide, but shallow; passing, with great rapidity, some hundred and fifty yards, over an inclined plane of solid stone, worn perfectly smooth by the action of the current, and presenting a silver-white appearance, of surpassing beauty. Above the Flume a fourth of a mile is the cataract, formed by the same rivulet, falling some rods over a precipice of cragged rocks. Just at the foot of the cataract proper, the descending current enters an opening in a massive rock, about one rod wide, twenty feet deep, and a hundred yards long; the side walls being perpendicular, and smooth as if the channel had been wrought by mechanical skill, though it was, no doubt, formed by the action of the water itself, in the course of many long centuries. Access to this point is obtained with difficulty, by clambering along the sides of the irregular cliffs, with scarce room for foothold, over the rapid stream. The whole scenery round the cataract, located in a ravine of the mountain side, is wild and strange.

Proceeding up the road, perhaps a mile or more from the tavern, and off to the right, as we understood, is the Pool, a large body of water far down in a deep cavity, among the rocks. This place is much resorted to by visitors; but want of time, and the difficulty of descending to the Pool, prevented our turning aside to examine it. But the most beautiful object in the vicinity is the Basin, immediately by the way on our left. It is formed by the Pemegewasset tumbling, in wild confusion, down a precipice of projecting rocks; so that, in the descent, the water is thrown to the left with violence, against a curving stone, then forced to the right, giving it a whirling motion, which has worn a basin in the rock that forms the bed of the river, of an oval shape, about thirty by twenty feet, and perhaps eight or ten feet deep. The Basin is always full, and running over. The troubled element, after whirling round in a circle, passes off at one corner, and pursues its wonted zigzag course, amid the obstructing fragments of rock below. The water is pure mountain spring, clear as crystal, sufficiently cold for comfort, and delicious to the taste; of which we had ample proof, by slaking our thirst at the Pool on a hot afternoon.

Above the Basin, some two or three miles, the scenery changes from the beautiful to the sublime. Here the valley becomes more narrow, and the mountains, on either side, more elevated, abrupt, and imposing. Just below the Notch House, kept by Mr. Gibbs, a place of much resort, on account of its romantic location, and the splendor of the surrounding scenery, is the Pond. Perhaps this is nothing more than a collection of mountain waters, detained by obstructions on a small level, similar to a large canal basin. On the north side, near the road, is a post, from which projects a finger-board, on which is inscribed, "Profile." This points across the water, and directs attention to "The Old Man of the Mountain." Viewed from this position, the projecting points of rock on Mount Jackson are so arranged as to form an exact profile of a man's face on a large scale—forehead, eyes, nose, mouth, chin, and all. He, however, does not conform to the modern style of hat, with high crown and narrow rim, but wears a kind of patriarchal cap, with an ample shade in front, and looks as though he defied all the revolutions of time. He is surmounted on a nearly-perpendicular cliff, or pinnacle of rocks, at an elevation of about one thousand feet, in an easy-sitting position, as if occupying a chair of state, looking, I believe, north-east, with his eye firmly fixed on the loftiest summit of Mount Lafayette, where he has probably remained a faithful sentinel ever since Noah's Flood, and perhaps for a longer period. Had he taken his position on a mountain, in some heathen land, no doubt but millions of the human family would have worshiped him as a supernatural being.

The next object of note is the Lake, situated between the mountains, being a collection of clear water supplied by mountain springs, with a sand and gravel bottom, covering, perhaps, some forty acres. On this lake is a pleasure-boat, which, at the time we passed by, was filled with visitors, amusing themselves with a speaking trumpet, and hearing themselves mocked by the mountain echo, which, in that confined location, was very distinct, and rather startling, as though some one was speaking from the caves of the mountain.

Soon after leaving the Lake, we reached the main mountain pass, wild and desolate, though rather inviting than repulsive. From this point we began to descend, but not rapidly, or abruptly; for the road through the Franconia Notch is pleasant for carriage-riding all the way. As we came down, one chasm on our left made an imposing appearance. It was a dark ravine, shaded with birch and hemlock, but how deep we could not determine, as the boughs, with their thick foliage, were so interlocked as to exclude the sun's rays, and, consequently, obstructed our vision, and, not being able to see the bottom, rendered it the more terrific. So far as we could obtain a distinct view from the carriage, the moss-covered rocks, resting under a dense forest, gave a somber and venerable air to the whole. Reaching the valley, and crossing the South Amonoosuc, we soon gained the elevation called Sugar Hill, some seven miles from the Franconia Notch. It was that hour of peculiar interest, when the luminary of day was about to disappear below the western horizon. Some of his last rays were faintly resting on the mountain side, while flitting clouds flung their moving shadows over other parts: we paused, and turned round to enjoy a last, lingering view of the mountain scenery, which had just left such a deep impression upon our minds. The sight was magnificent beyond description. Lafayette and Jackson loomed up toward heaven; fragments of their vapor clouds were floating up through the gorge, and embracing the bosoms of those mountains, but leaving their heads uncovered to look out on the vast expanse below.

Now let us resume our route up the Amonoosuc proper, and head toward the White Mountains. Here we are again in a fertile vale, some parts highly cultivated, others in nature's wildness, along the banks of a beautiful little river, now gliding gently and silently through the plain, then dashing with impetuosity over declining ledges, overhung with pine and fir-trees, here veering off, and leaving us in an extensive, smooth meadow, and there returning to the base of the hill, and crowding us into rocky narrows The main valley, through which this crooked stream flows, is several miles wide. Off to our right, in the distance, Mount Lafayette rears its proud summit, like a spacious dome—for that is the form of it—while, in our front, the whole series of White Mountains would be visible from a favorable position; but Mount Washington, like Saul among the armies of Israel, stands head and shoulders above all the rest. In the evening, after a journey of exceeding interest, we arrived at Mr. Fabian's Hotel, a large, commodious establishment, capable of boarding and lodging a hundred and fifty visitors; and, at the proper season, every room is full, but constantly changing between comers and goers. It is a white frame building, with long wings of double rooms, and halls and porticos; stands alone, and, in that lonely retreat, makes a fine appearance. Fortunately for us, Mrs. Morris and I obtained a comfortable room, which had just been vacated, and remained till after breakfast next morning. From the upper piazza, the view of Mount Washington was fair, though to the summit, by any practicable route, was nine miles. It was a pleasant evening, and nearly clear, excepting some light clouds of fog or mist, which are generally visible about those mountain hights. When these would come square against the mountain, then break, and pass in fragments on either side, the sight was, to us, both novel and sublime. No one needs to doubt this, when it is remembered that the hight of Mount Washington is six thousand and four hundred feet above the level of the sea, or about one mile and a quarter. Yet large parties, of both sexes, visit its summit almost every clear day in summer. They go partly on horses, walking over the most difficult places, and attended by a guide familiar with the "bridle-path," which leaves the road a short distance above the hotel. Each visitor, furnished with horse and guide, pays three dollars. A party of nineteen returned to Fabian's from such an expedition just after we arrived. They brought up in double file, swinging their hats and white handkerchiefs over their heads, and shouting as if they had not only scaled the Alps, but conquered all the nations beyond. Such a procession, in that mountain retreat, was, of course, exciting; but it was pleasure dearly bought, for some of the female adventurers were heard to say, next morning, they were scarcely able to walk. We had not the temerity to imitate their exploits, but resumed our journey on wheels, in a comfortable carriage, drawn by two well-trained ponies, in care of a careful and pleasant young gentleman, who had joined us as a traveling companion.

We soon passed the Giant's Grave, a mound, such as are common in the west; but who would stop to survey a mound with a mountain in view? As we neared the elevated region, we saw proof of the humidity of the atmosphere in the pale-green moss growing on the boughs of the trees, not of luxuriant growth, like the long gray moss of the south, but shorter, and of a more sickly and delicate appearance. About five miles of an almost imperceptible ascent, by a lonely road, through unbroken forests, brought us to the Notch House, kept by Mr. Crawford, the younger, standing near a bluff point, in the north-east section of a small level plain, a part of which, to our left, was a shallow pond, which seemed to be the source of one branch of the Amonoosuc, and running west, whose meanders had marked our general course thither, while a marshy-looking meadow, on our right, appeared to be drained by forming the head-spring of the Saco river, running east; the two streams rather interlocked, or reaching into each other's territory, but both originating in that plain, which, perhaps, included some ten acres. But how the Saco, or we, could find any outlet, was, at first, a mystery; for all before us appeared to be solid mountain, and impassable. However, passing the hotel, and turning round a point of rocks, our road formed a short curve to the left, and suddenly brought us into a very narrow pass, between two perpendicular stone walls, very high, leaving just room for a carriage and the little foaming rivulet to pass. This was the "White Mountain Notch." These huge masses of solid stone, on either hand, one of which we judged to be over forty feet high, looked as if they had been sundered by some terrible convulsion of nature in days of yore; while heaps of fallen cliffs, in scattered fragments, partly filling up the chasms below, corroborated the same idea. The plain above described could never have been a lake, with sufficient weight of water to force a passage through this immense barrier of solid rock, some forty feet above the plain, and as thick as high, because there was nothing to prevent the water from passing off west by the way we came. If this gorge was ever forced open by the element of water, it must have occurred after "all the high hills that were under the whole heaven were covered;" after "fifteen cubits upward did the waters prevail, [above the summits,] and the mountains were covered;" we say, after all this, when the Flood had so far abated as to form currents through the lower parts or gaps of mountains, when moved by the winds, then the water, if ever, here broke through, and produced this opening and confusion of cliffs. One thing is certain; that is, some of these ponderous masses have been long since removed from their original positions; but whether by the Flood which destroyed the old world, or by earthquakes, who can tell? So soon as we got through this narrow defile, all language would fail to give any tolerable idea of the scene which was disclosed. On the right were hideous caverns, whose death-like silence was broken only by gurgling rivulets, struggling for outlet among ruined masses of stone, thrown in wildest disorder, and overhung by ponderous mountain steeps, while, on the left, one of the bluff peaks of the mountain towered some thousands of feet above us. On these sublime pyramids of nature one might gaze for hours; and the longer he surveyed them the more he would become overawed, and impressed with an idea of the infinite power of that God whose hand formed "the everlasting hills." Before these stupendous monuments of Omnipotence, Atheism itself would stand abashed.

Leaving these scenes of wonder, we descended by the only possible route, a well-wrought road, curving round the irregular base of mammoth cliffs, the mountains apparently rising higher and higher above us, as we approximated their lower foundations. After proceeding gradually downward, perhaps a half mile or more, we came to two cascades, coming in on the left, both passing under bridges, which formed parts of our road. How far up they burst out of the mountain we had no means of determining, but we could distinctly see one of them, some five hundred, and the other about eight hundred feet above us, and from that down to the ravine below us; for, descending over rocky beds, at an angle of about sixty degrees, and broken into foam as white as milk, it was easy to trace their rapid course, and delightful to hear their soft music tones. At the time we saw them they were flush of water, and made a splendid exhibition. Before we reached the "Willey House," three miles further down the gorge, a steady rain commenced falling, which shut us in the balance of the day, and all night, affording ample time for inquiry and reflection. This house derives its name from its former occupants, the excellent and lamented Willey family, who were overwhelmed, and suddenly destroyed by the great avalanche, on the night of August 28, 1826. Apprehensive of danger, they had erected a shanty further from the base of the mountain, a little lower down the valley, where the slope was more gradual, as a refuge in case of alarm. During heavy falls of rain, on the night above named, the whole side of the mountain in the rear, for an extent of some hundred and fifty or two hundred yards long, and more than a thousand feet high, suddenly gave way, and came down with a fearful crash, carrying earth, trees, and loose rocks, in one confused mass of destruction. Had the inmates remained within doors they would have been secure, for just behind the house was a huge block of granite, deeply imbedded in the plain, and inclining toward the mountain, sufficiently strong to resist the whole pressure, till it parted, so as to pass on either side of the house, and reunite below, crushing the barn, and filling the garden and small meadow in front, but leaving the house on its proper foundation, and uninjured. But the family, consisting of Captain Willey, wife, five children, and two hired men, attempting to gain the shanty, were, with it, suddenly overwhelmed and crushed by the desolating slide. No one of the nine escaped to tell the fate of the others; but, by excavation, most of the bodies were found, and collected into one general deposit at the lower extremity of the sand-bank formed by the slide, where a heap of loose stones serves as a rude monument to designate the ever-memorable spot, though the remains, we are told, have since been removed to a neighboring cemetery. In the same habitation where the Willeys once enjoyed life, to which, however, additions have been made, we took shelter, during a day and night of rain and storm, and felt it to be the safest place within reach, as there was nothing left above to fall on us, but the solid strata of stone. Next day was clear, calm, and exhilarating, when we slowly retraced our steps through the mountain pass, completing the observations before noted. They faintly reflect our own first impressions. The general appearance of these mountains is what Field, Vines, and others described it to be, when they first visited them, more than two hundred years ago, and reported them under the name of the "Crystal Hills;" and the fair inference is, that, in the main, they are now as they were when first formed by the great Creator. The chief range of mountain hights is twenty miles long, and ten miles wide at the base, situated sixty-five miles from the ocean; and yet it is said that, on a clear day in winter, their snow-capped summits are visible fifty miles from shore, resting, like a silvered cloud, in the western horizon.

We must of necessity omit all observations made in passing west through Vermont, till we reach Lake Champlain, and can only notice it briefly. It is one hundred and twenty-eight miles long, and its greatest width fifteen or twenty miles, interspersed with islands of various forms and sizes, which, together with the points and indentations of its ever-varying shores, give it an air of romance and beauty equal to any thing of the kind. While ascending that lake, views are often presented from the upper deck of a steamboat at once grand and delightful. To the left, the Camel's Hump, and other peaks of the Green Mountains, have a most commanding and exhilarating appearance; the rugged hights in the "empire state," to the right, are scarcely less so, while all between these extended ranges is apparently made up of gentle swells, fertile vales, cultivated fields, living streams, and white cottages, including the lake and its numerous villages along the shores. The scene is really enchanting. It is no cause of marvel, to one familiar with it, that Dr. Dixon, on first view of it, for awhile forgot his native land, home, and friends, and felt like pitching his tent, and remaining there forever. At Ticonderoga Point, New York, famous in the history of the American Revolution, we went ashore, and found a quiet and agreeable hotel, in a cool, shady forest, a little below the ruins of the old fort, where we rested two hours, and enjoyed a comfortable dinner. Five miles staging brought us to Lake George, which, by a narrow outlet, is connected with Lake Champlain. It is thirty-three miles long, and about two miles wide, through which, in a small steamboat, we softly glided, on a bright afternoon, amid numerous green islands of limited dimensions, but handsome cliffs and shrubbery. The lake is rather crooked, so that, after proceeding a few miles, and curving round the bold point of a hill, we soon lost sight of the narrow pass through which we came. From that to midway of the lake, the mountains became higher, steeper, and more magnificent on both sides. At one point, four of these, two on either side, nearly opposite, whose respective bases were washed by the deep and narrow channel, and formed its rock-bound shores, brought even their lofty summits into such proximity, that it seemed as though friends standing on each might hail each other, if not converse together, across this lovely little sea. From thence to the end of the voyage the mountains gradually receded. In the evening, toward sundown, we rounded to opposite the Lake House, a very delightful retreat, at the head of navigation, which we entered by an easy ascent, through a wilderness of shrubbery and flowers, of which we obtained a fuller view from the upper piazza, overlooking, at the same time, part of the lake and its surrounding objects. Upon the whole, the voyage up Lake George is not excelled, in real interest, by any of the same extent. Here this sketch of rural scenery, already too extended, must terminate.

www.ingramcontent.com/pod-product-compliance
Lightning Source LLC
LaVergne TN
LVHW020116110826
845151LV00001B/174